BONDS OF UNITY

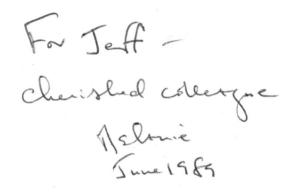

For Jeff –
Cherished colleague
Melanie
June 1989

American Academy of Religion
Academy Series

edited by
Susan Thistlethwaite

Number 65
BONDS OF UNITY
Women, Theology, and the Woldlwide Church

by
Melanie A. May

Melanie A. May

BONDS OF UNITY
Women, Theology, and the Worldwide Church

Scholars Press
Atlanta, Georgia

BONDS OF UNITY
Women, Theology, and the Worldwide Church

by
Melanie A. May

© 1989
The American Academy of Religion

Library of Congress Cataloging in Publication Data

May, Melanie A.
    Bonds of unity: women, theology, and the worldwide church/
Melanie A. May.
        p. cm--(American Academy of Religion academy series: no. 65)
        Bibliography: p.
        ISBN 1-55540-308-5 (alk. paper). -- ISBN 1-55540-309-3 (pbk.:
    alk. paper)
        1. Christian union--History--20th century. 2. World Council of
    Churches--History. 3. Women in Christianity--History--20th century.
    4. Church and minorities--History 20th century. 5. Theology,
    Doctrinal--History-20th century. I. Title. II. Series.
    BX6.5.M39 1989   88-3768
    262'.0011--dc19   CIP

Printed in the United States of America
on acid-free paper

BONDS OF UNITY:
WOMEN, THEOLOGY, AND THE
WORLDWIDE CHURCH

This dissertation is a study occasioned by the World Council of Churches' Community of Women and Men in the Church Study. The dissertation's method is informed by Michel Foucault, especially by his notion of the "insurrection of subjugated knowledges." Accordingly, the Community Study is presented as an uprising of voices against the effects of the theological discourse on unity formulated by the World Council Commission on Faith and Order. Voices heretofore silenced are privileged, particularly the voices of women who are engaged in theological conversation.

The voices of women are heard in two contexts. First, the voices of women who participated in the World Council of Churches from 1948-1975—from the First Assembly of the World Council to the Fifth Assembly when the Community Study was adopted—are heard. These women were clear that their role in the churches and in the council was not merely a "woman's question," but called into question the very foundations of the church and its unity. The voices of these women are the first sort of subjugated knowledge of which Foucault spoke—historical contents present but passed over in official documents—for these voices are not audible in the records of theological discussion during these years.

Foucault's reference to the second sort of subjugated knowledge informs the representation of voices of women inscribed in the local group reports of the Community Study. The voices of the local group reports articulate particular and very diverse knowledge. The differences among these voices are highlighted in an atttempt to hear and honor the uniqueness of each and every voice.

The dissertation does not draw conclusions, but seeks to draw readers into conversation with variegated voices. Conversation is claimed as a mode of theologizing and as an occasion when bonds of unity that celebrate rather than condemn differences may be created.

TABLE OF CONTENTS

ACKNOWLEDGMENTS

This dissertation is a corporate work. At the outset, therefore, I want to acknowledge the places and the people without whom I could not have written.

I am grateful to the libraries of the Ecumenical Centre, Geneva, Switzerland, and of the School of Theology at Boston University for making their resources available to me. They are well-endowed with the materials, especially the primary sources, I needed for research.

I thank Barbara Stewart for her careful eye, her skill, her patience and thoughtfulness, as she properly formatted and footnoted this dissertation from an assortment of floppy disks. I thank Kenneth Shaffer for ordering and formatting my bibliography—that nearly impossible final task in this project.

Krister Stendahl gave the guidance that was crucial in my decision to go to the World Council of Churches Graduate School of Ecumenical Studies, near Geneva, Switzerland. Constance F. Parvey extended an invitation to stay on at the World Council of Churches.

My conversations with Margaret R. Miles, Marilyn Chapin Massey, and Sharon D. Welch, on matters ranging from fourth-century African theology to feminist theory and the thought of Michel Foucault, were formative, indeed indispensible.

Gordon D. Kaufman taught me to think theologically and honed my critical capacities. Clarissa W. Atkinson, ever-present to this project, always asked *the* appropriate question and infused our conversation with humor. Richard R. Niebuhr emboldened me by discerning my perceptions from the outset, and taught me the fine art of appreciation. All three are integrally woven into my thinking and life.

Dorothy A. Austin and Diana L. Eck have provided a home for me and given me unqualified acceptance. Margaret R. Rose and Mark J. Baker have been family, amid crises and celebrations. With Lauree Hersch Meyer I first learned to converse and continue to enjoy conversation. Arlene and Russell May first taught me about *Bonds of Unity* and continue to extend those bonds into ever-widening circles of conversation.

Finally, I acknowledge my gratitude to the women and men who met in local study groups around the world, with whose voices I found my voice.

INTRODUCTION

> Our . . . past is mighty; the ghosts . . . of the selves that we
> have been haunt our days and nights though we refuse to
> acknowledge their presence.
>
> H. Richard Niebuhr[1]

> . . . we can best help . . . not by repeating . . . words and
> following . . . methods but by finding new words and cre-
> ating new methods.
>
> Virginia Woolf[2]

This dissertation is carved out of the quarry of my life.
Particular people and places, events and experiences, have informed the cast of my work. This dissertation is not, in this
sense, unique. It is unique insofar as I seek to acknowledge
that these words are an articulation of my own ancient and
ageless wrestling with *Bonds of Unity*.

Because the people and places, events and experiences,
that stand as waymarkers on my road toward this work are its
context, it is important to introduce them. Having made these
introductions, I will survey the chapters of the dissertation. I
will then state the posture from which I write.

My wrestling with bonds of unity began in the context of
my religious tradition—the Church of the Brethren. The
Church of the Brethren was founded at the confluence of Anabaptist and Radical Pietist streams in eighteenth-century Germany.[3] From the beginning, Brethren have embodied a high
doctrine of the church. The church, that is, has been viewed
not as a loose association of like-minded believers but as a
close-knit community whose life together is a means of grace.
The church is *Gemeinde* or *Gemeinschaft*.[4]

Unlike others who embody a high doctrine of the church,
therefore, Brethren have confessed the people are the church.
Neither a creed, nor a liturgy, nor an official hierarchy, nor a
building makes the church the church. The church is made
visible wherever and whenever members come together for
worship or for work dedicated to God.

Brethren have stressed obedience to the teachings of
Jesus and conformity to the life of early Christian communities.
On the basis of the New Testament, Brethren have practiced
believers' baptism by trine immersion, the washing of feet at
the Lord's Supper, the holy kiss, the anointing of the sick, rec-

onciliation of conflict according to Matthew 18, simplicity of life, and nonresistance.[5] This emphasis has led Brethren, particularly in the twentieth century, into service, peacemaking and ecumenical engagement beyond the boundaries of the community.[6]

But Brethren have not found it easy to live with diversity among members of the community. During the early eighteenth century in Germany, their illegal status called forth a careful determination of who was with them and who would report them to the authorities. During the Revolutionary War, Brethren refused to fight and were thus thought to be traitors, i.e., Loyalists. Brethren were, therefore, shunned, fined, and imprisoned. During the Civil War, particularly in the South, Brethren were again cast out because of their refusal to bear arms.[7] Many Brethren, consequently, were convinced that obedience to the teachings of Jesus was possible only when protected by a separatism and homogeneity. Nonconformity in relation to the surrounding culture, therefore, has often been maintained at the cost of conformity in relation to members of the community.

I lived in Church of the Brethren communities until I arrived at Harvard Divinity School. By then, I had learned very well the lessons and the limits of my formative community. I knew how to pattern my behavior according to expectations and, nonetheless, to excel. In search of anonymity and abstraction from the calling as well as the constraint of my formative community, I came to Harvard.

Before graduate school, I was formed by and identified with groups and perspectives named heretical by orthodox Christianity. At Harvard Divinity School, I learned to think thoughts unfettered by my earliest bonds of unity. I was nurtured by and came to appreciate the richness of Christian and other religious traditions. For example, I learned to appreciate, although not necessarily agree with, theologians in the classical Christian tradition. I came to see from within communities and cultures that I had heretofore only observed. However, as my critical capacity was honed, I stepped outside the confines of any and all traditions. I was compelled by the logic more than the life of my critical thoughts. At the end of three years, I realized that I had once more learned to pattern my thoughts according to established expectations. Yet again,

I bought bonds of unity with those around me at the cost of conformity.[8]

In 1979-1980, I studied at the Graduate School of Ecumenical Studies, near Geneva, Switzerland. The Graduate School of Ecumenical Studies, housed in the Chateau de Bossey, is affiliated with the World Council of Churches and the University of Geneva. I also was staff consultant to The Community of Women and Men in the Church Study of the World Council of Churches Commission on Faith and Order. As a student and as staff consultant I met people who embodied commitments and communities that were strikingly different from those with which I had wrestled thus far.

This year was marked by my engagement with issues raised by feminist theologians and theorists. Although I had read feminist writings at Harvard, I had reflected on them with regard to the logic of their critique of traditional theology. At Bossey, I read feminist writings with a handful of women among a host of men. I reflected on them, in this context, with regard to how women and men could live together in the same community.

Most of the feminist theology and theory I read was written by women from North America and Europe.[9] As staff consultant to the Community of Women and Men in the Church Study, however, I learned that although Western women have taken the lead in articulating a feminist critique they are not the only ones raising the issues. The Community of Women and Men in the Church Study was sponsored by the World Council of Churches in response to a call from women in its member churches around the world.[10]

At the Fifth Assembly of the World Council of Churches, held in Nairobi, Kenya, in 1975, the delegates discussed a study document on "The Community of Women and Men in the Church."[11] This document was drafted by women who had participated in a consultation on "Sexism in the 1970s: Discrimination Against Women" sponsored by the World Council in 1974.[12] Delegates at Nairobi "recommended that the churches participate fully in the study on the Community of Women and Men in the Church, with consideration of issues of theology, Scripture, tradition, and ministry. We ask the churches to engage in serious theological reflection on these issues, especially in relation to the issue of the nature of the unity we seek."[13]

The Community Study was lodged in the Sub-unit on Faith and Order, in cooperation with the Sub-unit on Women in Church and Society. The work of the study was dispersed into various settings— local study groups, regional consultations, and specialized consultations. A study booklet was prepared by the staff in Geneva for local study groups to use. Approximately 150 groups sent reports back to Geneva. I read these reports during my tenure as staff consultant to the Community Study.

As I listened to the voices in the reports, I began to ask questions about my own theological training. I had learned to think logically and abstractly. This mode of theological thought now threatened to silence the variegated voices conveyed in the reports by requiring consistency and coherence regardless of context. Moreover, I began to ask questions about the notion of "women's experience" in Western feminist theology and theory. Feminists had initially criticized male-oriented thought by attempting to minimize differences between women and men and to maximize similarity among women. Western feminist theology and theory had not yet moved to an appreciation of the diversity of women's experiences relative to factors such as race, class, age, geography, culture, and religion.[14]

With my questions unanswered, I returned to Harvard to search for new ways of working theologically. I was still attracted to feminist theology and theory because of its appeal to "women's experience" as resource and norm, as well as its analysis of traditional theology. But the voices articulated in the local group reports of the Community Study resounded relentlessly. Finding no way to hear them speak, my work was at an impasse.

When I read the writings of Michel Foucault, French philosopher and social critic, a way out of this impasse was illumined.[15] Foucault's work was fired in the crucible of the upheavals surrounding the Paris revolt of 1968. Foucault witnessed what he referred to as the "amazing efficacy of discontinuous, particular and local criticism."[16]

Foucault clarified this sort of criticism in a lecture delivered on 7 January 1976. He spoke of two discourses, the antipsychiatric and the discourse attacking the penal system, to exemplify the efficacy of "discontinuous, particular and local criticism." According to Foucault, these discourses or groups of statements "whose validity is not dependent on the approval of the established regimes of thought" are efficacious insofar as their emergence is a disclosure of "the inhibiting effect of global *totalitarian theories*."[17]

The emergence of such "discontinuous, particular and local criticism" is, according to Foucault, "a return of knowledge" that has been subjugated.[18] For example, the words spoken by the patient on the couch not the psychiatrist in the armchair, or by the prisoner behind bars not the jailer with the keys, articulate knowledge pressed down or passed over by unifying theoretical discourse. The return of such knowledge is not only a disclosure of the tyranny of unifying discourse; it is an insurrection against it.

I first read Foucault as I was convalescing after a time in the hospital. I brought to my reading of Foucault my sense of being a patient and, at times, a prisoner in my bed. Foucault gave me ways of seeing and words for speaking about the upheavals that accompanied this "return of knowledge" in my own world, this insurrection against the world of my own creation.

As Foucault spoke about the "*insurrection of subjugated knowledges*," he distinguished two sorts. The first is "the historical contents that have been buried and disguised in a functionalist coherence or formal systemisation."[19] Effective criticism excavates these historical contents, which are most often conflicts and struggles covered over by a theoretical order. Foucault referred to the second sort of subjugated knowledge as "particular, local, regional knowledge." This knowledge has not been disguised but disqualified as inadequate or insufficient for the sophisticated task of the systematizer. Its highly differential character cannot be entertained within "the hierarchy of knowledges" and so "particular, local, regional knowledge" is excluded.[20]

Foucault's reference to the second sort of subjugated knowledge gave me a way to read and represent the local group reports of the Community of Women and Men in the Church Study. The voices inscribed in these reports articulate knowledge that is "particular, local, regional knowledge," much of which is "beneath the required level of cognition or scientificity" on the hierarchy of theological thought and all of which is "incapable of unanimity."[21] Foucault's reference to the first sort of subjugated knowledge enabled me to uncover the conflicts and struggles surrounding the participation of women in the World Council of Churches. Although women had raised their theological voices since the World Council's inception, women's voices were not recognized by Faith and Order until the Community Study was begun.

When these two sorts of subjugated knowledges come together, what Foucault has called a "genealogy" emerges. A "genealogy" is not "an opposition between the abstract unity of theory and the concrete multiplicity of facts." Nor is it "a disqualification of the speculative dimension which opposes to it . . . the rigour of well established knowledges." "What it really does," Foucault clarified, "is to entertain the claims to attention of local, discontinuous, disqualified, illegitimate knowledges against the claims of a unitary body of theory . . ."[22] The "insurrection of subjugated knowledges," therefore, is an uprising against "the effects of the centralising powers" of a discourse that is linked to an institution.[23]

I will thus present the Community of Women and Men in the Church Study as an "insurrection of subjugated knowledges" against the effects of the theological discourse on unity formulated by the Commission on Faith and Order.[24] I do so in order that all members of the churches, particularly women as well as women and men of variegated colors and cultures be represented in this discourse. I do so in order that each member and member church, particularly those who have differed from dominant ecclesial doctrines and orders, be respected in this discourse. In short, I write this dissertation so that as many members who have been excluded from this discourse on unity may now enter and engage in conversation, so that difference is celebated in newly-created bonds of unity.

Chapter one is an account of women's participation in the World Council of Churches from 1948 to 1975—from the First Assembly to the Fifth Assembly where The Community Study was recommended to member churches. I feature the ways in which women were engaged in theological reflection. Women were clear that their role in the churches and in the World Council was not merely a "woman's question," but called into question the very foundations of the church and of church unity. Women's voices, however, are not audible in the theological discussions of unity that took place during these years. This chapter thus retrieves the first sort of subjugated knowledge of which Foucault spoke. It represents historical contents present but passed over in official documents and records.

In chapter two, I present the Community of Women and Men in the Church Study as an event in World Council history. It is an event, singular and significant, insofar as women were invited to reflect on their role and image in relation to theological understandings of church unity. The chapter ends with the Sixth Assembly of the World Council in 1983. At that Assembly, women's voices were once again muffled in the context of theological discussion. The Community Study is thus presented as a welling up of variegated voices, beset behind and before by a discourse bent on rendering these voices inaudible.

This unifying discourse is then analyzed in the third chapter. I present a history of the dominant theological discourse on unity: the discourse of the Commission on Faith and Order. I do not present a comprehensive history of the Commission on Faith and Order. Rather, I focus on the Commission's thinking about diversity in relation to the unity of the church, and on the split between theological and so-called "non-theological" that informs its thinking about diversity and unity, particularly with regard to the implications for the image and role of women in the church. It is my conviction that whoever or whatever has differed from the marks of visible unity as defined by dominant ecclesial doctrines and orders has been considered accidental or condemned as divisive.

I analyze, i.e., break up, the dominant discourse so the subjugated knowledge inscribed in the local group reports of the Community Study may be visible. Each of these reports is unique and singular. Each is also written in response to the same study book. I read these reports as theological texts written by women and men in various cultural and church contexts. In drawing a portrait of these women and men, I highlight the differences in an attempt to hear and honor each and every voice. I do not draw conclusions, but seek to draw the reader into conversation with the experiences and knowledges inscribed in these reports.

I refer to this chapter as a portrait because I assume that these reports are not altogether representative of their originating contexts. I also assume that my presentation is not altogether reflective of what was written. The lens of my own language and life predispose the decisions and delineations I have made.

In the fifth and final chapter, I shall articulate my theological vision of unity. I confess temptations that threaten to undermine my way of working. I then call each and every one to conversation. Conversation, as I will use the word, is not a means by which one person conveys her or his terms to another. Rather *con-ver-satio* is a turning with until satisfied, a giving and receiving of my words and your words until we are speaking our words, i.e., until all are changed. I name three moments in the midst of conversation—recognition, relinquishment, reception. These moments, which may not be captured by chronology, constitute conversation as an occasion when bonds of unity that celebrate difference may be created.

The titles of the chapters are significant. The titles of chapters one and three are taken from an address given at the First World Conference on Faith and Order in Lausanne, Switzerland, in 1927. "If Christ is the Head," declared Professor Dr. Friedrich Siegmund-Schultze, "then the Body must be one."[25] Chapter two is situated in the middle of this imperative. The title of chapter two, "A Chance to Change," was the sub-theme of the International Consultation on the Community of Women and Men in the Church Study.[26] Thus the titles of chapters one, two, and three signal that the Community Study was beset behind and before by a unifying discourse.

Taken together, the titles of chapters four and five extend an invitation. The titles are taken from the biblical text that is oft-cited at the moment of remembrance in the eucharistic celebration. The words—"This is my body which is [broken] for you"—are words of invitation: all are called to partake of Christ's body broken for the re-membrance of common life.[27]

The structure of the chapters is liturgical. The first three chapters constitute a testament of temptation, i.e., a confession. They confess the temptation to exclude the voices of women and of others who are different from those setting the terms of dominant discourse. The first three chapters prepare for the embodiment of excluded voices in chapter four. And chapter four anticipates the words of invitation articulated in chapter five. The chapters move toward the entertainment of variegated voices in conversation.

As I write, I assume that in Western culture we have been incapable of thinking without sharp distinctions between self and other, subject and object, the same and not-the-same-as, and without assigning one of the terms a positive value and the other a negative. This mode of thought has been particularly painful for women and others who have been objectified and identified as not-the-same-as those who have determined definitions and domains. I assume that the dominant order of things will not be subverted simply by the inclusion of women and others into now existing definitions and domains. As I write, I seek a way beyond the boundaries of the Same/Other, Subject/Object dichotomies diagnosed by Simone de Beauvoir more than thirty years ago.[28] I seek a way to live as well as to think that recognizes and receives differences for the sake of life together.

This dissertation is my contribution to the contemporary theological task. "The theology of any period" is called to hear "not only . . . the voices of the classical past, but . . . all the voices of the past" and to engage these voices in conversation with present voices.[29] I work toward theological conversation which engages all who reflect theologically, whether their education was earned in the academy or in living faith communities. I write, therefore, not to but "beyond the ending."[30]

Notes

/1/ H. Richard Niebuhr, *The Meaning of Revelation* (New York: Macmillan Co., 1941), p. 83.

/2/ Virginia Woolf, *Three Guineas* (Harmondsworth, Middlesex, England: Penguin Books, 1977), p. 164 [Originally published in London, 1938].

/3/ The degree of Brethren indebtedness to sixteenth century Anabaptism and to eighteenth century Radical German Pietism, respectively, is debated. Anabaptists were at least the antecedents of the Radical Pietists who directly influenced the early Brethren. And Anabaptists and Radical Pietists held a common understanding of the church, i.e., as a visible, disciplined local community of baptized believers maintained in nonconformity to the world. See Donald F. Durnbaugh, *European Origins of the Brethren: A Source Book on the Beginnings of the Church of the Brethren in the Early Eighteenth Century* (Elgin, Illinois: Brethren Press, 1958); *The Believers' Church: The History and Character of Radical Protestantism* (New York: Macmillan Co., 1968); Franklin H. Littell, *The Anabaptist View of the Church*, 2nd ed., rev. and enl. (Boston: Starr King Press, 1958).

/4/ "*Gemeinde, Gemeinschaft* are two German words that have a root meaning 'common,' just as the English word *community* is based upon the word *common*." See *Brethren Encyclopedia*, s.v. "*Gemeinde, Gemeinschaft*," by Vernard M. Eller (Philadelphia, Pennsylvania; Oak Brook, Illinois: Brethren Encyclopedia, 1983).

/5/ See Durnbaugh, *European Origins of the Brethren*, pp. 321-418; *The Brethren in Colonial America: A Source Book on the Transplantation and Development of the Church of the Brethren in the Eighteenth Century* (Elgin, Illinois: Brethren Press, 1967), pp. 425-596; Roger E. Sappington, *The Brethren in the New Nation: A Source Book in the Development of the Church of the Brethren, 1785-1865* (Elgin, Illinois: Brethren Press, 1976), pp. 123-251; Vernard M. Eller, "Beliefs," in *The Church of the Brethren Past and Present*, ed. Donald F. Durnbaugh (Elgin, Illinois: Brethren Press, 1970), pp. 42-45.

/6/ See Sappington, *Brethren Social Policy, 1908-1958* (Elgin, Illinois: Brethren Press, 1961).

/7/ See Rufus D. Bowman, *The Church of the Brethren and War, 1708-1941* (Elgin, Illinois: Brethren Publishing House, 1944); Durnbaugh, *The Brethren in Colonial America*, pp. 342-423; Sappington, *The Brethren in the New Nation*, pp. 329-404.

/8/ Robert N. Bellah, Richard Madsen, William M. Sullivan, Ann Swidler, and Steven M. Tipton speak about the "unencumbered" self "who must leave home and church in order to succeed in an impersonal world of rationality and competition" (*Habits of the Heart: Individualism and Commitment in American Life* [Berkeley: University of California Press, 1985], pp. 152-153). But, as Tocqueville observed and Bellah et al. recall, "when one can no longer rely on tradition or authority, one inevitably looks to others for confirmation of one's judgment. Refusal to accept established opinion and anxious conformity to the opinions of one's peers turn out to be two sides of the same coin" (Ibid., p. 146).

/9/ See for example Mary Daly, *Beyond God the Father: Toward a Philosophy of Women's Liberation* (Boston: Beacon Press, 1973); *Gyn/Ecology: The MetaEthics of Radical Feminism* (Boston: Beacon Press, 1978); Jean Baker Miller, *Toward a New Psychology of Women* (Boston: Beacon Press, 1976); Juliet Mitchell, *Psychoanalysis and Feminism* (New York: Pantheon Books, 1974); Elisabeth Moltmann-Wendel, *Liberty, Equality, Sisterhood*, trans. Ruth C. Gritsch (Philadelphia: Fortress Press, 1978) [Originally published under the title *Freiheit, Gleichheit, Schwesterlichkeit*, Munich, 1977]; Rosemary R. Reuther, ed., *Religion and Sexism: Images of Woman in the Jewish and Christian Traditions* (New York: Simon and Schuster, 1974); *New*

Woman/New Earth: Sexist Ideologies and Human Liberation (New York: Seabury Press, A Crossroad Book, 1975); Shelia Rowbotham, *Woman's Consciousness, Man's World* (London: Penguin Books, 1973); Letty M. Russell, *Human Liberation in Feminist Perspective--A Theology* (Philadelphia: Westminster Press, 1974); *The Future of Partnership* (Philadelphia: Westminster Press, 1979); Gerta Scharffenorth and Klaus Thraede, *"Freunde in Christus werden . . .": Die Beziehung von Mann und Frau als Frage an Theologie und Kirche* (Gelnhausen, Berlin: Burckhardthaus Verlag; Stein/Mfr.: Laetare-Verlag, 1977).

/10/ The World Council of Churches was constituted at its first Assembly in 1948. The seeds of the World Council had been sown at the World Missionary Conference in 1910. Two other ecumenical movements of the early twentieth century converged in the World Council of Churches, i.e., the Universal Christian Council on Life and Work, which was committed to united practical action in response to social, economic, and political problems, and the World Conference on Faith and Order, which discussed issues of doctrine and church order that have divided churches. See William Adams Brown, *Toward a United Church: Three Decades of Ecumenical Christianity* (New York: Charles Schribner's Sons, 1946), pp. 53-153. See also Barry Till, *The Churches Search for Unity* (Harmondsworth, Middlesex, England: Penguin Books, 1972).

The concerns of these originating movements can be seen in the present structure of the World Council of Churches. There are three Programme Units: Faith and Witness; Justice and Peace; Education and Renewal. The work of each Programme Unit is specified by their various sub-units. The Programme Unit on Faith and Witness has sub-units on World Mission and Evangelism, Dialogue with People of Other Living Faiths and Ideologies, Faith and Order, and Church and Society. The Programme Unit on Justice and Service has sub-units on Inter-Church Aid, Refugee and World Service, the Churches' Participation in Development, Churches and International Affairs, Programme to Combat Racism, and the Christian Medical Commission. The Programme Unit on Education and Renewal has sub-units on Theological Education, Renewal and Congregational Life, Women in Church and Society, and Youth. Staff for each of these units and sub-units is headquartered at the Ecumenical Centre in Geneva, Switzerland. The General Secretariat co-ordinates the work of the Programme Units and relates directly to the Communications Department, the Finance Department, the Library, the Ecumenical Institute at Chateau de Bossey, and the New York Office of the World Council of Churches.

The Programme Units carry out guidelines given by member churches of the World Council at an Assembly, a gathering of delegates appointed by over three hundred member churches in approximately 108 countries. An Assembly is held every seven years and is the governing body of the World Council. Each Assembly elects a Central Committee to be the interim governing body. The Central Committee, constituted of 150 members, meets annually and reports to the Assembly. See *What in the World is the World Council of Churches?*, 2nd ed., rev. (Geneva: World Council of Churches, 1983).

/11/   *The Community of Women and Men in the Church: A Proposal for Study Groups* (Geneva: World Council of Churches, 1975).

/12/   See *Sexism in the 1970s: Discrimination Against Women. A Report of a World Council of Churches Consultation, West Berlin, 1974* (Geneva: World Council of Churches, 1974).

/13/   *Breaking Barriers, Nairobi 1975: The Official Report of the Fifth Assembly of the World Council of Churches, Nairobi, 23 November-10 December, 1975*, ed. David M. Paton (London: S.P.C.K.; Grand Rapids: Wm. B. Eerdmans for the World Council of Churches, 1976), p. 69.

/14/   For an account of contemporary feminist thought that addresses the concern for an appreciation of difference see Hester Eisenstein, *Contemporary Feminist Thought* (Boston: G. K. Hall & Co., 1983).

/15/   I have been most influenced by: *Madness and Civilization: A History of Insanity in the Age of Reason*, trans. Richard Howard (New York: Vintage Books, 1973) [Originally published under the title *Histoire de la Folie*, Paris, 1961]; *The Archeology of Knowledge and The Discourse on Language*, trans. A. M. Sheridan Smith and Rupert Swyer (New York: Pantheon, 1972) [Originally published under the titles *L'Archeologie du savoir* and *L'ordre du discours*, Paris, 1969 and 1971, respectively]; *Language, Counter-Memory, Practice: Selected Essays and Interviews*, ed. Donald F. Bouchard, trans. Donald F. Bouchard and Sherry Simon (Ithaca: Cornell University Press, 1977); *Power/Knowledge: Selected Interviews and Other Writings, 1972-1977*, ed. Colin Gordon, trans. Colin Gordon, Leo Marshall, John Mepham, Kate S. Oper (New York: Pantheon Books, 1977); *Discipline and Punish: The Birth of the Prison*, trans. Alan Sheridan (New York: Vintage Books, 1979) [Originally published under the title *Surveiller et Punir: Naissance de la prison*, Paris, 1975]; *The History of Sexuality*, vol. I: *An Introduction*, trans. Robert Hurley (New York: Vintage Books, 1980) [Originally published under the title *La Volonte de savoir*, Paris, 1976]; *The Foucault Reader*, ed. Paul Rabinow (New York: Pantheon Books, 1984). See also Hubert L. Dreyfus and Paul Rabinow, *Michel Foucault: Beyond Structuralism and Hermeneutics*, 2nd ed. (Chicago: University of Chicago Press, 1983).

/16/   Foucault, *Power/Knowledge*, p. 80.

/17/   Ibid., p. 80. Emphasis his.

/18/   Ibid., p. 81.

/19/   Ibid. Emphasis his.

/20/   Ibid., p. 82.

/21/   Ibid.

/22/   Ibid., p. 83.

/23/   Ibid., p. 84. I draw on Foucault, as do most interpreters, in order to criticize the effects of a dominant and unifying discourse. However, in chapters four and five, I attempt to draw out the creative consequences of this critique.

/24/ I also present the Community of Women and Men in the Church Study as an "insurrection" against the unifying discourse of much twentieth-century theology, including much North American feminist theology. Cf. n. 14, pp. 78-79; n. 4, p.196; n. 8, p. 200 below.

/25/ *Faith and Order: Proceedings of the World Conference, Lausanne, August 3-21, 1927*, ed. H.N. Bate (New York: George H. Doran Co., 1927), p. 477.

/26/ See *The Community of Women and Men in the Church: The Sheffield Report*, ed. Constance F. Parvey (Geneva: World Council of Churches, 1983). See also Betty Thompson, *A Chance to Change: Women and Men in the Church* (Philadelphia: Fortress Press, 1982).

/27/ I Cor. 11:24 (RSV).

/28/ Simone de Beauvoir, *The Second Sex*, trans. and ed. H. M. Parshley (New York: Alfred A. Knopf, 1953) [Originally published in two volumes under the title *Le Deuxieme Sexe: I.* and *Les Faits et les Mythes: II. L'Experience Vecue*, Paris, 1949].

/29/ Karl Barth, *Protestant Theology in the Nineteenth Century: Its Background and History* (Valley Forge, Pennsylvania: Judson Press, 1973), p. 17 [Originally published under the title *Die protestantische Theologie im 19. Jahrhundert* in 1956].

/30/ I draw the phrase "writing beyond the ending" from Rachel Blau DuPlessis. DuPlessis takes "ending" as "a metaphor for conventional narrative, for a regimen of resolutions, and for the social, sexual, and ideological affirmations these make." She states: "Writing beyond the ending means the transgressive invention of narrative strategies, strategies that express critical dissent from dominant narrative. . . . Writing beyond the ending, 'not repeating your words and following your methods but . . . finding new words and creating new methods,' produces a narrative that denies or reconstructs seductive patterns . . . that are culturally mandated, internally policed, hegemonically poised" (*Writing beyond the Ending: Narrative Strategies of Twentieth-Century Women Writers* [Bloomington: Indiana University Press, 1985], pp. 21, 5). Cf. n. 6, p. 198 below.

CHAPTER I

"IF CHRIST IS THE HEAD": WOMEN IN THE WORLD COUNCIL OF CHURCHES

An at once sober and celebrative mood pervaded the First Assembly of the World Council of Churches. The year was 1948. Clouds of war still hovered over a devastated European landscape and cast shadows across the congregation in Amsterdam. East-West tension was palpable. John Foster Dulles, an American statesman, criticized Soviet Communism for its rejection of moral law and its denial of human rights, emphasizing the difference between Soviet and Christian presuppositions.[1] Josef L. Hromadka, member of the John Hus Theological Faculty at the Charles University in Prague, indicted the moral bankruptcy of the West, emphasizing the difference between the Soviet system and communism that "reflects . . . the Christian longing for the fellowship of full and responsible love."[2] Thus, midst fields of battle left barren, conflict now flared in the halls of conference.

Yet light was heralded on the horizon. The long process of the Council's formation had come to fruition. Delegates of 147 churches, representing forty-four countries, had come forth from war-reinforced isolation to confess their unity in Christ and to covenant with one another in the constitution of the World Council of Churches. Acknowledging the differences that had long divided them, they declared: "We intend to stay together."[3]

These words, which have resounded at ecumenical gatherings throughout the last thirty-five years, were written on behalf of the Assembly by a woman, Kathleen Bliss. Bliss had been a leader in the Student Christian Movement at Cambridge University, where she studied theology. She then served with her husband as a educator in India. Upon her return to England, Bliss, along with J.H. Oldham, edited a journal, *The Christian Newsletter*.[4] Wanting to convey the intent of the newly-formed Council to member churches, Assembly leaders asked Bliss to draft a message to be sent around the world. This powerful declaration of commitment appears in the opening paragraph of that message.

Bliss was not the only woman whose voice was heard at the Amsterdam Assembly. Sarah Chakko, Rena Karefa-Smart, Mildred McAfee Horton, and Anna Canada Swain, from India, Sierra Leone, and the United States, respectively, spoke from the platform of the Main Hall to the delegate body.[5] Other women spoke as well. One chronicler of the Amsterdam event remarked that some of the Assembly's most impressive speeches were made by women.[6]

Women began to contribute to the work of the World Council of Churches before the First Assembly. In response to their efforts, the image and place of women in the church was discussed at Amsterdam. The Assembly affirmed: "The Church as the Body of Christ consists of men and women, created, as responsible persons, together to glorify God and to do His will." The Assembly then acknowledged:

> This truth, accepted in theory, is too often ignored in practice. In many countries and churches it is evident that the full co-operation of men and women in the service of Christ through the Church has not been achieved. Yet the Church as a whole, particularly at the present time of change and tension, needs the contribution of all its members in order to fulfill its task.[7]

From the First Assembly came a call for the appointment of a World Council of Churches Commission to coordinate studies and activities related to women in the churches.

It is significant that the call for this commission was grounded theologically. Men and women were named as constituent members of "the Church as the Body of Christ," created together to be responsible to God. Indeed, "the full co-operation of men and women in the service of Christ" was affirmed as integral to church unity.[8]

During the years after the First Assembly, however, the theological ground for the consideration of women's role and image in the churches receded. The road leading beyond ecclesial divisions was charted in terms set by classical controversies defined by men of the classical traditions. Mutual recognition of baptism, eucharist, and ministry, and a common confession of faith, were identified as the marks of church unity. The role and image of women in the churches was regarded as one so-called "non-theological" problem among others to which the World Council of Churches would give attention.[9]

Despite this dominant perspective, women who were involved in the World Council of Churches during these years were clear that the question of their role and image in the churches was neither a "non-theological" problem nor a "woman's question" but a question integral to theological understandings of church unity.[10] In this chapter, I will recount the activities and thoughts of these women, thereby conjuring memories of conflict. To remember these activities and thoughts is thus an act of criticism: an act which widens cracks in the dominant perspective by entertaining other points of view.

Refugees or Partners?

Soon after the end of World War II, Twila McCrea Cavert, an American laywoman who was on the National Board of the YWCA and on the Executive Committee of the United Council of Church Women,[11] formulated a questionnaire on "The Life and Work of Women in the Church." Cavert, whose husband was General Secretary of the Federal Council of Churches in the United States and a leader in the formation of the World Council of Churches, had been impressed by information the World YWCA had gathered on the place of women in the church. She subsequently challenged W. A. Visser't Hooft, General Secretary of the World Council of Churches, to make use of the information as he planned the program of the World Council. Visser't Hooft responded with a challenge to Cavert: to formulate her own questionnaire.

Responses to the questionnaire were sent back to Geneva from approximately fifty-eight countries.[12] It was later reported: "Of all the enquiries sent by the World Council of Churches before the Amsterdam Assembly this questionnaire evoked by far the greatest number of serious, thoughtful and varied answers."[13] Because the responses to the questionnaire were so impressive, the French Reformed Church requested that the question of women's place in the church be placed on the Amsterdam agenda as one of the "Concerns of the Churches" to which a working committee at the Assembly would give its attention.[14]

In order to prepare the delegates who would discuss the question in Amsterdam, an Interim Report on the responses to the questionnaire was drafted. A portrait of the diversity of the women who wrote was drawn in the Introduction to the Report:

> Altogether many thousands of women, those living in the African bush, those who have emerged from the concentration camps of Germany, those who were friends of Burmese and Russian Orthodox, women martyrs for Christ's sake during the war, others who risked their lives and freedom for their Christian witness in Japan and the Philippines, some who live in the trailers. . . . these and countless others have in this study revealed their zeal, their activities, their concern for the Church and its witness, and an intention to listen for the voice of the Spirit of God guiding the steps of Christian womanhood in this new, dangerous and— potentially . . . glorious age.[15]

Many personal stories, letters, and diaries accompanied the responses to the questionnaire.

A new age had dawned for women with the outbreak of World War II. Consequent social upheaval shattered the boundaries delineating traditional spheres and made more diverse roles available to women.[16] Many of the women who were involved in the ecumenical movement after the war had been well trained by rescue and relief work during the war.[17]

Immediately following the proclamation of peace, these women began to fear that their energies, released and regenerated by the exigencies of a crisis situation, were threatened with confinement once again.[18] Madeleine Barot, for example, who had spirited Jewish and other political refugees across the border to Switzerland, recalled:

> Women, who during the war, had dealt with enormous responsibilities, and about whom there had been no question whatever of their being quite capable of carrying

out work as dangerous as any man's, suddenly found themselves pushed back into a definitely subordinated position in relation to men.[19]

Barot was convinced "that *the* struggle of the hour after the war was precisely the question of the future for women." In Barot's words, women had become another sort of "refugee."[20]

The women who attended the World Council of Churches Assembly in Amsterdam were well prepared not only by their work during the war. Many brought with them insights and convictions informed by years of theological reflection on the status of women. Henriette Visser't Hooft, for example, whose husband, W. A. Visser't Hooft, was the first General Secretary of the World Council of Churches, was convinced that economic and political discrimination against women was perpetuated by theological understandings. She corresponded with Karl Barth, challenging his interpretation of passages in Paul's epistles that prescribe the subordination of women to men.[21]

Henriette Visser't Hooft was particularly troubled by I Corinthians 11:5-9. In 1934, she wrote Barth to ask what Paul meant when he said: "For man was not created for woman, but woman for man" (I Cor. 11:8), especially in light of his subsequent statement about the interdependence of men and women. "It seems," she wrote, " . . . as if the first phrase were a law that is still valid. . . . Why ought we . . . let this law be valid and not conform ourselves to the second phrase, that more certainly has to do with God's grace?" She continued:

> . . . has not Christ made us free? Is not each human being, man or woman, directly related to God now? . . . That the woman was not created for God simply means: that Christ has nothing to say to her. It seems to me too cheap simply to say here that Paul was stuck in the prejudices of *his* time, the usual argument. Even then, it would be shocking that a person like Paul could so wantonly damn half the human race.[22]

In conclusion she stated: "Believe me, Professor, my inquiry . . . is not a pastime, rather it is forced by an inner necessity."[23]

Barth responded to her query with a lengthy letter in which he upheld Paul's hierarchical order of things: God, Christ, man, woman, the higher on the ladder being the head of the one lower down.[24] Not convinced by this response that Barth had understood her, Henriette Visser't Hooft wrote a second letter to him.

In this letter, Henriette Visser't Hooft made it clear that she did not agree with Barth's analogy of the headship of Christ over man with the headship of man over woman. The key question for women who have become conscious of their subordination, wrote Visser't Hooft, is how to make "their head" aware of the fact that he has "a body and a heart in the body" that limit the dominion of the brain.[25] At the end of the letter, Henriette Visser't Hooft admonished Barth:

> Do not think that I am a man-hater or that my husband is a terrible tyrant—the contrary is true. I hope that you have understood: I am only against decapitation and suicide.[26]

Barth did not answer this letter.

Barth attended the Assembly in Amsterdam. He delivered one of two addresses on its main theme, "Man's Disorder and God's Design."[27] Barth was also a member of the committee studying "The Life and Work of Women in the Church." W. A. Visser't Hooft later recalled the work of the committee:

> Most of the members of the committee were women in leading positions in Christian organizations or in the world of education. They had hoped that the Assembly . . . would speak out against male domination in church life. What they heard from Barth seemed to them simply a new version of the old story . . . . it appeared that Barth was merely advocating submission by women, in a slightly new form.[28]

Visser't Hooft defended Barth, heralding him as "first and foremost a pioneer in considering positively true dialogical relations between men and women." However, Visser't Hooft also acknowledged: "His [Barth's] reaction unfortunately was to make fun of those women who seemed to him to 'rush towards equality'."[29]

During the Assembly, a panel of those women debated with Barth at a press conference. Sarah Chakko, a member of the Syrian Orthodox Church of Malabar and Principal of Isabella Thoburn College, was one of these women.[30] The "Assembly News," published daily for all in attendance at Amsterdam, reported the event:

> Professor Barth believes with the Bible that there is equal-
> ity between men and women, but each has a different
> function in society . . . . He is not reconciled to the idea of
> a woman presiding at Holy Communion. A woman pre-
> siding at Communion would destroy the family idea of the
> meal. But to the delight of listening press-men, Miss Sa-
> rah Chakko began to instruct Dr. Barth in the ways of the
> East. Who cooks the meal and serves the family? The
> woman.[31]

On another occasion during the Assembly, several women invited Barth to meet with them and discuss this matter
at greater length. Years afterward, W. A. Visser't Hooft recalled Barth's response to this encounter:

> Later he confided to me that never in his life had he been
> so terrified as at that meeting with a group of women who
> he felt were ready to 'extort the last ounce of flesh from
> me.' He was *especially* scared of Sarah Chakko. . . . she
> really challenged him. She contended with the others
> that, having affirmed the woman and given such a beauti-
> ful exegesis of her place in the Genesis account of Crea-
> tion, he . . . 'pulled the rug out from underneath' when he
> turned to the Pauline teachings on the place of women.[32]

This formidable debater of Barth was appointed Executive
Secretary of the World Council of Churches Commission on
the Life and Work of Women in the Church at its first meeting
in 1950.[33]

Taking a sabbatical leave from her duties as Principal of
Isabella Thoburn College, Chakko traveled widely in Europe
and North America during the next year. Chakko was struck
by the contrast between the status of women in Western countries and that of women in India:

> One is very much intrigued by the concept of 'wo-
> man' underlying Church and public life in Europe. In a
> country like Switzerland, which claims to be the oldest de-
> mocracy in existence today, women are still unen-
> franchised. Even in countries where women have
> political rights they are not found in any significant num-
> bers in places of trust and responsibility. In some
> Churches where women were ordained to the ministry

during the war and did serve their congregations effectively, a reaction seems to have set in and women ministers are asked to confine their service to women and
children. Socially, while they are cherished and protected, they are often not treated as intelligent responsible persons. All this is very puzzling to one who has come
from a land where the Christian conception of womanhood has served as a dynamic in social and public life.
The Church in many so called 'mission lands' pioneered in
women's education, gave them their rightful place in society and offered them opportunities of service. Many of
the European missionary women workers find in these
lands greater opportunities for creative service than in
their own home countries.[34]

In light of these observations, Chakko asked: "Is the European
attitude on the status of women truly Christian? If not, when
and why did it stop moving in the right direction? Are we in
Asiatic countries on the wrong track?"[35]

When Sarah Chakko was appointed Executive Secretary,
Kathleen Bliss was asked to chair the Commission on the Life
and Work of Women in the Church. Chakko and Bliss were
determined that the commission should not be identified as "a
woman's commission." They were convinced that the congregation of women into groups of their own was an act of segre-
gation that perpetuated, rather than ameliorated, the problem
of women's subordinate status in relation to men. In the words
of Chakko, women's organizations, particularly those which
had proliferated in American churches since the late nineteenth-century, were "shadow churches."[36] Bliss agreed that,
although these organizations could function as "important
pressure groups," they did not facilitate the full participation
of women in the life of the churches. She commented:

"... in a place like Central Committee meetings, these ...
women said nothing. They sat scribbling, observing but
not participating, and simply waiting to take it to their
women's groups back home. These were merely token
women then, which I was never prepared to be."[37]

Thus, countering contemporary currents, the women who led
the commission during its formative years were committed to
enabling women to be partners with men at every level of
church life.

Bliss articulated her perspective in her book, *The Service and Status of Women in the Churches*. Drawing on the responses to the pre-Amsterdam questionnaire, Bliss documented the diverse ways in which women have served the churches: in voluntary associations, in parishes and on the mission fields, as teachers, nurses, deaconesses, and nuns, and occasionally as administrators and ordained pastors. Yet Bliss was clear:

> To say that women's powers . . . have found an outlet in an immense variety of ways is not the same thing as saying that the Church has made use of even a tithe of the vast reserve of talent and devotion which lay to hand in the persons of its women members. Often a woman's zeal has been damped down and discouraged by the Church, her gifts of mind and spirit refused, her devotion and labour frittered away on trifles.[38]

Bliss was also clear that the "nearer a service of women approaches to the ministerial function, the more on edge the Churches are about it."[39]

Accordingly, women's service has most often been for and with women. Bliss was convinced that this confinement of the work of women to the sphere of women is divisive to the life of the church. "Women," she stated, "constantly feel that in spite of what is said in preaching the men are really 'the Church' and their own participation is derivative from and dependent on, that of men."[40] Correlatively, women's organizations "*become* 'the Church' " for women. "Thus," according to Bliss, "there can arise in practice, although the theory of it is denied, a church within a church, or a church alongside a church."[41] Bliss concluded: "This is not a women's question, it is a Church question."[42]

While Bliss focused on women's work within the churches, she also took account of the social context of the churches. She accented the voices of women lamenting the way in which churches lag behind societies with regard to a wider range of roles for women. Bliss cited a report in which the contrast was sharply stated:

> Ministers and congregations are hidebound by tradition. Leading circles in the Church are disposed to be conservative, their view of society is *patriarchal* and their in-

clination towards the old ways affects their view of the
place of women in society and therefore in the
Church. . . . The patriarchal conception of the relation of
men and women is even stronger in parsonages than it is
among people generally.[43]

Bliss hastened to add that not all the reports were so strong.
But, she continued: ". . . in nearly every Church it remains
true that there is an underlying fear of the modern woman, of
her independence of character, her acceptance of herself as a
person in herself and not merely for man."[44]

Bliss reflected on the churches' slowness to respond to social change with reference to "the Christian ideal of marriage
as the life-long union of one man with one woman."[45] And,
she remarked, the growing economic independence of women
is often linked to rising divorce rates. Bliss did not criticize
"the Christian ideal of marriage" as such. She made it clear,
however, that until churches recognize women as workers
outside as well as within the home, churches will continue to
regard women as secondary beings in relation to men.[46]

In an address delivered to a conference on "Men and Women in Church and Society," held at St. Andrews, Scotland, in
1952, Sarah Chakko also reflected on the status of women relative to economic factors. She began by contrasting the active
role of women in agricultural societies with the passive posture
to which women were relegated with the rise of industry in
the West. As the sphere of economic activity shifted from
home to the factory outside the home, stated Chakko, woman
became "a decorative adjunct" to men's work.[47]

Chakko sketched three responses women can make to
their subordinate status in the society and the church. Women
can accept their subordination, supporting their husbands and
nurturing their children in the home. Women can imitate
men and endeavor to establish themselves as men's equals. Or
women can work as partners with men. From Chakko's point
of view, if women choose either subordination or imitation,
their contribution would be made on the terms and in the in-
stitutions established by men. Only partnership can enable
women to contribute with regard to their own unique and different capacities.[48]

Despite the conviction of Bliss and Chakko that the question of women's participation in the churches was not "a wo-

men's question" but "a Church question," that is, addressed to
men as well as women, the Commission on the Life and Work
of Women in the Church was never fully integrated into the
work of the World Council. Of the six men who were named
as members of the commission, only two attended the initial
meeting. Noting the absence of the men, Sarah Chakko, in her
report to the World Council of Churches Central Committee
meeting in 1950, declared: "The tendency of member
Churches has been to appoint women . . . But we shall be de-
feating our purpose if we have only the thinking of women and
Women's organizations."[49]

In 1953, the Commission on the Life and Work of Women in the Church was renamed the Department on the Co-
operation of Men and Women in Church and Society, in order
"to remove the impression that it [was] the 'Women's Department' of the World Council of Churches."[50] The steering committee was constituted by men and women and was jointly
chaired by a woman and a man.

The designation of this new name was also a request for a
new status. The First Assembly had recommended that a commission be appointed to continue the inquiry into the life and
work of women that had already been initiated. The Second
Assembly was being asked to create a department more fully
integrated into the structure and thus the scope of World
Council work.[51]

The Second Assembly of the World Council of Churches
met in Evanston, Illinois, during the summer of 1954. Political
differences, which had been articulated at Amsterdam, had deteriorated into sharp divisions during the years since the Assembly. The Cold War was so bitter that delegates to the
Second Assembly from Eastern European countries were denied entrance to the United States until John Fostor Dulles,
now United States Secretary of State, intervened on their
behalf.

Theological debate, focused on the Assembly theme,
"Jesus Christ—the Hope of the World," had also deteriorated
into sharp divisions. Europeans held to an eschatological view
of Christian hope, while North Americans hoped for change in
this world. Even though the Message of the Assembly to the
member churches proclaimed that Christ's promises enable
Christians to "face the powers of evil and the threat of death

with a good courage," the delegates also acknowledged: "We are not agreed on the relationship between the Christian's hope here and now, and . . . ultimate hope."[52]

The Second Assembly approved the new name and status recommended by the Commission on the Life and Work of Women in the Church. The Department on the Co-operation of Men and Women in the Church was charged "to help the churches to work towards such co-operation between men and women as may enable them both to make their full contribution to church and society."[53]

The Assembly's welcome to the newly-created department was, however, not hearty. Even before the Assembly, in the official report of the activities of the World Council since Amsterdam, it was remarked:

> It is difficult to say whether this re-examination . . . of the situation of women in the Church will procure for them wider openings in the service of the churches, or whether, on the contrary, it will result in a renewed and stricter subordination of woman's ministry to that of man's.[54]

At the Assembly, this statement seemed to have been a portent.

Madeleine Barot, who had been the Executive Secretary of the Commission on the Life and Work of Women since 1953, was to report on the newly-created department's program at the Second Assembly. Barot had been scheduled to speak during an evening session that was tightly-packed. The heat was oppressive. In the official report of the Assembly it was noted that even "the most sober and formal members in the Assembly" removed their coats.[55]

During the session, a message from the Oecumenical Patriarch of the Orthodox Church was received. Reports of the Assembly Credentials Committee and Nominations Committee followed and were followed by more reports: reports of the World Council Ecumenical Institute and of the World Council Study Department by Henrik Kramer, Henry P. van Dusen and Nils Ehrenstrom. W. A. Visser't Hooft then announced that Madeleine Barot had proposed that the Assembly "no longer be exposed to the excessive heat of this night." According to the official report, "the large audience breathed a sigh of gratitude."[56]

Madeleine Barot had acceded to Visser't Hooft's plea for postponement. She did not know, until later, that Greyhound busloads of American churchwomen had come on that evening to hear her speak. When Barot finally addressed the Assembly, she declared:

> As long ago as the 1850s, Florence Nightingale said: 'I offered the Church my heart, my mind and all my life, but it sent me to do crochet-work in my grandmother's parlor.' In many different forms, this is the response which the women of our day still receive to their offers of service in the Church.[57]

Barot later commented that this was not an isolated incident. The attitude, she continued, was often the same: "Oh, it's only the women. They can wait ... until after the more interesting and important issues are dealt with."[58]

After the Second Assembly, the Department on the Cooperation of Men and Women in the Church sponsored a series of consultations. Participants studied biblical and theological issues related to the co-operation of men and women, as well as psychological and technological obstacles to the co-operation of women and men in modern industrial societies.[59] Participants focused on the failure of the churches to witness to the liberating message of the Gospel in their own life and work, rather than on the ambiguity of Christian scripture and tradition with regard to roles appropriate for women and men.

Madeleine Barot traveled widely during these years. A memorandum drafted by the department to the 1959 World Council of Churches Central Committee bears witness to her conversations in locales as diverse as Madagascar, India, Greece, Argentina, Morocco, and Indonesia:

> We do not expect that the Western expressions of the right status of women, or of just and mutual relations of men and women, will be those found most expedient or relevant to other areas of rapid social change. Our understanding of the right ordering of society will reflect local and historical circumstances and there can be no thought of imposing cultural patterns externally or of requiring a uniformity of behavior.[60]

This appreciation of different patterns of cooperation in different contexts was grounded in a theological affirmation: "Our

common obedience before God is consistent with a plurality of
expressions of that obedience, guided by the spirit of the love
of Christ."[61]

Barot also cultivated working relationships with the UN
Commission on the Status of Women, the Department of Adult
Education for Women of the UNESCO, and the International
Labor Organization. Reporting on the contribution of the De-
partment on the Co-operation of Men and Women in Church
and Society to these organizations, Barot remarked:

> The philosophy of the Department, and indeed its
> very name, intrigues everybody with whom we work.
> The WCC is the only organization, as far as I know, which
> stresses the idea of *cooperation*. All other organizations
> have either a department concerned with women's ques-
> tions or a group of women so as to segregate them, or
> have totally integrated women by trying to have at least
> one woman on the executive staff whose duties could just
> as well be entrusted to a man.[62]

Barot was often asked whether the Department's accent on co-
operation was a feminist affirmation or assent to the idea of the
subordination of women to men. Both sides, said Barot, were
baffled.

Barot articulated her own perspective in an article, "Considerations on the Need for a Theology of the Place of Women
in the Church." Citing the work of Karl Barth and Emil Brunner, she declared: "Anything which tends to deny or to belittle
the difference between the sexes is an attack on God's will for
His creation."[63] "However," she hastened to add, "it is not
enough merely to accept the differences between the sexes
and to be a real man *or* a real woman . . . We have all to be
both men and women."[64] Thus Barot shattered a stereotypic
identity for women and for men as she declared the differences between the sexes. Stereotypic identity was the foundation for a hierarchical ordering of men over women. Respect
for differences, among as well as between women and men,
was the basis for cooperation.

Her respect for the differences between women and
men, as well as her accent on cooperation, distinguished Barot
from feminists of her day. She agreed with the perception that
women's participation in church and society had been limited

because they were different from men. But Barot was convinced that the women would become partners with men, not as their God-given gifts were forfeited by the claim that women were like and thus equal to men, but as their gifts were appreciated.

The same year Barot's article was published, the Department drafted a statement of its philosophy at a meeting in Davos, Switzerland. The so-called Davos Statement proclaims that Christianity has "something revolutionary" to say about men and women: "It is that men and women, created by God as two different sexes, with diversity of gifts, can have a new relationship to each other by having a living relationship with Jesus Christ."[65] Although the liberating changes taking place in women's roles are affirmed in the statement, the Department's work is distinguished from "a feminist battle for 'women's rights' or even for 'equal opportunities'."[66] The statement declares that women and men "are truly themselves as they continually respond to each other in partnership, a partnership of equal grace and equal responsibility."[67] For the Department, therefore, the crucial question was not the place of women alone, but the cooperation of women and men in church and society.

In the Davos Statement, the cooperation of women and men is not viewed as "a special or separate issue." Rather, cooperation is viewed as integral to the unity of the church: "To be true to its nature, the Church is obliged to be a living expression of this complementary and completing relationship between the sexes, since fulness and unity must be embodied in the Church."[68]

The concern for the unity of the church, stated at Davos, was matched by a call for renewal. In 1957, Walter Meulder, co-chair of the committee that supervised the work of the Department, stated:

> . . . it seems that more effort must be made to use creative imagination in setting new criteria of efficiency in order to be able to consider the possible contribution of women not only in relation to masculine patterns of work but in relation to a new set of values.[69]

Women, Meulder declared, "can bring a new dimension to the renewal of the Church."[70]

Just prior to the Third Assembly of the World Council, held in 1961, it became evident that the vigor of the Department testified to the irrepressible energy and ingenuity of Madeleine Barot, rather than to the institutional support of the World Council of Churches. The World Council was re-examining its structure and program, in order to incorporate the International Missionary Council at the Third Assembly. Some departments were being consolidated; some were being eliminated.

The Department on the Co-operation of Men and Women in Church and Society was in a particularly vulnerable position. Its diverse activities appeared to overlap with the work of other departments. The fact that only a few men had contributed to the Department's work called its ability to carry out its mandate into question. And, according to Barot, some women's organizations had not supported the Department because they "resented" the presence of men on committees and at events related to the Department.[71]

In 1960, the Committee on Program and Finance, charged with the task of proposing a new structure for the World Council, reported to the Central Committee meeting in St. Andrews, Scotland. Eugene Carson Blake, chairman of the Committee on Program and Finance, presented the report. Referring to the incorporation of the International Missionary Council, Blake declared: "Responsible growth implies choice between the many possible tasks . . . Responsible growth also presupposes pruning."[72] In the interest of such economy, Blake recommended that the Department on the Co-operation of Men and Women in Church and Society be reduced to the status of a secretariat. He further recommended that this secretariat, with one staff member, be subsumed in the Department on Work for the Laity.[73]

This recommendation was forecast by a statement made at the Second Assembly in Evanston. According to a committee that reviewed the work of the Department on the Co-operation of Men and Women in Church and Society during the Assembly, the Department was concerned with "certain quite special problems of dislocation and unbalance in the life of the Church, now seen as urgent in many areas, but which we dare to hope may prove to be transitional."[74] The Davos Statement, which the Department drafted the year after the Assembly, both confirmed and refuted this perspective on the Department's work:

> If the implications of the co-operation of men and women in all doctrinal and practical issues of the Church were generally recognized by the member churches and the World Council of Churches, there would be no further need for this Department. For the good of the Church and the effectiveness of its witness, . . . it is necessary, for the present, to continue to emphasize this special concern.[75]

The Department agreed, as has been noted, that the cooperation of women and men ought not remain "a special or separate issue." However, at Davos the Department made it clear that, until cooperation was embodied in the World Council and its member churches, its work was not done. At the meeting of the Central Committee in St. Andrews, representatives of the Department thus declared: "Although considerable progress has been made in the past five years, we believe that the time has not yet come to discontinue the Department."[76]

Eugene Carson Blake replied, commenting that the recommendation to change the Department's status was not "motivated by any underestimation of the importance of the work or of the faithfulness and competence of its working committee and staff-members but by the opinion that the work should be related to that of the Department of the Laity." Blake then reiterated "that there would be real value in permeating the work of the Laity Department by the concerns of the Department on the Co-operation of Men and Women."[77]

The Central Committee was more responsive to the Department's declaration than to Blake's reply. Moreover, the Central Committee was admonished that a change in the Department's status "might well be interpreted as an indication that the World Council of Churches had lost interest in the question of the service and status of women."[78] The Central Committee finally voted to continue the Department on the Co-operation of Men and Women, with two staff members rather than one.[79]

The Central Committee also voted to make an addition to the list of Departmental functions and to rename the Department in light of this addition. The Department on the Co-operation of Men and Women in Church, Family and Society was asked to "assist churches and Christian councils to discover and express the significance of the Christian faith in the realms of marriage and family life particularly in the context of other religions and secularism."[80] Issues related to marriage and family life were brought to the World Council by the International Missionary Council and were assigned to the Department by the Committee on Program and Finance, charged with the task of restructuring.

The Third Assembly of the World Council, which ratified the extended mandate of the Department on the Co-operation of Men and Women, met in New Delhi. This was the first Assembly of the World Council not held in the West. The New Delhi Assembly was thus not dominated by political and theological debate as at Amsterdam and Evanston. Indeed, East-West tensions were ameliorated as the Orthodox Churches of Eastern Europe were welcomed as members of the World Council. A number of so-called "younger churches" from Africa, Asia, and Latin America also became members of the World Council at this Assembly. The perspective of the World Council widened with the reception of new members in New Delhi.[81]

After the Third Assembly, the attention of the Department on the Co-operation of Men and Women was taken over by issues that had been peripheral. Most of the consultations held during the 1960s studied issues related to marriage and family life.[82] One consultation sponsored by the Department considered women's work outside the home.[83]

Madeleine Barot resigned her position as Executive Secretary of the Department on the Co-operation of Men and Women in Church, Family and Society in 1966. In her Christmas letter that year, she wrote that she wanted to continue to work for cooperation "in a . . . post which need not necessarily be filled by a woman, but in which a woman could make a special contribution and to which she could perhaps add a new dimension."[84] Matti Joensuu, a Finnish Lutheran pastor and Barot's associate on the staff of the Department, was appointed to be the new Executive Secretary.[85] Barot joined the staff of the World Council of Churches' Division of Inter-Church Aid, Refugee and World Service.

"Gladly We Rebel"

The Fourth Assembly of the World Council of Churches met in Uppsala, Sweden, in 1968. The event marked a turning point for the Department on the Co-operation of Men and Women, indeed for the entire World Council. The event pulsated with political affairs from around the world. Although political affairs had influenced earlier Assemblies, particularly at Amsterdam and at Evanston, the terms of discussion at those gatherings had been theological. Reports of the Fourth Assembly agree that the world set the agenda at Uppsala.[86] This is dramatically signaled by the opening sentence of the "Message of the Fourth Assembly." In contrast to the theological affirmations at the beginning of other Assembly messages, this message begins: "The excitement of new scientific discoveries, the clash of wars: these mark the year 1968. In this climate the Uppsala Assembly met first of all to listen."[87]

Crisis situations worldwide were then recited in the "Message of the Fourth Assembly." The recital was punctuated by the phrase: "But God makes new."[88] In response to the turmoil of the time, the World Council of Churches meeting at Uppsala acknowledged the irrelevance of its ways of working toward church unity and affirmed its call to renew the church as well as the world.

There were more women at Uppsala than at any previous Assembly. The delegate body was 9 percent women, compared to 3.37 percent at Amsterdam, 3.4 percent at Evanston, and 6 percent at New Delhi.[89] A woman, Pauline Webb, was elected Vice-Moderator of the World Council of Churches Central Committee. Pauline Webb, a Methodist laywoman and Director of Religious Broadcasting in the External Services of the British Broadcasting Corporation, was attending her first Assembly. Later, she reflected on her election:

> I realized very much that I had been made Vice-Chairman because I was a woman and found this humiliating at first. Everything in me rebelled against being a token woman. I would have liked to think that I was made Vice-Chairman because I was *me*. But I knew that wasn't so and I had to accept that."[90]

Six of the 119 members of the Central Committee appointed at Uppsala were women.[91]

Despite the greater number of women delegates, Pauline Webb recalled how few women delegates were at Uppsala:

> . . . I hadn't realized how few, until a little woman from the Philippines interrupted one of the sessions and asked that the women who were there representing their churches as fully appointed delegates should stand up. I remember Archbishop Wood from Australia, a great tall man, who looked at this little lady and said, 'I don't think that's necessary. There are plenty of women here when you look around.' And there were quite a lot of advisors, people like Margaret Mead, very distinguished women. So I, too, had been impressed by the women there. Then the actual representatives did stand; and you suddenly realized as you looked around the hall how very few we were.[92]

Later, the Assembly passed a resolution expressing "great dissatisfaction" that so few women, laymen, and youth were official delegates.[93]

Three of the six reports adopted by the Fourth Assembly brought the role of women to the attention of member churches. The report on "Renewal in Mission" called for a release of "the people of God . . . from structures that inhibit them in the Church" and declared:

> We need to explore how, in the diverse roles in which we find ourselves, we can creatively and with integrity express our full humanity—whether it be as young people, or women, or members of minority groups, or people in positions of authority, and so on.[94]

At the end of a paragraph decrying white racism, the report on "World Economic and Social Development" noted: "Discrimination against women is another pervasive impediment to personal and community development."[95] Finally, the report on "Towards New Styles of Living" included a discussion of creative partnership between women and men.[96] One chronicler of the Fourth Assembly remarked with regard to this report: "This was certainly not a report of conservative or reactionary temper. It was poorest, perhaps, in the passages dealing with the relations between the sexes."[97]

At Uppsala, talk of cooperation between women and men, based on the theological affirmation of sexual difference, receded. The emphasis was on equalizing the participation of women and men, "irrespective of their sex." The Assembly asked the Department on the Co-operation of Men and Women to study problems preventing the partnership of women and men in the churches, particularly at administrative levels and in decision-making contexts. The ordination of women was also identified as a question urgently in need of study by the Department.[98]

The Assembly also directed the Department's attention to the world in which the churches are situated. Departmental study of family issues was extended to the social policies that affect family life. A study of inter-confessional, inter-faith, and inter-racial marriages, their problems and opportunities, was proposed. Finally, the Department was encouraged to work on improving the status of women in developing countries, in cooperation with other international organizations.[99]

Just prior to the Fourth Assembly, the Department had drafted a statement on the nature and significance of its work. This statement, which was presented to the Central Committee meeting in 1967, anticipated the directives given at Uppsala:

> Earlier statements and declarations on man-woman relationship were dealt with mostly in terms of theology as for example the Davos-Statement, which was accepted by the Central Committee in 1955.
>
> Now, we are emphasizing the urgency of the main concerns of the Department on Cooperation in light of the social revolution of our times . . .[100]

The Department, therefore, asked the Central Committee to allow "greater freedom and flexibility" in its work. "The emphasis," declared the Department, "is on the message and the messengers, and not on the structures."[101]

During the decade that followed the Fourth Assembly, the Department's most zealous messenger was Brigalia Bam. Bam joined the staff in 1967, after winning a lengthy battle with the South African government for the return of her passport. Her passport had been seized in 1962 when she became outspoken for human rights and kept company with people such as Winnie and Nelson Mandela, who were considered threats to the South African system of apartheid.[102] Brigalia Bam's perspective, formed by her South African experiences and later informed by her contacts among Blacks and feminists in North America and the poor in Latin America, shaped the Department anew.

In a report of the Department's work to the 1969 Central Committee meeting, it was declared: "There is . . . conflict between women and men in a man-made world. Premature harmonizations in concepts like 'complementarity' have not solved the conflict; they have dimmed it."[103] The shift in the perspective of the Department was made manifest in the new structure of the World Council of Churches. The work of the Department on the Co-operation of Men and Women was redistributed. Family life issues were assigned to a newly-created sub-unit on education. A Sub-unit on Women in Church and Society was created in place of the Department.[104]

Bam was convinced that the conflicts rampant in "a manmade world" would be resolved only as women, together with men, make decisions about the structures of church and society. Recognizing that most women have not been prepared to assume such responsibility, Bam organized consultations to enable women to become leaders. Most of these consultations were for women only. Madeleine Barot, reflecting on these years after Uppsala, remarked:

> . . . when the WCC's work ceased to be dominated by the western world, it became apparent that, to give effective support to women in their quest for liberation, there was still a need for a place where women could be together, where they could, without being subjected to pressure or coopted for other purposes, discover their own identity, work out their own contribution, show what they could do and express their hopes for justice, peace and unity in the world in their own way.[105]

These consultations were not primarily occasions for discussion of study papers on theological, psychological, and sociological issues, as those organized by Barot had been. Instead, the insights and experiences with which women came from their own contexts were articulated and affirmed.[106]

In 1970, Brigalia Bam convened a consultation on the

most controversial issue relative to women's leadership in the church: ordination. Bam organized the consultation in direct response to the recommendation from Uppsala. The question of women's ordination, however, had been hovering in the background of World Council discussions since Amsterdam. Indeed, at the First Assembly, the churches' position relative to the ordination of women was assessed:

> The churches are not agreed on the important question of admission of women to the full ministry. Some churches for theological reasons are not prepared to consider the question of ordination; some find no objection in principle but see administrative or social difficulties; some permit partial but not full participation in the work of the ministry; in others women are eligible for all offices of the Church. Even in the last group, social custom and public opinion still create obstacles. In some countries a shortage of clergy raises some urgent practical and spiritual problems. Those who desire the admission of women to the full ministry believe that until this is achieved the Church will not come to full health and power. We are agreed that this whole subject requires further careful and objective study.[107]

In the early 1950s, however, Mrs. Geoffrey Fisher, wife of the Archbishop of Canterbury, made clear to Kathleen Bliss what would continue to be clear for years to come: if the question of the ordination of women were brought to the forefront of discussion, the goal of church unity would recede.[108]

Despite a tacit ban on discussion, a consultation on the ordination of women was held in 1963. The New Delhi Assembly had instructed the Department on Faith and Order, in conjunction with the Department on the Co-operation of Men and Women, to study "the theological, biblical and ecclesiological issues involved in the ordination of women."[109] At this jointly-sponsored consultation, eight study papers on women's ordination were prepared for the upcoming Fourth World Conference on Faith and Order. In the report of the conference, there are three brief references to the topic. One of the three references is a footnote proposing further study of the question of women's ordination.[110]

The consultation organized by Brigalia Bam met in Cartigny, Switzerland. The ordination of women was considered

in depth and from multiple perspectives. Theological, psychological, and sociological issues shaping attitudes and practices
relative to the ordination of women were explored. Case studies, which described possibilities and problems pertaining to
women's ordination in the churches from which the women at
the consultation came, were considered.

Voices from Africa articulated a perspective from their
context that characterized the discussion:

> Where, in parts of Africa, women assume positions
> of leadership in religious movements, this is often the re-
> assertion of a prophetic role which once characterized
> their tribal tradition. It is in conflict with, rather than an
> interpretation of, forms of Christianity imported from the
> West.[111]

Understandings of ministry and ordination that have prevailed
in mainline Western denominations were called into question
by many women at the consultation. These women were seeking far more than ordination to an already existing church office. Echoes from Uppsala could be heard as the women at
Cartigny envisioned new models of ministry in a transformed
church.

"*Gladly We Rebel!*" appeared the next year.[112] The
opening words exclaim:

> *They* will say it is ridiculous. Surely the issues of ra-
> cism, development, and world peace are far more crucial?
> Is it not just a debate confined to a comparatively small
> group of middle class women in the affluent societies? Is it
> not just an American thing? Is it not sheer exaggeration
> to talk about oppressor and oppressed when referring to
> the relationships between men and women? That is what
> *they* will say. We come with no apologies. The answers to
> such questions will be as many as the attitudes to the
> issue.[113]

In the articles that follow, the diversity of women's struggles
for liberation is depicted.

Davida Foy Crabtree, from the United States, considered
certain factors that make the church "one of the chief oppressors of women."[114] Josina Machel, a political commissar in the
Women's Detachment of FRELIMO, discussed how women's
involvement in that organization has begun to redefine their

role in the whole of society.[115] Laila Khaled, a notorious fighter in the Popular Front to Liberate Palestine, envisioned a society in which women and men are no longer imprisoned by stereotypes.[116] Gabriele Dietrich, a German free-lance writer, presented a comparative study of women's movements for liberation in Holland and in the United States, ending with a call for women to organize in her own country.[117] In an "Unscientific Postscript," Anna Marie Aagaard, professor of theology at the University of Aarhus, Denmark, disclosed the discrimination still entrenched despite legal equality in her country.[118] The word "sexism," used with reference to the subordination of women in church and society, was introduced to the ecumenical vocabulary in these articles.

The images portrayed on the pages of "Gladly We Rebel" are as compelling as the words. Women are marching in the streets, armed with placards: "Women Unite." Finely etched faces of Russian Orthodox nuns are framed in folds of black cloth. A woman, nailed to a cross and noosed at the neck, is displayed against shadowed draperies. Veiled, save a slit for her eyes, a Muslim woman squats amidst a bustling marketplace to sell wares spread before her. Belly-naked dancers on billboards beckon to extravagant consumption. The power of images, either to exploit or to empower, is thus presented.

At a consultation on "Sexism in the 1970s: Discrimination Against Women," held in Berlin in 1974, the power of images was considered. Nelle Morton, Associate Professor Emeritus of Drew University's School of Theology, addressed the matter most directly. She declared:

> . . . just changing words from the masculine to the feminine is not the answer because of the images the words have conjured up. . . .
> So we see that theologizing as women becomes top agenda for a consultation such as this. It involves dealing with images . . . and recognizing how much more difficult it is to change an image that operates underground than it is to change a concept, and that many images in our various cultures mark the styles of life of our children long before they come to the age of conceptualization.[119]

From Morton's perspective, patriarchal structures are perpetuated by the theological images articulated by men and ascribed universal status. Women will become fully human,

according to Morton, only when "a whole theology" emerges:
a theology that emerges when "men can begin to hear women,
and to listen to women, and when men and women together
can participate fully and equally and joyfully in bringing faith
to expression."[120]

"A whole theology," continued Morton, cannot come
"through the Western world alone, nor through the Eastern
world, nor from any control group speaking out of its own experience as if it were the whole experience of all the people."
'A whole theology' can come when all the people of the world
"speak freely out of their own experiences, can hear and be
heard, can touch one another to heal and be healed."[121] 'A
whole theology' thus is articulated by "hearing one another to
speech. . . . to new creation."[122]

The consultation on "Sexism in the 1970s" was convened
to consider the place of Christian women in the context of women's struggles for liberation around the world. It was convened in 1974 to prepare for two significant events the
following year: the UN International Women's Year and the
Fifth Assembly of the World Council of Churches.

The theme of the Fifth Assembly, to be held in Nairobi in
1975, had already been chosen: "Jesus Christ Frees and
Unites." Brigalia Bam posed the question that reverberated
throughout the gathering in Berlin: "Can we continue to talk
about unity in the Church or in the world while discrimination
exists against women, poor people, and other oppressed
groups?"[123] Pauline Webb addressed this question, particularly with regard to discrimination against women. She spoke
about "sexism," defining it as "any kind of subordination or de-
valuing of a person or group solely on the ground of sex."
Webb declared:

> It is not just a matter of acknowledging the physical differ-
> ence between men and women and saying, as most of us
> would, '*Vive la difference!*' It is rather recognizing that
> alongside this difference there have been different histo-
> ries, different expectations, a different sense of identity,
> and an association with the structures of power that have
> created a male-dominated order in almost all human soci-
> ety and certainly within the Church, making it impossible
> for the Church to foreshadow the truly human commu-
> nity. So it is for the sake of that community that we Chris-
> tian women come now to examine the heresy of sexism

and to explore ways of overcoming it that will liberate both men and women for a new partnership in the gospel.[124]

As she called sexism a heresy, Webb made clear the theological significance of the issues women were raising with regard to their role in the church: the unity of the church would be made manifest only as all members of the church freely participated in its life and work.

Despite this clarity about the relationship between unity and liberation, it was not easy for the women gathered in Berlin to speak with a united voice. Approximately 150 women came from forty-nine countries. Their perspectives were informed by different social, economic, and political situations. At the consultation, nine women were chosen at random and asked: "How do you feel your church and your society value you as a woman?" The women's responses to this question bear witness to the diversity represented in Berlin.

Leila Shaheen da Cruz, editor for a Lebanese publishing house and member of the Greek Orthodox Church, said:

> I don't think I have ever had to stop and think about the question you have asked. I have always been valued in my own right as a woman for what I am worth. . . .
>
> Women have always had a place in society in Lebanon. . . . The Lebanese woman . . . is a very important person in the family.
>
> Maybe this is because we still are the traditional family of old where the woman shared in the responsibility, brought up the children—and when I say 'brought up the children' I give it another dimension than the chore which some women seem to think it is. It meant educating the new generation, handling the economics of the home and seeing to it that things went smoothly.
>
> The same is true of the church. Churches in Lebanon . . . have always relied on women. I recall as a child that almost every Christian village had a church or a school, often both, that had been built solely through the efforts of the women of the community. . . . The church of that day was the place around which the activities of the village revolved.
>
> Now, today, woman is side by side with man in the business world. . . .
>
> I think to serve the cause of true liberation it is for us to liberate not only ourselves but the communities around us . . .[125]

"I don't go to church anymore," said Zanele Dlamini, member of the women's section of the African National Congress in exile from her homeland, South Africa. "My father left the Methodist Church much earlier than I decided to leave," she continued. "I left the church because I found it racist in its administration and controlled through the missionaries from overseas . . ." Dlamini acknowledged that South African society is "oppressive by class, by race, and by sex," but hastened to add:

> . . . there is something else—that when you are on the other side of the oppression, of capitalism, apartheid—you attain a certain kind of equality under oppression.
>
> We have our history—which is patriarchal—with a patriarchal division of roles. . . . But it doesn't hurt me. I don't feel any deprivations from it; I don't feel any of the men humiliating me. . . .
>
> I've never felt any bitterness because these men do not wish it upon their women to be un-fed or anything else. . . .
>
> Among the oppressed I like to use the phrase 'a deformed kind of equality.' It is not a healthy equality—but I feel a certain unity in the problem that we will have to work through.[126]

Joan Anderson, convener of the Ecumenical Affairs Committee of the Presbyterian Church of New Zealand, responded with reference to the legal and economic situation of women in her country:

> In theory—under the law—women are becoming much more looked after and much less discriminated against. The practice of this is a different matter. It's 'slowly, slowly.' . . .
>
> And when I listen here to some of the discrimination in other countries, I say to myself, 'Who am I to feel unliberated in the secular society?'
>
> I think that the church lags behind the secular society in discrimination against women.[127]

According to Helen Hee-Kyung Chung, the principal of a girl's high school in Korea, the church in Korean society has been and still is the institution that gives a place to women outside the home. She also acknowledged: "I feel that Korean women in the church—to use the American phrase—take care of all

the 'trash' in the church."[128] Hee-Kyung Chung went on to
say that, because family structures in Korea are different from
those in the West, that is, women are not left alone with children, many women prefer to stay at home: "There are aunts,
uncles, and other relatives in the family with whom the child
can identify and with whom the wife can have dialogue whenever she feels the urge to do so." She then remarked:

> Our total picture looks quite different from that of
> the Western world. Here at this consultation, I feel there
> is a cry from Western women who are totally isolated into
> the core family; in their isolated apartments from which
> they cannot escape, with unhappy children and their own
> frustrated ambitions. They have been conditioned by the
> education given them—an education that was not origi-
> nally designed for the benefit of women but was struc-
> tured instead around the interests of men.
> I see that the future of our women in Korea may
> soon face a similar kind of situation and we must work on
> this before it is too late.[129]

"I receive full recognition as a woman in my church," said
Christa Lewek, Secretary for the Department of Church and
Society of the Federation of Protestant Churches in the Ger-
man Democratic Republic:

> I am employed by a central church office. . . .
> This office is a good model of partnership in the
> church. However, I have to admit that this is, generally
> speaking, still an exception. In principle our church still
> possesses a traditional hierarchy with a patriarchal struc-
> ture which does not grant women the same opportunities
> as men. . . . The church's expectations of women are pat-
> terned as in the past primarily on the traditional feminine
> virtues: humility, modesty, selflessness, willingness to
> sacrifice.[130]

Even though equality has been legislated in the German Democratic Republic, Lewek declared, difficulties for women and
men persist. Men, according to Lewek, have difficulty "sur-
rendering toward true partnership," while women fall back
into their "customary, seemingly comfortable pattern of behavior: submission, or at least conformity."[131]
The diversity to which these statements bear witness was

"so great," declared the women in Berlin, that "at times . . . we could hardly hear each other's shouts of joy or cries of pain:"[132]

> We came from almost too many situations, with the usual prejudice, our own ideas, our exaggerated hopes, many of us tired of conferences, all of us full of our own preoccupations.
> Then we shared our biographical materials, struggling to express our thoughts, groping for words that might communicate, hurting each other by hasty reactions, being hurt when not heard, showing some of the frustrations we have in our work back home, sharing our fear for the future of our world, our feeble faith.[133]

Although the women acknowledged their inability to speak with one accord, they did not despair. Instead, the women affirmed that, in the midst of difference and even disagreement, they had been "met by God" and "experienced the . . . force of God's invitation to continuous conversation."[134]

At the consultation on "Sexism in the 1970s," working groups met to discuss the status of women in political and economic structures, in educational settings, in the family, and in the church. There was also a working group on women and theology. This group, unlike the others, had not been planned prior to the consultation.

Constance F. Parvey, a pastor in the Lutheran Church of America and co-moderator of the working group on women and theology, recalled how the group was gathered: ". . . I was asked to co-chair a meeting on women in politics. I had never studied political science . . . and had never worked as a practical politician. But I had studied theology and . . . served for years as a pastor on the local congregational level." Parvey therefore asked Brigalia Bam and other consultation leaders about the possibility of organizing a group on women and theology. "The reply I got," remembered Parvey, "was 'theology is not relevant to the lives of women, but if you want to organize one, go ahead and see what happens'." Twenty-three women, all of whom had studied theology, came to the group. Three of these women were employed by the church. One was a seminary professor from North America. Another woman, from Latin America, was a seminary lecturer, but without pay. Parvey, the only pastor, remarked, "all of us talked of the difficulties we had encountered in the church, no matter what church, area of the world, or economic system."[135]

This working group recommended that the Fifth Assembly initiate a World Council of Churches study of "God-language," which would address "the problems of speaking about the action of God in ways that communicate the gospel to all races, sexes, and cultures."[136] According to Madeleine Barot, the other co-moderator of the working group, this "was really the beginning of the Faith and Order study 'on The Community of Women and Men in the Church'."[137]

Nearly two decades had passed since women had called for theological study relative to their role and image in the church. In 1952, Kathleen Bliss wrote:

> A danger lies in the very virtues of women, their ability to make sacrifices and raise money and the thorough-going nature of much of their organized work. Few of them think theologically and few theologians turn their minds to the enormous work done by women and ask what it all means in terms of a doctrine of the Church.[138]

Bliss lamented the lack of theological reflection on the rapidly changing role of women in society as well. Noting the work of Margaret Mead and Simone de Beauvoir, Bliss stated: "What is needed is that there should start within the Churches . . . a process of thought about women in modern society, an imaginative act of understanding, an entering into, a total experience."[139]

In 1955, Madeleine Barot recalled Bliss' concern and underscored "the real urgency of such a theological study . . ."[140] She declared:

> . . . the Church is bound to ask itself . . . whether it has not forgotten part of its message of liberation. And the very worst thing that could happen would be for women to remain passive and the men indifferent to this question, as has for so long been the case. It is better if women are rebellious and men incoherent—as now seems to happen more frequently. All are then forced to reflect anew and to re-examine the traditional ways of thinking and acting.[141]

Barot called for study of two theological issues that, from her perspective, are significant relative to the role of women: understandings of the church and of humanity.[142]

The call for theological study that came from the women gathered in Berlin was different, in at least one way, from these earlier calls. Bliss and Barot had reflected on traditional texts and doctrines.[143] The working group on women and theology in Berlin began with their own situations as well as struggles for liberation, affirming lived experiences as the context for reflecting theologically.[144]

Women spoke about their life experiences and struggles for liberation at the Fifth Assembly in Nairobi. One of the plenary sessions was on "Women in a Changing World." Kiyoko Takeda Cho, a member of the Presidium of the World Council of Churches at Uppsala, was the moderator of the session. She sketched the history of women in the World Council, recalling the names of early women leaders. "In the life of the WCC," Cho noted, "this is the first time that a plenary has been held in which women can speak clearly, fully, and radically out of our concrete situations to the whole Assembly."[145]

Thus the silence was broken. Voices of women welled up, "filled up and spilled over" the time allotted. One chronicler remarked: "It was as though having waited twenty-seven years in the World Council's life for such a session their eyes were on the calendar rather than the clock."[146]

Voices of women are recorded in some of the reports adopted by the Fifth Assembly. The report on "What Unity Requires" echoes words spoken at Berlin, as well as at Amsterdam: "The unity of the Church requires that women be free to live out the gifts which God has given to them and to respond to their calling to share fully in the life and witness of the Church."[147] The report on "Structures of Injustice and Struggles for Liberation" declared:

> Despite efforts of the WCC in the past, the position of women in both the Church and the world, has not changed significantly. As long as women are largely excluded from decision-making processes, they will be unable to realize a full partnership with men and therefore the Church will be unable to realize its full unity.[148]

In this report, member churches are encouraged to give attention to women's ordination, as well as to the relationship between cultural contexts and interpretations of "the Word of God."[149]

Delegates at the Fifth Assembly received a document for their consideration: "The Community of Women and Men in the Church: A Proposal for Study Groups."[150] This document was drafted by women who had participated in the Berlin consultation together with representatives of the Commission on Faith and Order. Recognizing the Commission on Faith and Order's responsibility for theological reflection on church unity, women from the Berlin consultation had taken their recommendation for study of "God-language" to the commission meeting in Accra, Ghana, later in 1974. Once again, women were enacting their conviction that their concerns belong to the entire church.

At the Faith and Order meeting in Accra, some members of the commission considered the issues raised in Berlin to be "non-theological matters" and some thought the "woman problem" had nothing to do with the church. There was much debate about whether or not the questions being raised by women are integrally related to theological discussions of church unity.[151]

A working group at Accra considered the recommendations brought from Berlin. The group drafted a statement that begins: "Our Christian faith leads us to hope for a renewed and transformed man-woman relationship."[152] The distortion of "man-woman relationship" is then discussed. Particular attention is given to the ways in which theological language and images contribute to the obstacles women encounter in churches and societies. The statement concludes:

> Theology entails watching our language in the presence of God. Both generic language and the conventional use of male and female language in speaking about God and the Church stand in the way of a Christian community in which all can participate fully. Both present theological problems which urgently need Faith and Order's attention.[153]

The Commission on Faith and Order adopted this statement and agreed to sponsor a study, in cooperation with the Sub-unit on Women in Church and Society.

The Secretariat on Faith and Order and the Sub-unit on

Women called a consultation to draft a working paper for presentation to the Fifth Assembly. Representatives of the Commission on Faith and Order and representatives of the Berlin consultation met in February, 1975. Keenly aware that no one model for study would be appropriate for groups throughout the world, these women and men urged regional and local study groups to engage in "a process of reflection and action according to the needs and challenges of the local and regional situations:"

> It is hoped that women and men of all church traditions and cultures will find ways to participate in this study. There is no limitation on the types of groups to be formed for action and reflection. All groups must feel free to react to this study according to the cultural patterns in which they find themselves and which vary greatly from country to country and church to church. Some may concentrate on a particular theme, others may choose a particular action for change and reflect on its implications for theology and church life. Others again will work through larger regional groupings which divide into smaller study and action groups dealing with selected issues.[154]

All groups were asked to send reports of their reflection and of their process to the Faith and Order Secretariat in Geneva.

The method of this study is reminiscent of the pre-Amsterdam questionnaire regarding the service and status of women in the churches. For both studies, questions were formulated and sent to churches throughout the world for reflection and response. This similarity is signaled by a report adopted at Nairobi. In this report, the statement made at Amsterdam is quoted: "The Church, as the Body of Christ, consists of men and women, created as responsible persons to glorify God and to do God's will."[155]

However, the drafters of the Nairobi report made one revision in the Amsterdam statement: the masculine pronoun for God was eliminated. This revision points to the difference between the study formulated in the 1940s and the one formulated in 1975. In the 1940s, women were asking for recognition of their service and for fuller participation in the life of the churches. In the 1970s, women were aware that, until the theological language and imagery that forms the life of churches are recast, they would not be partners with men.

Notes

/1/ John Foster Dulles, "The Christian Citizen in a Changing World," in *Man's Disorder and God's Design*, 5 vols., vol. 4: *The Church and International Disorder*. The Amsterdam Assembly Series (New York: Harper & Bros., Publishers, 1948), pp. 73-114.

/2/ Joseph L. Hromadka, "Christian Responsibility in Our Divided World," in *The Church and International Disorder*, p. 132. Cf. Harold E. Fey, "Amsterdam Strikes Middle Way In Discussing Economic Order," *Christian Century* 65 (22 September 1948):980; John C. Bennett, "Capitalism and Communism at Amsterdam," *Christian Century* 65 (15 December 1948):1362-64.

/3/ *Man's Disorder and God's Design*, 5 vols., vol. 5: *The First Assembly of the World Council of Churches, held at Amsterdam, August 22nd to September 4th, 1948*, ed. W. A. Visser't Hooft. The Amsterdam Assembly Series (New York: Harper & Bros., Publishers, 1948), p. 207.

/4/ See *The Christian Newsletter* (London), nos. 1-341 (1939-1949).

/5/ See *The First Assembly of the World Council of Churches*, pp. 40, 176, 180.

/6/ H. G. G. Herklots, *Amsterdam 1948: An Account of the First Assembly of the WCC* (London: S.C.M. Press, 1948), p. 42.

/7/ *The First Assembly of the World Council of Churches*, p. 146.

/8/ Ibid.

/9/ For discussion see chap. III, esp. pp. 131-132 below.

/10/ See for example pp. 29-34 below.

/11/ See Gladys Gilkey Calkins, *Follow Those Women: Church Women in the Ecumenical Movement. A History of the Development of United Work Among Women of the Protestant Churches in the United States* (New York: National Council of the Churches of Christ in the U.S.A., 1961); See also William J. Schmidt, *Architect of Unity: A Biography of Samuel McCrea Cavert* (New York: Friendship Press, 1978).

/12/ *Revised Interim Report of a Study on the Life and Work of Women in the Church, including Reports of an Ecumenical Conference of Church Women, Baarn, Holland, and of the Committee on "The Life and Work of Women in the Church: of the Assembly of the World Council of Churches, Amsterdam, 1948* (Geneva: World Council of Churches, 1948), pp. 11-12.

/13/ *The First Six Years, 1948-1954: A Report of the Central Committee of the World Council Churches on the activities of the Departments and Secretariats of the Council* (Geneva: World Council of Churches, 1954), p. 54.

/14/ For the report of this working committee see *Revised Interim Report of a Study on the Life and Work of Women in the Church*, p. 71-76.

/15/ Ibid., p. 12.

/16/ For examples see Ibid., pp. 37-48. This significant shift in the history of women's work has not been thoroughly researched. How-

ever, there are a number of books that document various aspects of
the shift. See Susan B. Anthony II, *Out of the Kitchen and into the
War: Women's Role in the Nation's Drama* (New York: Stephen Day,
1943); Leila J. Rupp, *Mobilizing Women for War: German and American Propaganda, 1939-1945* (Princeton: Princeton University Press,
1978). Maureen Honey, *Creating Rosie the Riveter: Class, Gender,
and Propaganda during World War II* (Amherst, Massachusetts: University of Massachusetts Press, 1984). A similar shift in women's role
has often occurred at the outbreak of war. See for example Maurine
Weiner Greenwald, *Women, War and Work: The Impact of World
War I on Women Workers in the U.S.* (Westport, CT: Greenwood
Press, 1980) for documentation of the shift at the outbreak of World
War I.

/17/ See, for example, Jeanne Merle d'Aubigne and Violette
Mouchon, *God's Underground*, trans. William and Patricia Nottingham (St. Louis, Missouri: Bethany Press, 1970) [Originally published
under the title *Le Clandestine de Dieu*, Paris, 1968]. d'Aubigne and
Mouchon tell the story of C.I.M.A.D.E. (*Comite Inter-Mouvements
aupres des Evacues*), formed in 1939 by young French Protestants to
help refugees from Germany. Madeleine Barot, later Executive Secretary of the World Council Department on the Co-operation of Men
and Women, was the first General Secretary of C.I.M.A.D.E. See
Marc Boegner, *The Long Road to Unity: Memories and Anticipations*,
trans. Rene Hague, with an Introduction by W. A. Visser't Hooft
(London: Collins, 1970), pp. 170-181 [Originally published under the
title *L'Exigence oecumenique: Souvenirs et Perspectives*, Paris, 1968].
See also Margaret L. Rossiter, *Women in the Resistance* (New York:
Praeger Publishers, 1986).

/18/ For example see Sibylle Meyer and Eva Schulze, "Trummer-
Frauen," *Emma: Das Magazin von Frauen fur Frauen* (Cologne), May
1985, pp. 30-34. This significant shift in the history of women's work
has been even less thoroughly researched than the shift at the beginning of World War II.

/19/ Susannah Herzel, *A Voice for Women: The Women's Department of the World Council of Churches* (Geneva: World Council of
Churches, 1981), p. 131.

/20/ Ibid.

/21/ See Henriette Visser't Hooft, "Aus den Briefwechsel mit Karl
Barth 1934," in Gundrun Kaper, Henriette Visser't Hooft, u.a. *Eva
wo bist du? Frauen in internationalen Organisation der Okumene:
Eine Dokumentation* (Gelnhausen, Berlin, Stein Mfr.:
Burckhardthaus-Laetare Verlag, 1981), pp. 14-19.

/22/ Ibid., p. 14. My translation.

/23/ Ibid. My translation.

/24/ Ibid., pp. 15-17.

/25/ Ibid., p. 18. My translation.

/26/ Ibid., p. 19. My translation. See Henriette Visser't Hooft, "Eva
wo bist Du?—Aufsatz von 1934" and "Briefe an Karl Barth 1941,
1946, 1948" in Kaper and Visser't Hooft, *Eva wo bist du?* pp. 20-32,

32-36. Cf. W. A. Visser't Hooft, *The Fatherhood of God in an Age of Emancipation* (Philadelphia: The Westminster Press, 1982). W. A. Visser't Hooft, who has been called "a truly international apostle of the Barthian theology," upheld the fatherhood of God in the face of contemporary critique in this book (Adolf Keller, *Karl Barth and Christian Unity: The Influence of the Barthian Movement Upon the Churches of the World*, trans. Rev. Manfred Manrodt, rev. Dr. A. J. MacDonald, with an Introduction by Luther A. Weigle [New York: The Macmillan Company, 1933], p. 128).

/27/ "First things first," Barth declared to the delegates, "*first* God's Design, which is His and not ours, and must never be confused with any sort of 'Christian Marshall Plan'. . . . I do not wish to weaken the earnestness, the goodwill and the hopes that have brought us here, but only to base them on their proper foundation, when I now say: we ought to give up, even on this first day of our deliberations, every thought that the care of the Church, the care of the world, is our care . . ." Barth called the Assembly to begin with "our Lord's will for His Church, and put all our conceptions into the 'testing fire of His Word'. . . . All we can do is to 'point to God's Kingdom'—not some earthly kingdom of our own" (*The First Assembly of the World Council of Churches*, pp. 32-33).

/28/ Visser't Hooft, *The Fatherhood of God*, p. 58.

/29/ Ibid.

/30/ See Mary Louise Slater, *Future-maker in India: The Story of Sarah Chakko* (New York: Friendship Press, 1968). Isabella Thoburn College was named in memory of the first women sent by the Methodist Women's Foreign Missionary Society. Thoburn was sent to India in 1869. See Calkins, *Follow Those Women*, p. 8. See also James M. Thoburn, *Life of Isabella Thoburn* (Cincinnati: Jennings and Pye, 1903).

/31/ Alan Brash, *Amsterdam 1948: Being a Report on the First Assembly of The World Council of Churches, August 22-September 4, 1948* (Christchurch & Dunedin, New Zealand: Presbyterian Bookroom, 1948), pp. 9-10.

/32/ Herzel, *A Voice for Women*, p. 23.

/33/ The Commission on the Life and Work of Women was appointed by the World Council of Churches Central Committee in 1949. The Commission was charged to continue work on the Interim Report on the Life and Work of Women; to study the men-women relationship in light of biblical teaching and church tradition; to stimulate study and action on women's place in the church; to collect and disseminate information on women's activities, as well as opportunities for service and training; to discover well qualified women to serve in the structures of churches and in ecumenical organization. See *Minutes and Reports of the Second Meeting of the Central Committee of the World Council of Churches, held at Chichester (England), July 9-15, 1949* (Geneva: World Council of Churches, 1949), pp. 33-34.

/34/ Sarah Chakko, "Reflections on Recent Travels in Europe and North America," *The Ecumenical Review* 3 (January 1951):148-149.

/35/   Ibid.

/36/   Herzel, *A Voice for Women*, p. 14. Many of these women's organizations were missionary organizations. See Patricia R. Hill, *The World Their Household: The American Woman's Foreign Mission Movement and Cultural Transformation, 1870-1920* (Ann Arbor, Michigan: University of Michigan Press, 1985). See also Robert Pierce Beaver, *All Loves Excelling: American Protestant Women in World Mission* (Grand Rapids: Wm. B. Eerdmans, 1968).

/37/   Ibid.

/38/   Kathleen Bliss, *The Service and Status of Women in the Churches* (London: S.C.M. Press, 1952), pp. 13-14.

/39/   Ibid., p. 79.

/40/   Ibid., pp. 30-31.

/41/   Ibid., p. 30.

/42/   Ibid., p. 31.

/43/   Ibid., p. 187.

/44/   Ibid.

/45/   Ibid., p. 196.

/46/   Ibid., pp. 197-201.

/47/   David A. Gaines, *The World Council of Churches: A Study of Its Background and History* (Peterborough, N.H.: Richard R. Smith, 1966), p. 516.

/48/   Ibid., p. 517.

/49/   *Minutes and Reports of the Third Meeting of the Central Committee of the World Council of Churches, Toronto (Canada), July 9-15, 1950* (Geneva: World Council of Churches, 1950), p. 119.

/50/   Gaines, *The World Council of Churches*, p. 517. According to the minutes of the Working Committee of the Commission on the Life and Work of Women, "The first name given to the Commission, 'Life and Work of Women in the Church,' indicated only one of the areas of work and sounded feministic and segregative. Therefore, it was decided to adopt the present title, stressing the other and less considered aspect of our work. Another aspect of our present name is that the men may now be certain that they are concerned with this department" ("Report of Minutes of the Working Committee, meeting 1-3 September 1953." A statement drafted 11 March 1954 in preparation for the Second Assembly of the World Council of Churches. [Unpublished document. Archives, Library of the Ecumenical Centre, Geneva, Switzerland]).

/51/   The work of the Department was defined as follows: "promoting the study, by both men and women, of questions affecting the relationship, the co-operation and the common service of men and women in church and society" and "helping women to make their contribution to the total life of the churches and at the same time encouraging the churches to accept the contribution of women to a fuller extent and in more varied ways" ("Report of Minutes of the Working Committee, meeting 1-3 September 1953").

/52/   *The Evanston Report: The Second Assembly of the World*

Council of Churches, 1954, ed. W. A. Visser't Hooft (London: S.C.M. Press, 1955), pp. 2, 70.

/53/   Ibid., p. 207.

/54/   *The First Six Years, 1948-1954*, p. 55.

/55/   *The Evanston Report*, p. 48.

/56/   Ibid., p. 50.

/57/   James Hastings Nichols, *Evanston: An Interpretation* (New York: Harper & Bros., Publishers, 1955), p. 116.

/58/   Herzel, *A Voice for Women*, p. 133.

/59/   See *Report of the Consultation held by the Department on the Co-operation of Men and Women in Church and Society, at Herrenalb, Germany, 15th-19th July, 1956* (Geneva: World Council of Churches, 1956); *The Renewal of the Church: Report of a Consultation of the World Council of Churches, Yale Divinity School, New Haven, Connecticut, U.S.A., July 15-20, 1957* (Geneva: World Council of Churches, 1957); *Report of the Consultation on the Christian Approach to Women's Questions: Freedom of Marriage-Freedom of Work, held at The John Knox House, Geneva, Switzerland, March 27-30, 1958* (Geneva: World Council of Churches, 1958); *Report on Two Consultations in Africa: Ibadan, Nigeria, 4th to 10th January 1958, Nkongsamba, Cameroons, 21st to 23rd February, 1958* (Geneva: World Council of Churches, 1958); *Report of the Consultation on Obstacles to the Cooperation of Men and Women in Working Life and in Public Service: Implications for the Work of the Department, held at Odense, Denmark, August 8-12, 1958* (Geneva: World Council of Churches, 1958); *Report of the Consultation held at "Uplands," High Wycombe, Bucks, England, July 27-August 2, 1960, on "Towards Responsible Cooperation Between Men and Women, Our Christian Responsibility"* (Geneva: World Council of Churches, 1960); *Report of the Consultation held at Women's Christian College, Madras, India, November 13-17, 1961, on "Changing Patterns of Men-Women Relationships in Asia"* (Geneva: World Council of Churches, 1961).

/60/   *Minutes and Reports of the Twelfth Meeting of the Central Committee of the World Council of Churches, Rhoades (Greece), August 19-27, 1959* (Geneva: World Council of Churches, 1959), p. 172.

/61/   Ibid.

/62/   Ibid., p. 166.

/63/   Madeleine Barot, "Considerations on the Need for a Theology of the Place of Women in the Church," *The Ecumenical Review* 7 (January 1955):156. Cf. Karl Barth, *Church Dogmatics*, III/1, 2, 3, 4, ed. G. W. Bromiley and T. F. Torrance (Edinburgh: T. & T. Clark, 1958-1961) [Originally published under the title *Kirchliche Dogmatik*, III/1, 2, 3, 4 (Zollikon-Zurich: Evangelischer Verlag A.G., 1948)]; Emil Brunner, *The Christian Doctrine of Creation and Redemption*, vol. 2: *Dogmatics*, trans. Olive Wyon (London: Lutterworth Press, 1952) [Originally published under the title *Die christliche Lehre von Schopfung und Erlosung*, vol 2: *Dogmatik* (Zurich: Zwingli-Verlag, 1952)].

/64/   Ibid., p. 157.

/65/ *Men and Women in Church and Society: A Statement Commended to the Churches by the Central Committee of the World Council of Churches* (Geneva: World Council of Churches, 1956), p. 6.

/66/ Ibid., p. 12.

/67/ Ibid., p. 8.

/68/ Ibid., p.9

/69/ *Minutes and Reports of the Tenth Meeting of the Central Committee of the World Council of Churches, Yale Divinity School, New Haven (Connecticut, U.S.A.), July 30-August 7, 1957* (Geneva: World Council of Churches, 1957), pp. 97-98.

/70/ Ibid.

/71/ Madeleine Barot, "What *Do* These Women Want?," in *Faith and Faithfulness: Essays on Contemporary Ecumenical Thought. A Tribute to Philip A. Potter*, ed. Pauline Webb (Geneva: World Council of Churches, 1984), p. 79.

/72/ *Minutes and Reports of the Thirteenth Meeting of the Central Committee of the World Council of Churches, St. Andrews (Scotland), August 16-24, 1960* (Geneva: World Council of Churches, 1960), p. 195.

/73/ Ibid., p. 18.

/74/ *The Evanston Report*, p. 227.

/75/ *Men and Women in Church and Society*, p. 5.

/76/ *Minutes and Reports of the Thirteenth Meeting of the Central Committee of the World Council of Churches, St. Andrews (Scotland), August 16-24, 1960*, p. 143.

/77/ Ibid., pp. 18-19.

/78/ Ibid., p. 143.

/79/ Ibid., p. 51.

/80/ Ibid., p. 198.

/81/ See *The New Delhi Report: The Third Assembly of the World Council of Churches, 1961*, ed. W. A. Visser't Hooft (New York: Association Press, 1962).

/82/ See *Report of the Consultation held at Cite Universitaire, Paris, France, July 25-30th, 1963, on "Marriage and Family Life"* (Geneva: World Council of Churches, 1963); *Report of the Consultation held at the College Protestant Romand at Founex, Switzerland, July 6-10, 1964, on "Sexual Ethics Today"* (Geneva: World Council of Churches, 1964); *Report of the Consultation held at St. Cergue, Switzerland, 1967, on "International and Inter-Church Counseling and Family Education"* (Geneva: World Council of Churches, 1967); *Report on the Consultation on Developing Relations of Men, Women and Children and Their Meaning for the Mission of the Church in Our Changing World, held at Sita Katharinastiftelsen, Osterskar, Sweden, from June 28th-July 2nd, 1968* (Geneva: World Council of Churches, 1968).

/83/ See *Report of the Consultation on "Relationships of Men and Women at Work," held at the College Protestant Romand at Founex, Switzerland, 1964* (Geneva: World Council of Churches, 1965). Cf. p. 32 above.

/84/ Herzel, *A Voice for Women*, p. 48.

/85/ Matti Joensuu was a pastor in the Lutheran Church of Finland, one of the last Protestant churches to ordain women, beginning only in March, 1987. See abstracts from the "Minutes of the 1963 Assembly of the Church of Finland," in Margaret Sittler Ermarth, *Adam's Fractured Rib: Observations on Women in the Church* (Philadelphia: Fortress Press, 1970), pp. 90-91.

/86/ For example see *The Uppsala Report 1968: Official Report of the Fourth Assembly of the World Council of Churches, Uppsala, July 4-20, 1968*, ed. Norman Goodall (Geneva: World Council of Churches, 1968), p. xvii.

/87/ Ibid., p. 5.

/88/ Ibid., pp. 5-6.

/89/ Ibid., p. 191.

/90/ Herzel, *A Voice for Women*, p. 52.

/91/ *The Uppsala Report 1968*, pp. 459-461.

/92/ Herzel, *A Voice for Women*, p. 52.

/93/ *The Uppsala Report 1968*, p. 191.

/94/ Ibid., p. 33.

/95/ Ibid., p. 50.

/96/ Ibid., pp. 92-93.

/97/ Kenneth Slack, *Uppsala Report: The Story of the World Council of Churches Fourth Assembly, Uppsala, Sweden, 4-19 July 1968* (London: S.C.M. Press, 1968), p. 59.

/98/ *The Uppsala Report 1968*, p. 250.

/99/ Ibid., p. 251.

/100/ *Central Committee of the World Council of Churches, Minutes and Reports of the Twentieth Meeting, Heraklion, Crete (Greece), August 15th-26th, 1967* (Geneva: World Council of Churches, 1967), p. 221.

/101/ Ibid., p. 226.

/102/ See Nelson Mandela, *The Struggle Is My Life* (London: International Defense and Aid Fund for South Africa, 1978). See also Hilda Bernstein, *For Their Triumphs and For Their Tears: Conditions and Resistance of Women in Apartheid South Africa*, rev. ed. (London: International Defense and Aid Fund for South Africa, 1978).

/103/ *Central Committee of the World Council of Churches, Minutes and Reports of the Twenty-Third Meeting, University of Kent at Canterbury, Canterbury (GB), August 12th-22nd, 1969* (Geneva: World Council of Churches, 1969), p. 167.

/104/ See "Revised Report of the Structure Committee approved by Central Committee, 1971," in *Central Committee of the World Council of Churches, Minutes and Reports of the Twenty-Fourth Meeting, Addis-Ababa, Ethiopia, January 10th-21st, 1971* (Geneva: World Council of Churches, 1971), pp. 136-188.

/105/ Barot, "What *Do* These Women Want?" p. 80.

/106/ See *Half the World's People: A Report of a Consultation of Church Women Executives, Glion, Switzerland* (Geneva: World Council of Churches, 1978); *Consultation of European Christian Women, Brussels* (Geneva: World Council of Churches, 1978); *Report on*

Middle East Consultation on Women in Church and Society, Cairo, Egypt (Geneva: World Council of Churches, 1978); *"We Listened Long before we spoke": A Report of the Consultation of Women Theological Students, Cartigny, Switzerland* (Geneva: World Council of Churches, 1978); *Report of Conference on Women, Human Rights and Mission, Venice, Italy* (Geneva: World Council of Churches, 1979); *Choose Life-Work for Peace, an International Workshop, Nassau, Bahamas* (Geneva: World Council of Churches, 1981).

/107/ *The First Assembly of the World Council of Churches*, p. 147.

/108/ Herzel, *A Voice for Women*, p. 17.

/109/ Foreword to *Concerning the Ordination of Women* (Geneva: World Council of Churches, 1964).

/110/ *The Fourth World Conference on Faith and Order, Montreal, 1963*, ed. P. C. Rodger and L. Vischer. Faith and Order Paper No. 42 (London: S.C.M. Press, 1964), p. 65n. See also pp. 25-26.

/111/ *What is ordination coming to? Report of a Consultation on the Ordination of Women, held in Cartigny, Geneva, Switzerland, 21st-26th September, 1970*, ed. Brigalia Bam (Geneva: World Council of Churches, 1971), p. 8.

/112/ *Gladly We Rebel! Risk*, no. 1 (1971). *Risk*, at that time, was published four times a year by an editorial group within World Council of Churches Programme Unit on Education and Communication (Unit III).

By 1971, a number of books calling for women's liberation from structures of church and society had been published, particularly in the United States of America. For examples see Mary Daly, *The Church and the Second Sex* (New York: Harper & Row Publishers, 1968); Sarah Bentley Doely, ed., *Women's Liberation and the Church* (New York: Association Press, 1970); Margaret Sittler Ermarth, *Adam's Fractured Rib: Observations on Women in the Church* (Philadelphia: Fortress Press, 1970); Betty Friedan, *The Feminine Mystique* (New York: W. W. Norton & Co., 1963); Valerie Saiving Goldstein, "The Human Situation: A Feminine View," *Journal of Religion* 40 (April 1960):100-112; Elizabeth Janeway, *Man's World, Woman's Place: A Study in Social Mythology* (New York: William Morrow & Co., 1971); Kate Millett, *Sexual Politics* (New York: Doubleday & Co., 1970); Nelle Morton, "Women's Liberation and the Church," *Tempo* (1 October 1970).

/113/ *Gladly We Rebel*, p. 11.

/114/ Davida Foy Crabtree, "Women's Liberation and the Church," p. 12.

/115/ Josina Machel, "Revolutionary Women," pp. 21-23. FRELIMO is the abbreviation for Frente de Libertacao de Mozambique.

/116/ "Laila Khaled Answers Some Questions," pp. 38-43.

/117/ Gabriele Dietrich, "Liberating Women: A Comparative Survey," pp. 44-57.

/118/ Anna Marie Aagaard, "Unscientific Postscript," pp. 59-63.

/119/ Nelle Morton, "Towards a Whole Theology," in *Sexism in the 1970s: Discrimination Against Women. A Report of a World Council of Churches Consultation, West Berlin, 1974* (Geneva: World Council of Churches, 1975), pp. 60, 63.

/120/   Ibid., p. 57.

/121/   Ibid., p. 58.

/122/   Ibid., p. 64. At the beginning of her address, Morton made it clear that she would speak as a woman formed by her own culture and context. The printed text evidences her engagement with feminism as expressed in the United States as that time. For example see Morton's reference to Mary Daly (*Beyond God the Father: Toward a Philosophy of Women's Liberation* [Boston: Beacon Press, 1973]) on pp. 58, 65. A revised version of "Toward a Whole Theology" is published in Morton, *The Journey Is Home* (Boston: Beacon Press, 1985), pp. 62-85.

/123/   *Sexism in the 1970s*, p. 5.

/124/   Ibid., p. 10.

/125/   Interview with Leila Shaheen da Cruz, in *Words to the Churches: Voices of the Sisters, Risk*, no. 2 (1974), pp. 36-37.

/126/   Interview with Zanele Dlamini, in *Words to the Churches*, p. 37.

/127/   Interview with Joan Anderson, in *Words to the Churches*, p. 38.

/128/   Interview with Helen Hee-Kyung Chung, in *Words to the Churches*, p. 38.

/129/   Interview with Helen Hee-Kyung Chung, p. 39. The Western women in Berlin were middle-class women. Their "cry" was given a language by the women whose books are cited in n. 112, p. 55 above, among others.

/130/   Interview with Christa Lewek, in *Words to the Churches*, p. 40.

/131/   Interview with Christa Lewek, p. 40.

/132/   *Sexism in the 1970s*, p. 5.

/133/   "An Affirmation of Faith," in *Words to the Churches: Voices of the Sisters*, p. 32.

/134/   Ibid.

/135/   Constance F. Parvey, "Journey of a Dream: Beginning Again," in *Report of Regional Consultation on Community of Men and Women in the Church Study* (Nairobi, Kenya: An All-Africa Conference of Churches Production, n.d.), p. 6.

/136/   *Sexism in the 1970s*, p. 100.

/137/   Herzel, *A Voice for Women*, p. 76.

/138/   Bliss, *The Service and Status of Women in the Churches*, p. 30.

/139/   Ibid., p. 185. Cf. Margaret Mead, *Male and Female: A Study of the Sexes in a Changing World* (New York: William Morrow & Co., 1967) [Originally published in 1949]; Simone de Beauvoir, *The Second Sex*, trans. and ed. H. M. Parshley (New York: Alfred A. Knopf, 1953) [Originally published in two volumes under the title *Le Deuxieme Sexe: I.* and *Faits et Les Mythes: II. L'experience Vecue*, Paris, 1949].

/140/   Madeleine Barot, "Considerations on the Need for a Theology of the Place of Women in the Church," p. 153.

/141/   Ibid., p. 152.

/142/   Ibid.

/143/   Cf. Suzanne de Dietrich, *Free Men: Meditations on the Bible Today*, trans. Olive Wyon (Philadelphia: The Westminster Press, n.d.) [Originally published in London, 1961]. de Dietrich was a colleague of Madeleine Barot at the Sorbonne and was later a member of the faculty of the Ecumenical Institute, Chateau de Bossey, as well as a participant in many of the consultations sponsored by the Department on the Co-operation of Men and Women.

/144/   "For the purposes of discussions, the group used a working description of liberation theology as: *reflection on experiences of oppression in the light of human-divine action on behalf of the creation of a more human society.* . . . we tried to view liberation theology, not as one uniform schoool to which all must conform, but as a possible tool for affirming the radical differences in the way we hear, receive, and act upon the gospel in concrete situations." *Sexism in the 1970s*, p. 97. Emphasis theirs.

/145/   *Breaking Barriers, Nairobi, 1975: The Official Report of the Fifth Assembly of the World Council of Churches, Nairobi, 23 November-10 December, 1975*, ed. David M. Paton (London: S.P.C.K.; Grand Rapids: William B. Eerdmans for the World Council of Churches, 1976), p. 19.

/146/   Kenneth Slack, *Nairobi Narrative: The Story of the Fifth Assembly of the World Council of Churches, 23 November-10 December 1975* (London: S.C.M. Press, 1976), p. 44.

/147/   *Breaking Barriers*, p. 62.

/148/   Ibid., p. 107.

/149/   Ibid.

/150/   *The Community of Women and Men in the Church: A Proposal for Study Groups* (Geneva: World Council of Churches, 1975). Also published in *The Ecumenical Review* 27 (October 1975):386-393.

/151/   See "Conspectus of Studies and Programme," in *Accra, 1974: Meeting of the Commission on Faith and Order. Minutes and Documents*. Faith and Order Paper No. 71 (Geneva: World Council of Churches, 1974).

/152/   Ibid., p. 107.

/153/   Ibid.

/154/   *The Community of Women and Men in the Church: A Proposal for Study Groups*, p. 3.

/155/   *Breaking Barriers*, p. 107. See p. 67 above.

CHAPTER II

"A CHANCE TO CHANGE": THE COMMUNITY OF WOMEN AND MEN IN THE CHURCH STUDY

In the first chapter, the activities and thoughts of women involved in the World Council of Churches were recounted. The clarity of these women with regard to the theological implications of their role and image, as well as the conflict, often subtle, that ensued, was featured. When the Community of Women and Men in the Church Study began, this conflict surfaced. The Community Study thus heralded "a chance to change."

"A Chance to Change" was the sub-theme of the International Consultation on the Community of Women and Men in the Church, held in Sheffield, England, in 1981.[1] At the opening ceremony, Philip Potter, General Secretary of the World Council of Churches, delivered an address.[2] In his address, Potter recalled an event at the First World Conference on Faith and Order. Seven women were among the hundreds of men who had gathered to discuss church unity in Lausanne, Switzerland, in 1927. These women declared:

> In this great Conference assembled to try to discover the will of God for His Church, it has been laid upon the hearts of the women delegates to ask the Conference to realize the significance of the fact that out of nearly 400 delegates only seven are women. We do not wish to raise any discussion on the subject, but we believe that the right place of women in the Church and in the councils of the Church is of grave moment, and should be in the hearts and minds of all.[3]

The Sheffield Consultation bore witness to the fact that, since 1927, discussion had been raised "on the subject [of] the right place of women in the Church and in the councils of the Church."[4]

The women, as well as men, who gathered in Sheffield came with a sense of conviction similar to that of the women among the men in Lausanne. The women in Lausanne had also declared:

> The signatories of this document make no claim to state what is the right place of women in the Church, and in fact not all of them are agreed on all points. But on one they are agreed—that this is a matter that cannot be decided by men or by women alone. It is not for women to claim and for men to give, but as the Church unitedly sets out on a quest for deeper spiritual unity, we believe that in this matter also we shall unitedly see fresh light and a fresh revelation of God's will. . . .
>
> We believe that the call must go out from this Conference to all men and women alike, for faithfulness in giving the message, lest the differing gifts and opportunities be unused. . . .
>
> We . . . ask the prayers of all, that the gifts of women as well as of men may be offered and used to the full in the great task that lies before us . . .[5]

From the point of view of the women and men who gathered in Sheffield the task no longer lay before them; it was at hand.

During the years between the Fifth Assembly of the World Council of Churches and the Sixth Assembly, held in Vancouver, British Columbia, in 1983, the Community Study heralded hope for transformation in the World Council and in member churches. The report of the Central Committee to the Sixth Assembly noted: "The study directly touched more people and encouraged more grassroots participation during its four years of existence (1978-1981) than any previous Faith and Order-related programme."[6] This participation was called forth by the Community Study's method: a method primarily concerned not with access to already existing church structures or stances, nor with the articulation of an ideological position to be upheld, but with the cultivation of conversation, about so-called "non-theological" as well as traditionally theological matters, in local study groups.

Following the Sheffield Consultation, however, hope for transformation had already begun to fade. When a letter to the churches from Sheffield, along with recommendations from the delegates at the consultation, was presented to the World Council Central Committee, the discussion threatened to become disruptive. Then, at Vancouver, the split between issues raised by women and issues related to church unity opened once more. Questions being raised by women were received as "non-theological": as psychological or sociological or cultural or economic or political or racial or gender-related, but not related to theological discussion of unity.[7]

In this chapter, I will consider the significance of the Community Study in the context of the life and thought of the World Council. I will give particular attention to the Community Study process. I intend thereby to make visible the vision of unity that inspired the Community Study. It is a vision strikingly different from the vision of unity to which Faith and Order has borne witness.[8]

Liberation or Unity?

The drafters of the 1975 working paper on the Community of Women and Men in the Church Study stated: "Obviously we cannot approach the question of unity in the Church and among humankind without dealing specifically with what this means for women, and the ways in which both women and men can enter into a fully committed community."[9] This was not obvious to everyone, however. Even after the Commission on Faith and Order meeting at Accra and the Fifth Assembly at Nairobi, debate about the Community Study continued. The debate had a particular focus: the lodgment of the Community Study within the structure of the World Council.

Debate about the lodgment of the Study—whether it would be in the Secretariat on Faith and Order or in the Subunit on Women—resurfaced questions about the character of the Community Study. Is the Community Study primarily a women's study, concerned with women's liberation from male-dominated structures in church and society? Or is the Community Study concerned with issues integral to the goal of church unity? Some who debated the questions were reluctant to identify the Study with church unity and thus did not want to lodge it in the Secretariat on Faith and Order. These people, women and men alike, considered the Study to

be a women's study. For many men, this meant that the issues
being raised were not relevant to the work of Faith and Order.
For some women, this meant that the issues would be disre-
garded in Faith and Order discussions. Two underlying assumptions were present in this debate: church unity is made
manifest by the resolution of the classical controversies, particularly those over baptism, eucharist, ministry, and a common
confession of faith; and the issue of women's participation requires singular attention.

The 1976 Central Committee finally voted to lodge the
Community Study in the Secretariat on Faith and Order.[10]
The character of the Study was thus clarified; it was a study of
church unity with particular regard to the experience of women. According to Constance F. Parvey, who became the Director of the Study, this clarity was "part of the breakthrough"
of the Community Study:

> . . . the issues being raised by women and by feminist the-
> ology are no longer only 'women's issues' but, like Black
> theology and Latin American liberation theology, they are
> issues concerning the church and its wholeness. Though
> our program does deal with a broad spectrum of issues af-
> fecting women, it deals with them in relation to the impli-
> cations these topics have for women and men in the
> renewal of theology, teaching, and moral/ethical practice
> affecting their lives. Put negatively, this Study is a pro-
> gram to rescue the church from its masculine barriers,
> and, put positively, it is a pioneering venture of women
> and women, and women and men, struggling to 'image
> God' in humankind and in the church in a more true way.
> It is a new approach to unity, through an inner disunity—
> the imbalance in the relationships of women and men—
> that permeates every aspect of the life of the church.[11]

The Community Study was officially launched in January,
1978, when Parvey joined the Secretariat on Faith and Order
in Geneva.

During 1978, work on each part of the Community Study
process was begun. There were four parts: local study groups
within and among churches and church-related organizations,
regional consultations in the major continental and oceanic areas, specialized consultations on issues integral to Faith and
Order discussions of church unity, and an international consultation. The international consultation was planned to be the

culmination of the Community Study process, that is, to be the occasion when women and men who had participated in the Study in local and regional contexts would gather for conversation and celebration.

Local study groups were guided by a study booklet which was submitted to the Commission on Faith and Order for approval in August, 1978.[12] The study booklet was distributed to member churches of the World Council as well as to interested individuals and organizations. From the initial printing of nine thousand copies, the circulation grew to an estimated sixty-five thousand copies. The booklet was originally published in French, German, and English. It was translated by local initiative into at least thirteen additional languages.

The booklet set forth personal and cultural questions: about identity, sexuality, marriage, family life, and alternative lifestyles. Other questions addressed church teachings: exploring scripture and tradition in relation to a community of women and men in the church. The last set of questions concerned church structures: inquiring into renewal, worship, theological education, and ministry with regard to women's participation. Questions that ask participants to describe their particular contexts were also posed: What is the present situation in your church? Why are things the way they are? What is your vision of the community of women and men in the church? How can you move from where the church is to your vision of community? Throughout the study booklet, personal and corporate experience was taken as the starting point for reflection.[13]

Groups met to reflect on these questions in every continental and oceanic region of the world. Approximately 150 groups sent reports to Geneva. Reports came from South and Southeast Asia, Africa, the Middle East, the Caribbean, Latin America, Australasia, and the Pacific. The vast majority, however, were sent from countries on both sides of the North Atlantic. This distribution is, in part, a reflection of the disparity between communication technologies in the so-called "developed" and "developing" worlds.

The distribution may also be an indication that some of the questions posed by the Community Study were not accessible or relevant to some regions of the world. As an example, on 15 July 1981, at the International Consultation on the Com-

munity of Women and Men in the Church, some of the Third
World participants read a statement from the plenary floor.
The statement began:

> There has been a growing feeling of frustration
> among a large number of third world delegates that the
> concerns and issues expressed so far in the plenaries have
> had little relevance to where we are and where we come
> from. . . .
>
> As representatives not only of the church but also of
> our own particular societies, we feel we cannot confine
> our concerns to speaking of wholeness and community
> within the church. There is a larger struggle for the reali-
> zation of human wholeness, for liberation from wide-
> spread oppression that is classist and racist. . . .
>
> Our sense of priorities constrains us to speak from
> within and to this larger struggle.[14]

The statement continued with a call to participants to keep the
global context in mind during discussions of the community of
women and men in the church.

The reports received in Geneva testify to the diverse contexts whence they came. Some are printed, illustrated, and
bound documents. Some are short statements handwritten on
sheets torn from children's school tablets. Individual testimo-
nies, sermons, prayers, and poems are woven into many pages.
Rather abstract theological reflection fill other pages. Philip
Potter remarked, the reports are "a sort of algebraic sign of a
very great depth of well-buried meaning."[15]

The regional consultations brought together women and
men who had participated in local study groups. The first regional consultation was held just prior to the Commission on
Faith and Order meeting in Bangalore, India, in August, 1978.
In 1980, there were regional consultations in Beirut, Lebanon,
in the Federal Republic of Germany, and in Ibadan, Nigeria.
The Latin American and United States consultations were held
in 1981, in San Jose, in Costa Rica and in Stony Point, New
York, respectively.

Reports document the distinctive character of the discussion at each consultation. At the Middle East consultation, Orthodox theologians led an exploration of the image of
"woman" in scripture and tradition. Analysis of economic and
political situations was the starting point at the Latin American

consultation. African women recalled strong women role models from their tribal traditions and thus criticized the "the European image of womanhood" that came with Christianity. The European meeting was fraught with conflict, not between women and men so much as between people whose nations had been at war.[16]

The first of four specialized consultations was held in July, 1978. The task of this consultation was to explore ways in which long-standing Faith and Order issues could be addressed within the context of the Community Study. Three topics—ministry, Mariology, and biblical hermeneutics—were discussed in light of questions being raised by women. Mariology, in particular, posed difficulties. The divergence between Mary as portrayed by feminist theologians and as portrayed by Orthodox and Roman Catholic icons and doctrines seemed irreconcilable.[17]

A consultation on the "Ordination of Women in Ecumenical Perspective" met at Chateau Klingenthal, near Strasbourg, France, the next year. It had been nearly ten years since the first World Council consultation on the ordination of women had been held.[18] In the interim, notes regarding the need for further consultation had been made in statements issued by the Commission on Faith and Order as well as by the Sub-unit on Women in Church and Society.[19] The deepest disagreements, however, were neither acknowledged nor addressed.

At Klingenthal, 30 participants—theologians, pastors, biblical scholars, church leaders, administrators, and teachers—represented Orthodox, Roman Catholic, Old Catholic, and Protestant traditions. Admitting ancient differences, these women and men discussed a range of topics related to the ordination of women. God-language in biblical writings and church traditions, women's experiences as ministers or priests, women's ministry and priesthood in relation to ongoing Faith and Order work toward the mutual recognition of ministry, were among the topics discussed.[20]

A consultation on "Towards a Theology of Human Wholeness" was held at the Niederaltaich Benedictine Abbey near Munich, in 1980. Participants from five continents and from Protestant, Roman Catholic, and Orthodox traditions gathered around the affirmation that women and men are created in the image of God. Even so, the consultation did not begin with this vision of wholeness, but with statements of brokenness experienced in the cultures and churches whence the participants came: Latin America, Thailand, New Zealand, the Kongo society in Zaire, the Church of Greece, the Orthodox Church in France, the Roman Catholic Church in Italy, and the Lutheran and Roman Catholic Churches of Scandinavia. Thus "the disparity between what women have been taught about 'being woman' and what women experience their lives to be" was the starting point for the consultation.[21]

Having discussed this disparity and its consequences, participants in the Niederaltaich consultation reaffirmed the potentially transforming power of the theological teaching of *Imago Dei*. Participants interrelated the work of social scientists, their experience, and traditional teachings as they attempted to articulate a theological anthropology to heal the brokenness.[22]

The final specialized consultation on "The Authority of Scripture in Light of the New Experiences of Women" was held in December, 1980, in the Amsterdam Tropical Museum. Among the questions addressed were: "To what extent, and on what basis, is the Bible authoritative for Christian reflection and action today? Can the Bible's authority, at times unquestioned, be reaffirmed in the face of legitimate challenges from contemporary experience, including the new experiences of women?"[23]

As at Klingenthal and Niederaltaich, participants' experience was a vital part of the discussion. The women and men at Amsterdam acknowledged that their experience was diverse. They also acknowledged an experience that was common to them: the subordination of women in the name of biblical authority as defined by male-dominated biblical interpretation.

The interaction of biblical authority and experience, with particular regard to the experiences of women, was discussed in terms of text in relation to context. Participants from Africa, China, the Carribean, and Latin America, spoke about the use of biblical texts to reinforce rigid sexual stereotypes and patterns. Participants were convinced that part of the ecumenical task is "to delineate what is intrinsically 'Christian' through ages of intermingling Christian experience with various cultures, values, and traditions."[24]

Participants did not agree about the extent to which this

delineation is possible. Some argued that biblical texts are thoroughly conditioned by their originating patriarchal context and so are irrevocably oppressive of women. Some affirmed that despite this patriarchal cast "the central themes of God's revelation in Scripture call for an inclusive community and a liberation of all humanity." This difference of perspective was not resolved. Participants did agree, however, that "the churches have often used scriptural texts to reinforce the subordination of women."[25]

This discussion posed further questions for the women and men at Amsterdam: "Can we accept some passages and reject others? Does this not undermine the authority of the Bible as a whole?"[26] As participants discussed biblical authority, various points of view were expressed. Some asserted that authority as such is oppressive. For these women and men, authority was associated with hierarchical or legalistic church structures, as well as with repressive or militaristic political structures. Some, however, associated the word with continuity and stability within community and thus affirmed authority. As the report of the consultation remarks: "The different cultural, political and confessional backgrounds of participants made neat definitions of the term impossible. Connotations ranged from those of personal authority to authoritarianism to benevolent authority."[27] Participants affirmed together, however, that "the final test of authority" is transformation of life in community.[28]

The experiences of women and men, wrought in diverse contexts, were recognized as vital for theological reflection in local groups, at the regional consultations, and at the specialized consultations. The reports of the groups and consultations reveal, however, that the appeal to experience was as fraught with problems as it was full of possibilities. Participants in the Community Study most often appealed to experience to call into question long-assumed structures and concepts and point to liberating alternatives. Those structures experienced as life-giving, however, were not called into question. Thus awareness that the same structure or event may be experienced and valued differently became increasingly acute. It was acknowledged that the experience of no one person or group could be definitive for another. Neither experience nor tradition provided a clear vision of a global community of women and men.

"the whole people of God"

A rainbow of color transfigured the chilly, grey industrial city as women and men came to Sheffield for the International Consultation on the Community of Women and Men in the Church Study. Indian saris, Ghanaian headdresses, and Thai silks announced the homelands of their wearers. They, along with delegates from one hundred member churches of the World Council representing fifty-five countries, constituted the 250-member body that gathered in July, 1981.

It was the summer of the Royal Wedding in Great Britain. Shop windows were stuffed with memorabilia bearing the images of Charles and Diana. It was also the summer of riots among the ranks of the unemployed in England's northern industrial cities. A festive spirit and raging anger charged the atmosphere.

The consultation partook of both moods. The women and men who came to Sheffield were ladened with the fruits of study in local groups, in regional and in specialized consultations. They came to celebrate the Community Study and their participation in it. However, the differences that were represented threatened to divide the congregation. The vision of a community of women and men began to be visible in Sheffield only as both anguish and hope were articulated.

Dr. Robert Runcie, Archbishop of Canterbury, came into this congregation to deliver an address at the opening ceremony. Decrying "a highminded neutrality which hides a commitment to the status quo,"[29] Runcie addressed the issue of women's ordination. He recalled Luther's remark about women having "broad hips and a wide fundament to sit upon, keep house, bear, and raise children" and then reflected:

> In the first place ministry has become a masculine professional status occupation. It has become largely a matter of priesthood. . . .
>
> It is therefore imperative for the churches to regain a wide concept of ministry which is not narrowed by the jurisdictional inhibitions of those who cannot recognize a ministry unless it is institutionalized by the formal authorization of a bishop, a presbytery, or a congregation. Indeed, there is a real danger that an overconcentration on the issues involved in the ordination of women may rein-

force a clericalist view of the church: the only ministry worth exercising is an *ordained* one.[30]

Runcie paid tribute to "female minister": to "the contemplative nun, the nurse, the teacher, and social worker." "Women do not simply need to be trained for ordination for these roles," Runcie declared. "Indeed, some of the more imaginative courses for them," he continued, "are those which train them in spirituality . . . or in the recognition of their own selves, body, mind, and spirit, wombs and wit . . ."[31] Runcie concluded with a word of warning: "The 'ecumenical argument' on the ministry of women can be a two-edged sword, and I am convinced we must patiently listen to all the churches."[32]

Philip Potter, who spoke immediately after the Archbishop, departed from his prepared text in order to respond. Potter paid tribute to the work of Kathleen Bliss and Madeleine Barot, as well as to the women who spoke at the First World Conference on Faith and Order. Potter then told the congregation what he had learned as he read the reports from local study groups:

> I have read these reports, but I have also read between the lines, because as an old ecumenic I know that reports are only a sort of algebraic sign of a very great depth of well-buried meaning. What I have learned from this decoding exercise is that, compared, for example with the anger and frustration of the 1974 Berlin conference on sexism, I felt here through this enormous study which has gone on in so many parts of the world, the incredible pain and agony of it all—and with it the extraordinary love and patient endurance and perserverance which lie behind it.
>
> I perceived also the tremendous insights and wisdom—which have been lying there wasted for so many years and which are still emerging, thank God, for our enrichment—which have come out of this common effort largely by women. I have been aware, reading these reports, of the impotence of our male-dominated churches to see, hear, feel, decide, and act. And incensed with this impotence, I wait for the potency which God's Spirit can bring to us. For me, this study is a veritable test of our faith and of the ecumenical movement which is concerned about the unity of the whole people of God, as a sign and sacrament of the unity of all the peoples of the world.[33]

Potter then spoke about some specific issues that the Community Study raised as "urgent and inevitable for our attention as churches and Christians."[34]

Potter spoke first about biblical authority and interpretation. "We have systematically," *systematically*, Potter emphasized as he spoke, " . . . clung to all the things that strengthen and confirm out attitudes of domination and of hierarchical oppression. . . . this discovery challenges the way in which we deal with the Scriptures, and we shall have to do some hard thinking about this."[35] Secondly, said Potter, understandings of the church need to be rethought. "What *do* we mean," he thundered, "when we speak of the church as 'the whole people of God,' as we have been saying in the ecumenical movement for the past nearly forty years?"[36]

Potter's recital of issues continued as he challenged church historical records. He lamented the dearth of accounts about women's work and lauded the leadership women have given to renewal movements at various times in the history of the church. Potter also confessed that the reports had deepened his theological understanding of what it means to be human. "The heart of God's revelation of humanity," said Potter, "was male and female." Thus, Potter declared, God "indicated to us that there is no homogeneous, uniform way by which God wills that we should live, but rather in full recognition of our diversities and through these diversities we find our unity and community."[37]

Potter concluded: ". . . what I have learned from these studies has been a fresh impetus for our call to justice and peace."[38] He lifted up the figure of Mary, "that . . . person who has been used and abused by the churches concerning the role of woman." Mary came, said Potter, "to teach us . . . the beauty of holiness, . . . but also the power of healing and renewing love for a chance to change men and women toward one family in justice and peace."[39]

At subsequent plenary sessions, speakers addressed issues of justice and peace in community. The first of these four sessions was a dialogue between two theologians from the Federal Republic of Germany. Elisabeth Moltmann-Wendel and her husband, Jurgen, spoke about "Becoming Human in New Community." Tissa Balasuriya, a Roman Catholic priest from Sri Lanka, addressed oppression on the basis of gender, race, and class. Jean Baker Miller, a psychiatrist from the United States, reflected on "The Sense of Self in Women and Men: In Relation to Critical World Questions." At the final plenary session, Elisabeth Behr-Sigel, a theologian in the Orthodox Church in France, and Rose Zoe-Obianga, a theologian and member of the Presbyterian Church in the Cameroon, asked whether tradition, both cultural and ecclesial tradition, obliges restraint or offers resources for the community of women and men within the church.[40]

Delegates from the Third World read their statement at the end of the last plenary session. These women and men challenged the limited churchly context of the consultation, as of the Community Study:

> We are here, representing two-thirds of the world's women; they are the most exploited people on earth. We are from nations in Africa and Asia where the Church is a minority among other faiths and ideologies. Most of us have come here with no prior opportunity to share our concerns. When we did so here, we realized that they are not confined to women and men in community in the Church only, and that our perceptions about the global context are affirmed as urgent. We felt that dealing with such problems in section [rather than in plenary session] has precluded an overall view of our concerns. . . .
>
> While we seek to remedy conscious or unconscious sexual discrimination within the fellowship of the churches, let us also look to ways of ending the equally sinful exploitation of the powerless by the powerful, whenever that is found . . ."[41]

These women and men cited examples of exploitation in their countries: the employment of cheap labor by multinational corporations, the dumping of products not deemed fit for consumption in the West, the proliferation of a tourist industry based on the prostitution of women and young men.[42]

In response to this statement of Third World concerns, regional meetings were held. The Europeans drafted a written response to the Third World participants. They confessed:

> Our struggle is not merely for equality within the old structures which we experience as rigid, oppressive, alienating and destructive. We have experienced their destructiveness at the local level, as well as at the national and international levels. They destroy the identity of

adults and children, the relationship between individuals
and peoples. They alienate people at work, orient people's minds to capital, militarization and the exploitation
of the earth's resources.[43]

The Europeans also acknowledged the need to "reconsider
whether we have really accepted that each continent and each
cultural group has an identity of its own."[44]

A delineation of the oppressed and the oppressors
blurred during this exchange. Some women from the Third
World confessed that their churches are social ghettos and that
they are thus part of a privileged minority in their countries.
Some white, Western, middle-class women confessed their
complicity in the oppression of men, as well as women, in the
Third World. Delegates to the consultation considered the in-
terrelatedness of their struggles and spoke about a "web of oppression," woven with threads of race and class as well as
gender.[45]

As this exchange continued, it became evident that there
was more consensus on issues of economics, social, and political
justice than on the ordination of women.[46] Women and men
from diverse situations together deplored dehumanization and
deprivation relative to the distribution of governance and
goods around the globe. Then a woman seeking ordination in
the Church of England asked Roman Catholics and Orthodox
whether they would wield the "bludgeon of unity" to prevent
the ordination of women.[47] A woman delegate from the Orthodox Church in America asked whether the style of the consultation was to be "You say your theology and I'll say mine
and we'll see who gets points on the screen."[48] These questions resounded as the delegates moved from plenary sessions
to sections.

Delegates discussed issues raised in local, at regional, and
at specialized consultations, in seven sections: Identity and Relationships in New Community; Marriage, Family, and Life
Style in New Community; Scripture in New Community; Ministry and Worship in New Community; Authority and Church
Structures in New Community; Tradition and Traditions—A
Chance for Renewal?; Justice and Freedom in New Community. Each of the sections drafted a report that describes the
situations whence the delegates came, analyses obstacles to
change for women and men, and proposes steps toward trans-

formation. The work done in these sections, as during the consultation, "underlined the necessity to overcome the web of oppression—of sex, race and class—which veils and blocks that 'fruitful agony of travail' we anticipate when we confess the Christ who lives though crucified."[49]

The "fruitful agony of travail" was also expressed in a Letter from Sheffield to the Churches and in recommendations addressed to various units and sub-units of the World Council. The Letter and the recommendations were presented to member churches of the World Council at the Central Committee meeting in August, 1981. The presentation began with an affirmation:

> At Sheffield the Community of Women and Men in the Church Study was born. Not a program *against* sexism, *for* more participation of women; that was Berlin 1974. Sheffield 1981 is about *women and men becoming human in a new community* and the means to bring that about. Since the beginning of the Study process in 1978 its framework has not been illness, but health and healing, not brokenness, but new community.[50]

After a review of the Community Study's process, the Letter and recommendations were delivered to the Central Committee for approval and then for transmission to member churches and appropriate units and sub-units of the World Council.[51]

The Central Committee approved all but two recommendations. One of these two recommended that at the Sixth Assembly "50% of all membership elected to sub-units and committees of the WCC be women" and "three of the six Presidents of the WCC elected at the Assembly be women."[52] Debate on this recommendation raged for days. Orthodox Church members of the Central Committee, in particular, were opposed to its adoption. The World Council of Churches, they declared, is "not a church but a fellowship of the churches and has no right to legislate for its members."[53] Finally, a compromise resolution was adopted. This resolution affirmed "a principle of equal representation" as a goal or criterion rather than a quota or mandate to member churches.[54]

The other exception was a recommendation that the Central Committee endorse the Sheffield Letter and send it to

member churches of the World Council. Messages or letters
written on behalf of World Council Assemblies or consultations
are most often sent to member churches without comment or
criticism. Two paragraphs in this Letter, however, were ques-
tioned. The first paragraph stated:

> . . . for many women and men there is real pain in
> the frustration of a church life controlled by male leader-
> ship, where, for instance, women feel called to the minis-
> try of word and sacraments and ordination is not open to
> them or where the Church has not responded to creative
> developments in society.[55]

The second paragraph was a brief statement that affirmed
"sexuality is not opposed to spirituality but . . . Christian spirituality is one of body, mind and spirit in their wholeness."[56]

Once again, the Orthodox members of the Central Committee led the opposition to the Letter's endorsement. They
asked that a phrase be included in order to express the pain
felt by those whose Holy Tradition is threatened by the ordination of women. The Central Committee finally agreed to send
the Sheffield Letter, but not until a cover letter acknowledging
the Dresden debate could be drafted to accompany it.[57]

The Sheffield recommendations, along with a report of
the Community Study, were presented to the Commission on
Faith and Order meeting in January, 1982. Four people who
had contributed to the Community Study addressed the commission. Constance F. Parvey, the first speaker, gave "an impression" of the study, reflecting on issues of identity, life in
community and in the church as they had arisen in the study
process.[58] The issue of identity, she stated, emerged as most
important. Parvey noted that the cross-cultural approach of
the study had disclosed the way in which social and economic
situations determine identity. No universal patterns for women and men could be pointed out, she concluded.[59]

Nicolas Lossky, Lecturer in Western church history at the
University of Paris and a member of the Orthodox Church in
France, challenged members of the commission to incorporate
the concerns of the Community Study into their reflection on
all Faith and Order issues. Lossky then focused his attention
on ministry, speaking from his Orthodox point of view. He
clarified two presuppositions at the outset: "all members of the

eucharistic community have a gift of the Spirit, a ministry, a *diakonia*" and "sexual distinctions are not abolished in the body of Christ, but their distortions are overcome."[60] Thus, stated Lossky, women can and do fulfill diverse ministries in the Orthodox Church. Most significant among these ministries, he noted, are those of iconographer and of teacher in theological academies.[61]

Lossky then clarified the Orthodox conviction that women may not be ordained to the presidency of the eucharistic community:

> The absence of such ordination in our tradition has to do with the maleness of Christ. In Orthodox liturgy, the bishop (priest) is at certain times regarded as image or type of Christ. This is no mere allegory; typology or symbolism in the Orthodox tradition is no mere imagery, no mere evocation of another reality. A symbol is not merely something suggested, it is participation in the true reality, the disclosing of God's plan, of the eternal in the transitory, the discovery of 'the point of intersection of the timeless with time' (T.S. Eliot, *Four Quartets*, Dry Salvages, V).[62]

This understanding of symbolism calls for serious theological study, Lossky stated. "Such a study," he concluded, "has not been made as yet and it will probably take a long time. But in the meantime, be patient with us and give the possibility of effecting this reflection."[63]

Mary Tanner, Moderator of the Community Study's Advisory Committee and then Lecturer at the Anglican Theological College, Cambridge University, was the next speaker. Tanner identified "the issue of right scriptural interpretation" as the most challenging issue raised by the Community Study. The study, Tanner noted, broadened the community of interpreters beyond "professional (male) experts" to "the whole people of God." Tanner recognized that diverse interpretations resulted from this method of study. Difficult questions about norms for interpretation have been raised for the Commission on Faith and Order, she concluded.[64]

The last speaker was Letty Russell, Associate Professor of Theology at the Yale Divinity School. Russell contrasted a "paradigm of domination" and a "paradigm of doxology" as she spoke. Life in the church, Russell declared, has been ordered according to a "paradigm of domination." This paradigm is challenged in the reports of local groups who participated in the Community Study. The women and men who wrote the reports envision life in a community in which "people value the possibility of diversity and inclusiveness even when this tends to break the pyramid of values open into a rainbow spectrum of colours, people and ideas." This way of life, said Russell, expresses the "paradigm of doxology." According to this paradigm, church unity is made manifest not by consensus on doctrine and polity but "in trying to reach out to the outsiders in order to discover a more inclusive consensus."[65] Russell concluded: "The Community Study has not concluded because its method is now essential to all the work of Faith and Order."[66]

The future of the Community Study was a matter of much debate at the meeting of the Commission on Faith and Order. William H. Lazareth, the new Director of Faith and Order, stated:

> The Community of Women and Men in the Church Study has now come to an end. . . .
> Originally a three-year programme, extended to four, the purpose of the Study was to investigate the implications for the ecumenical movement of the new levels of participation of women in many dimensions of church life, as part of the search for the new community we seek. It was expected that the Study would do intensive biblical and theological work on issues such as the interpretation and authority of the Bible, the understanding and roles of women and men in God's saving history, styles of participation of women in ministry, including the ordination of women in an ecumenical context. Since the method of work had a broad base, inviting all member churches to participate, and the style of the study was contextual, inviting groups to speak from within their own cultural and church traditions, it was also anticipated that the range of issues to emerge would have widespread implications, not only for the future work of Faith and Order but for the overall work of the World Council of Churches.[67]

Lazareth ended his remarks with reference to the final report of the Community Study that would be available for study prior to the Sixth Assembly, "where it will contribute to the discussions on churches seeking unity and the renewal of the life of the whole human family."[68]

According to the minutes of the Commission on Faith and Order meeting, "plenary discussion revealed broad and deep appreciation for the Community Study": "In spite of fears that the study would be perceived as . . . a 'women's study,' the development of the project has genuinely been as a 'community study'."[69] During this discussion, two alternatives for further reflection on the issues raised by the Community Study were debated: study of specific issues or infusion of all Faith and Order studies with the perspectives of the Community Study. The accent fell on the second alternative. It was then "observed that the three studies on Faith and Order's present agenda which must be infused by the perspective of the Community Study are The Unity of the Church and the Renewal of the Human Community, Towards a Common Expression of the Apostolic Faith Today, and Baptism, Eucharist and Ministry."[70]

The Lima meeting of the Commission on Faith and Order is already a landmark in ecumenical history. From this meeting a document, *Baptism, Eucharist and Ministry*, was transmitted to member churches of the World Council. In the preface to this document this judgment was ventured: " . . . that theologians of such widely different traditions should be able to speak so harmoniously about baptism, eucharist and ministry is unprecedented in the modern ecumenical movement."[71] Since the First World Conference on Faith and Order, the mutual recognition of baptism, eucharist and ministry had been listed among the requirements for visible church unity. *Baptism, Eucharist and Ministry* is thus a monument to long-standing Faith and Order agenda set by the classical church controversies.

When the Commission on Faith and Order sent *Baptism, Eucharist and Ministry* to member churches, the churches were asked to study the document and to make an official response. Members of the commission made several proposals to insure that the perspective of the Community Study would be part of the churches' study. Specifically, they called for a section in the document study guide that would elucidate the ways in which mutual recognition of baptism, eucharist and ministry is related to the community of women and men.[72] It was also proposed that "the volume of theological essays on the BEM text should include one or two essays on the theme, especially as it relates to the ordination of women to diaconal and eucharistic ministries."[73] Finally, it was suggested that a special study on the ordination of women be undertaken by Faith and Order.[74]

More proposals were made with regard to the Community Study. A working group at the meeting of the Commission on Faith and Order recommended that a member of the Faith and Order staff be assigned to represent the concerns of the study, especially to the World Council Staff Task Force responsible for planning the Sixth Assembly; that the concerns of the study be a vital part of the visitation and consultation program preceding the Assembly; and that the story of the study be told at the Assembly. More specifically, the working group recommended that a full plenary session be allotted to telling the story of the Community Study; that a resource center be set up at the Assembly to provide information on the study; that Bible studies at the Assembly represent the perspectives of women; that worship materials be prepared according to World Council guidelines for non-sexist language; and that speakers and worship leaders include women familiar with the study.[75]

The sermon at the opening worship service of the Sixth Assembly of the World Council of Churches was preached by Pauline Webb. Expounding I John 1, Webb emphasized the lively character of the word of God: "The word of God is never just a spoken or a written word. It is always a happening, a real life event." Webb recalled the Fifth Assembly in Nairobi to illustrate her point:

> . . . Nairobi 1975, the year the U.N. decreed was to be International Women's Year. For some of us a new dimension was given to the theme 'Jesus Christ frees and unites' by the event that became known as the 'Women's session', a session in which women from many parts of the world opened their hearts and gave expression to the pain they'd felt in being excluded from a full partnership with men in the life and leadership of the church. It was as though we were at last free to be heard and recognized for our own worth and with our own gifts. And again it's not the words that were spoken nor the resolutions that were passed that I recall now but the event in itself, an

event that led to the whole study process on the Community of Women and Men in the Church which for some of us has been life-changing.[76]

Webb then spoke about the living word as "the word communicated through the body and a word written in blood." She affirmed the shedding of blood as "a symbol of creation and life rather than of destruction and death" in the experience of women.[77]

People brought "symbols of life" to place upon the altar during the opening worship service. These symbols were expressions of the Assembly's theme: "Jesus Christ—the Life of the World." The last symbol brought to the altar was a baby girl, seven-month-old Miriayi Mvuselelo of Zimbabwe. Miriayi was lifted by her mother, Sithembiso Nyoni, over the altar and into the arms of the presiding minister, Philip Potter. This moment became a symbol of the Sixth Assembly.

A host of women were among the presenters of the Assembly's theme and sub-themes to plenary sessions. Among these women were Dame Nita Barrow, a Methodist laywoman from Barbados and formerly on the staff of the Christian Medical Commission; Sithembiso Nyoni, an Anglican laywoman from Zimbabwe; Domitila Barrios de Chungera, president of the miner's human rights organization in Bolivia; Dorothee Solle, professor at Union Theological Seminary in New York; Mother Euphrasia, Mother Superior of the Dealu convent of the Romanian Orthodox Patriarchate; Helen Caldicott, Australian medical doctor and member of Physicians for Social Responsibility; and Frieda Haddad, Orthodox laywoman from Beirut.[78]

More women were present at the Sixth Assembly than at any previous Assembly. They came as official delegates, advisors, observers, accredited visitors, press, and staff. Barbel von Wartenberg, who succeeded Brigalia Bam as Director of the Sub-unit on Women in Church and Society, commented: "The Vancouver meeting was marked by the numerically greatest participation of women ever—29 per cent of the voting delegates. It was the aim in all planning procedures to give about one third of Assembly leadership to women." Von Wartenberg then added a word of caution: "But the numerical argument often hides the real difficulties behind the issue of women's participation."[79]

Reports of the Vancouver Assembly testify to the participation of women. Women's exclusion from church structures, the ordination of women, economic factors related to the sexual exploitation of women, are noted. In the report on "Taking Steps Toward Unity" there is a paragraph on the Community Study:

> . . . through the study of the Community of Women and Men in the Church, many have discovered that life in unity must carry with it the overcoming of division between the sexes, and have begun to envision what profound changes must take place in the life of the Church and the world. The participants at the Sheffield conference of the Community of Women and Men in the Church emphasized that one form of oppression is interwoven with others. The inter-relatedness of racism, classism and sexism calls for a combined struggle since no one form of renewal will, by itself, accomplish a renewal of ecclesial community. Such insights would be deepened and built upon with the study on the Unity of the Church and the Renewal of Human Community. Further, the specific challenges contained in the Sheffield recommendations should be taken up in the process of response to 'Baptism, Eucharist and Ministry', the work on confessing the apostolic faith, and the quest for common ways of decision-making and teaching authoritatively.[80]

This paragraph did not appear in the first draft of the report, which reflected on the work of the Commission on Faith and Order. It was added after Margaret Sonnenday, a Methodist laywoman and member of the Community Study's Advisory Committee, stood up on the floor of plenary session and called for explicit expression of commitment to continued reflection on the issues raised by the study.

In this paragraph on the Community Study, and in every other paragraph from Vancouver that mentions women, the primary reference is the renewal of the church. In reports from the Berlin, Accra, Nairobi, and Sheffield gatherings, the primary reference is the unity of the church, as well as the significance of so-called "non-theological factors." Indeed, the Community Study was initiated at Berlin by a call to address "the problems of speaking about the action of God in ways that

communicate the gospel to all races, sexes, and cultures."[81]
And Philip Potter declared at Sheffield:

> For me, this study is a veritable test of our faith and of the
> ecumenical movement which is concerned about the
> unity of the whole people of God, as a sign and sacrament
> of the unity of all the peoples of the world.[82]

In the Berlin, Accra, Nairobi, and Sheffield statements, the inseparability of theological and so-called "non-theological factors," of unity and renewal, of the church and the world, is
articulated. In the reports from Vancouver, that inseparability
is strained.

In the guidelines for future work of the World Council,
the report of the Assembly's Programme Guidelines Committee, the strain gives way to separation. One of the "priority
areas" listed in the guidelines is "theological work." Under
work named theological, Faith and Order studies such as "Baptism, Eucharist and Ministry" and "The Unity of the Church
and the Renewal of Human Community" are noted.[83] The
Community Study is mentioned in another priority area,
under the heading "concerns and perspectives of women."[84]
In this priority area, the issues of "women and work, women in
poverty, violence against women, sex tourism, and women as
initiators and participants in social change" are listed. Women's "concerns and perspectives" relative to theology or to
understandings of church unity are not mentioned.

To relegate the Community Study to the priority area
under the heading "concerns and perspectives of women" was
to dismiss the implications of its method. In the report of the
Lima meeting of the Commission on Faith and Order it was
remarked:

> In expressing appreciation for the Community Study, it
> was observed that theologians like to receive new data,
> but then to absorb this data in a way that does not require
> any change in the basic theological position. This study,
> however, requires that our theologies be adapted to re
> spond to the voices which have been heard.[85]

At Vancouver it was clear that theologians did not intend to
change the basic position out of which the Commission on
Faith and Order has worked.

Before the Amsterdam Assembly, the women who met in
Baarn to write the report of their study on women in the
church concluded:

> The . . . most important thing which all this discussion ap-
> pears to reveal is that the arrangements for a relatively
> full service of women in the Church have been character-
> ized by a rhythm of advance, retreat, advance, etc. . . . A
> recalcitrant and sceptical frame of mind about women's
> place in the Church has, in fact, never been completely
> overcome.[86]

In the next chapter, I will investigate the "recalcitrant and
sceptical frame of mind" of which these women spoke and to
which the retreat at Vancouver must be referred.

Notes

/1/ "A Chance to Change" is also the title of a brief, popular ac-
count of the International Consultation. See Betty Thompson, *A
Chance to Change: Women and Men in the Church* (Philadelphia:
Fortress Press; Geneva: World Council of Churches, 1982).
/2/ See Philip Potter, "The Community of Women and Men in the
Church," *Mid-Stream: An Ecumenical Journal* 21 (July 1982):279-284.
Potter's address is also published under the title "A Chance to
Change," in *The Community of Women and Men in the Church: The
Sheffield Report*, ed. Constance F. Parvey (Geneva: World Council of
Churches, 1983), pp. 23-28.
/3/ *Faith and Order: Proceedings of the World Conference, Lausanne, August 3-21, 1927*, ed. H.N. Bate (New York: George H. Doran
Co., 1927), p. 372.
/4/ Ibid.
/5/ Ibid., pp. 372-73.
/6/ *Nairobi to Vancouver, 1975-1983: Report of the Central Committee to the Sixth Assembly of the World Council of Churches* (Geneva: World Council of Churches, 1983), p. 85.
/7/ See p. 105 below.
/8/ For discussion of that vision see chap. III, pp. 107-154 below.
/9/ *The Community of Women and Men in the Church: A Proposal
for Study Groups* (Geneva: World Council of Churches, 1975), p. 1.
Also published in *The Ecumenical Review* 27 (October 1975):386-393.
/10/ *World Council of Churches Central Committee, Minutes of the
Twenty-Ninth Meeting, Geneva, Switzerland, 10-18 August 1976* (Geneva: World Council of Churches, 1976), p. 28.
/11/ Constance F. Parvey, "Reflections on the questions asked at
the Task Force meeting of August 5, 1980," Geneva, World Council

of Churches, August 7, 1980. Unpublished Memorandum, Personal
Files of Melanie A. May, Lombard, Illinois.
/12/   For a record of the discussion at this meeting, see *Sharing in
One Hope: Reports and Documents from the Meeting of the Faith and
Order Commission, 15-30 August, 1978, Ecumenical Christian Centre, Bangalore, India.* Faith and Order Paper No. 92 (Geneva: World
Council of Churches, n.d.), pp. 263-270.
/13/   *Study on The Community of Women and Men in the Church*
(Geneva: World Council of Churches, 1978).
/14/   "A Statement from Third World Participants," 15 July 1981,
Sheffield, England. Unpublished Document, Personal Files of Melanie A. May, Lombard, Illinois. A revised version of this statement,
along with the European response to it, is published in *The Community of Women and Men in the Church: The Sheffield Report*, ed.
Parvey, pp. 96-101. Cf. pp. 90-91 below.

One set of questions in the study booklet that evidences a Western cast and concern is: "Do your responsibilities inside and outside
the home conflict with one another? How is this conflict different for
men than for women? What makes it possible for you to cope with
that conflict? How can the community of women and men in the
church help you with your struggle for personal fulfillment?" (*Study
on The Community of Women and Men in the Church*, p. 16).

Although not explicit, this formulation assumes a distinction between two spheres: the domestic/private/female and the eco-
nomic/public/male. Erika Bourguigon, in her introduction to the
anthology *A World of Women: Anthropological Studies of Women in
the Societies of the World* (New York: Praeger Publishers, 1980), suggests that because this distinction seems self-evident in the West we
should be alert to the possibility that it is an unexamined cultural ax-
iom. The case studies presented in this anthology evidence that in
some societies the domestic sphere is public and in some societies the
market place is the world of women. Definitions of domestic and economic, private and public, women's world and men's world, thus begin to shift when the self-perceptions of people in different contexts
are taken seriously. Indeed, the distinctions may blur in some sociocultural settings.

The drafters of the study booklet intended to ask not to answer
questions. Insofar as the questions evidence a Western cast, they testify to the embeddedness of some of the drafters in Western sociocultural contexts.

Much Western feminist analysis has assumed this sharp distinction of spheres and even argued that the distinction is universal. For
example see Sherry Ortner, "Is Female to Male as Nature is to Culture?" in *Women, Culture, and Society* (ed. Michelle Zimbalist
Rosaldo and Louise Lamphere [Stanford: Stanford University Press,
1974], pp. 67-87). Some recent studies of women in Western societies,
however, have called this distinction into question. Eugenia Kaledin,
for example, attempts to present a view of American women in the
1950s that modifies the prevailing assumption that women were sim-

ply rejected from the public sphere after World War II and relegated
to the domestic sphere during the decade that followed (*Mothers and
More: American Women in the 1950s* [Boston: Twayne Publishers,
1984]). Cf. pp. 23-24 above.

　　　Kaledin, like most Western feminist analysts, focuses her attention on the lives of white, middle-class women. For a study of how
the lives of white women and men influenced the lives of black working women see Jacqueline Jones, *Labor of Love, Labor of Sorrow:
Black Women, Work and the Family from Slavery to the Present*
(New York: Basic Books, 1985).

/15/　Philip Potter, "The Community of Women and Men in the
Church," *Mid-Stream: An Ecumenical Journal* 21 (July 1982):281.

/16/　See *The Community of Women and Men in the Church: Re-
port of the Asian Consultation held at the United Theological College,
Bangalore, on 11-15 August 1978* (Bangalore: Printers India, 1978);
*Report of the Middle Eastern Council of Churches Consultation on
The Community of Women and Men in the Church, Beirut, Lebanon,
January, 1980* (Geneva: World Council of Churches, 1981); *"A Space
to Grow In. . .": Report of the European Regional Consultation of The
Community of Women and Men in the Church Study, Bad Segeberg,
Federal Republic of Germany, 20th-24th June, 1980* (Geneva: World
Council of Churches, 1981); *Report of the All-Africa Regional Consul-
tation on Community of Women and Men in the Church Study, Iba-
dan, Nigeria, 15-19 September 1980* (Nairobi: An All-Africa
Conference of Churches Publication, 1981); *Communidad de Mujeres
y Hombres en la Iglesia: Encuentro latinamericano de mujeres, 15-18
marzo de 1981* (San Jose, Costa Rica: Sebila, 1981); *A Gathering to
Share Our Hope: Report on the National Consultation U.S. Section of
the World Council of Churches Study of the Community of Women
and Men in the Churches, Stony Point, New York, March 25-26, 1981*
(New York: National Council of Churches, 1981).

/17/　See "Notes on *Ministry, Mariology and Biblical Hermeneutics*
Consultation, sponsored by The Community of Women and Men in
the Church Study, June 26-29, 1978, Foyer John Knox, Geneva, Switzerland." Unpublished Document, Personal Files of Melanie A. May,
Lombard, Illinois.

/18/　See *What is ordination coming to? Report of a Consultation
on the Ordination of Women, held in Cartigny, Geneva, Switzerland,
21st-26th September 1970*, ed. Brigalia Bam (Geneva: World Council
of Churches, 1971).

/19/　See *One Baptism, One Eucharist and a Mutually Recognized
Ministry: Three Agreed Statements.* Faith and Order Paper No. 73
(Geneva: World Council of Churches, 1975), pp. 45-49; *Orthodox Women, Their Role and Participation in the Orthodox Church: Report on
the Consultation of Orthodox Women, Agapia, Roumania, September, 1976* (Geneva: World Council of Churches, 1977), p. 5; *Towards
An Ecumenical Consensus on Baptism, the Eucharist and the Ministry: A Reply to the Replies of the Churches.* Faith and Order Paper
No. 84 (Geneva: World Council of Churches, 1977), pp. 17-19; *Consul-*

tation of European Christian Women, Brussels, 29 January to 4 February 1978 (Geneva: World Council of Churches, 1978), p. 10; *Sharing in One Hope: Reports and Documents from the Meeting of the Faith and Order Commission, 15-30 August 1978*, pp. 269-270.

/20/ See *Ordination of Women in Ecumenical Perspective: Workbook for the Church's Future*, ed. Constance F. Parvey. Faith and Order Paper No. 105 (Geneva: World Council of Churches, 1980).

/21/ "Human Wholeness," in *In God's Image: Reflections on Identity, Human Wholeness and the Authority*, ed. Janet Crawford and Michael Kinnamon (Geneva: World Council of Churches, 1983), p. 50.

/22/ Ibid., pp. 70-77.

/23/ "The Authority of Scripture," in *In God's Image*, p. 82.

/24/ Ibid., p. 89.

/25/ Ibid.

/26/ Ibid., p. 94.

/27/ Ibid., p. 96.

/28/ Ibid., p. 104.

/29/ Robert Runcie, "The Community of Women and Men in the Church," in *The Community of Women and Men in the Church Study: The Sheffield Report*, ed. Parvey, p. 20.

/30/ Ibid., p. 21.

/31/ Ibid., pp. 21-22.

/32/ Ibid., p. 22. It is astonishing that Runcie, the highest-ranking Archbishop of the Church of England, chose this occasion to address the dangers of clericalism. Runcie's choice affiliates the dangers of clericalism with women, while in his church only men can be clerics!

/33/ Philip Potter, "The Community of Women and Men in the Churches," *Mid-Stream: An Ecumenical Journal* 21 (July 1982):281.

/34/ Ibid.

/35/ Ibid.

/36/ Ibid., pp. 281-282.

/37/ Ibid., p. 283.

/38/ Ibid.

/39/ Ibid., p. 284.

/40/ For the full text of the plenary presentations see *Mid-Stream: An Ecumenical Journal* 21 (July 1982). For a summary report of the plenaries see *The Community of Women and Men in the Church: The Sheffield Report*, ed. Parvey, pp. 20-73.

/41/ "Women and Men in Community for Humanity," in *The Community of Women and Men in the Church: The Sheffield Report*, ed. Parvey, pp. 96-97.

/42/ Ibid., pp. 97-98.

/43/ "A European Response," in *The Community of Women and Men in the Church: The Sheffield Report*, ed. Parvey, p. 99.

/44/ Ibid., pp. 99-100.

/45/ See the section report on "Justice and Freedom in New Community," in *The Community of Women and Men in the Church: The Sheffield Report*, ed. Parvey, pp. 145-154.

/46/   Cf. Kathleen Bliss, *The Service and Status of Women in the Churches* (London: S.C.M. Press, 1952), p. 79. Quoted on p. 31 above.

/47/   Thompson, *A Chance to Change: Women and Men in the Church*, p. 73.

/48/   Ibid.

/49/   Preface to "The Community of Women and Men in the Church: The Sheffield Recommendations." As presented to the World Council of Churches Central Committee, meeting in Dresden, German Democratic Republic, August, 1981. Unpublished Document, Personal Files of Melanie A. May, Lombard, Illinois. Cf. *World Council of Churches Central Committee, Minutes of the Thirty-Third Meeting, Dresden, German Democratic Republic, 16-26 August 1981* (Geneva: World Council of Churches, 1981), pp. 14-30.

/50/   Constance F. Parvey, "The Journey from the Sheffield International Consultation to Dresden: Plenary Report on the Sheffield International Consultation, The Community of Women and Men in the Church Study." World Council of Churches Central Committee, meeting in Dresden, German Democratic Republic, August 1981. Unpublished Document, Personal Files of Melanie A. May, Lombard, Illinois.

/51/   See "The Community of Women and Men in the Church: The Sheffield Recommendations" and "A Letter from Sheffield," in *The Community of Women and Men in the Church: The Sheffield Report*, ed. Parvey, pp. 83-90, 91-93. For responses to the recommendations and to the Letter by the World Council of Churches Central Committee see *Minutes of the Thirty-Third Meeting*, pp. 16-30.

/52/   Ibid., p. 90.

/53/   *World Council of Churches Central Committee, Minutes of the Thirty-Third Meeting*, p. 27. Cf. "The Church, the Churches and the World Council of Churches: The Ecclesiological Significance of the World Council of Churches," in *A Documentary History of the Faith and Order Movement, 1927-1963*, ed. Lukas Vischer (St. Louis, Missouri: Bethany Press, 1963), pp. 169-171. This statement, which addresses the issue of legislation relative to the World Council and its member churches, was adopted at the Central Committee meeting in Toronto in 1950. See *Minutes and Reports of the Third Meeting of the Central Committee of the World Council of Churches, Toronto (Canada), July 9-15, 1950* (Geneva: World Council of Churches, 1950).

/54/   Ibid., pp. 26, 29.

/55/   "A Letter from Sheffield," in *The Community of Women and Men in the Church: The Sheffield Report*, ed. Parvey, p. 92.

/56/   Ibid.

/57/   *World Council of Churches Central Committee, Minutes of the Thirty-Third Meeting*, p. 30.

/58/   *Towards Visible Unity: Commission on Faith and Order, Lima, 1982*, vol. I: *Minutes and Addresses*, ed. Michael Kinnamon. Faith and Order Paper No. 112 (Geneva: World Council of Churches, 1982), p. 126.

/59/ For the full text of Parvey's address see "The Community of Women and Men in the Ecumenical Movement: Held Together in Hope and Sustained by God's Promise—A Personal Reflection," in *The Community of Women and Men in the Church: The Sheffield Report*, ed. Parvey, pp. 156-183.

/60/ *Towards Visible Unity*, vol. I, p. 126.

/61/ Thompson, *A Chance to Change: Women and Men in the Church*, p. 85.

/62/ Ibid., p. 86.

/63/ Ibid.

/64/ *Towards Visible Unity*, vol. I, p. 127.

/65/ Ibid.

/66/ Ibid. For the full text of the addresses delivered by Lossky, Tanner, and Russell see *Mid-Stream: An Ecumenical Journal* 21 (July 1982).

/67/ Ibid., p. 21.

/68/ Ibid., p. 23.

/69/ Ibid., p. 128.

/70/ Ibid., p. 129.

/71/ *Baptism, Eucharist and Ministry*, Faith and Order Paper No. 111 (Geneva: World Council of Churches, 1982), p. ix.

/72/ *Towards Visible Unity*, vol. I, pp. 86-87.

/73/ Ibid., p. 129. There is only passing reference to the ordination of women in the volume of theological essays. See *Ecumenical Perspectives on Baptism, Eucharist and Ministry*, ed. Max Thurian. Faith and Order Paper No. 116 (Geneva: World Council of Churches, 1983), pp. 119-120, 136.

/74/ Ibid., p. 130.

/75/ Ibid., pp. 116-117.

/76/ Pauline Webb, "The Word of Life," *The Ecumenical Review* 35 (October 1983):345.

/77/ Ibid., p. 348.

/78/ For a summary of the presentations on the Assembly theme and sub-themes see *Gathered For Life: Official Report, VI Assembly, World Council of Churches, Vancouver, Canada, 24 July-10 August 1983*, ed. David Gill (Geneva: World Council of Churches; Grand Rapids: Wm. B. Eerdmans, 1983), pp. 21-26.

/79/ Barbel von Wartenberg, "Participation in the Oikoumene: Reflections on Women's Participation in the Sixth Assembly—Vancouver: A Model," *The Ecumenical Review* 36 (April 1984):156.

/80/ *Gathered for Life*, pp. 49-50.

/81/ *Sexism in the 1970s: Discrimination Against Women. A Report of a World Council of Churches Consultation, West Berlin, 1974* (Geneva: World Council of Churches, 1975), p. 100. See p. 64 above.

/82/ Philip Potter, "The Community of Women and Men in the Church," *Mid-Stream: An Ecumenical Journal* 21 (July 1982):281.

/83/ *Gathered for Life*, pp. 253-254.

/84/ Ibid., p. 256.

/85/ *Towards Visible Unity*, vol. I, p. 129.

/86/   *Revised Interim Report of a Study on the Life and Work of Women in the Church, including Reports of an Ecumenical Conference of Church Women, Baarn, Holland and of the Committee on "The Life and Work of Women in the Church" of the Assembly of the World Council of Churches, Amsterdam* (Geneva: World Council of Churches, 1948), p. 25.

CHAPTER III

"... THEN THE BODY MUST BE ONE": THE FAITH AND ORDER MOVEMENT

In chapter two, the Community of Women and Men in the Church Study was presented as "a chance to change." Women had contributed to the life of the World Council of Churches since its inception and they had clarified the theological dimensions of their involvement. Only with the inception of the Community Study, however, were women received as participants rather than as problems to theological discussion of church unity.

The Community Study was founded in the affirmation that all the people of God are called to engage in theological conversation about church unity. Women and men were invited to gather in local groups to reflect on traditional teachings in light of their own experience and on their own experience in light of traditional theological teachings. Experiences rather than classical ecclesial controversies shaped the conversation. Cultural, national, economic, racial, gender-related and other so-called "non-theological" factors were recognized as significant for theological reflection. Diverse experiences and perspectives were thus acknowledged and appreciated by the Community Study. The end of the study signaled the resurgence of another vision of unity, a vision represented by the ongoing work of Faith and Order.

The Faith and Order movement was inspired at the 1910 World Missionary Conference held in Edinburgh, Scotland. The World Missionary Conference was called in order to address the problems of dissension and division on mission fields. Discussion of matters related to doctrine and polity was prohibited at the Edinburgh conference, so that as many missionary societies as possible would participate. However, Charles

H. Brent, Anglican bishop of the Philippines and later of Western New York, foresaw another step on the road to unity while he was at the Edinburgh conference.[1] Brent began to envision church unity built not on cooperation but on agreement with regard to doctrine and order.[2]

Bishop Brent gave a report of the World Missionary Conference to the General Convention of the Protestant Episcopal Church of the United States meeting in Cincinnati, Ohio, in October, 1910. The General Convention passed a resolution that initiated the Faith and Order movement:

> WHEREAS, There is today among all Christian people a growing desire for the fulfillment of our Lord's prayer that all His disciples may be one; that the world may believe that God has sent Him:
> RESOLVED, That a Joint Commission be appointed to bring about a Conference for the consideration of questions touching Faith and Order and that all Christian Communions throughout the world which confess our Lord Jesus Christ as God and Saviour be asked to unite with us in arranging for and conducting such a Conference.[3]

A Joint Commission of the Protestant Episcopal Churches in the United States, appointed to arrange for a World Conference on Faith and Order, later issued a statement to clarify the purpose of such a conference:

> The Conference is for the definite purpose of considering those things in which we differ, in hope that a better understanding of divergent views of Faith and Order will result in a deepened desire for reunion and in official action on the part of the separated Communions themselves.[4]

The statement concluded: "It is the business of the Conference not to take such official action, but to inspire and to prepare the way for it."[5]

These statements calling for a conference convey a spirit similar to that which inspired the Lambeth Conferences of Anglican bishops. The first Lambeth Conference was called in 1867 to attend to affairs that were divisive within the Anglican communion. The third Lambeth Conference turned its attention to division between the Anglican communion and the Free Churches in England. This conference, held in 1888, adopted a basis for "Home Reunion."[6] The bishops who assembled at Lambeth in 1920 expanded their vision of reunion beyond their own realm, issuing "An Appeal to All Christian People."[7]

The vision of unity articulated in the "Appeal to All Christian People" is ambivalent. On one hand, there is the vision of "a Church . . . within whose visible unity all the treasures of faith and order, bequeathed as a heritage by the past to the present, shall be possessed in common, and made serviceable to the whole Body of Christ."[8] On the other hand, there is the declaration that "the visible unity of the Church will be found to involve the whole-hearted acceptance of:

> The Holy Scriptures, as the record of God's revelation of Himself to man, and as being the rule and ultimate standard of faith; and the Creed commonly called Nicene, as the sufficient statement of the Christian faith, and either it or the Apostles' Creed as the Baptismal confession of belief:
>
> The divinely instituted sacraments of Baptism and the Holy Communion, as expressing for all the corporate life of the whole fellowship in and with Christ:
>
> A ministry acknowledged by every part of the Church as possessing not only the inward call of the Spirit, but also the commission of Christ and the authority of the whole body.[9]

The vision of unity expressed in "An Appeal to All Christian People" acknowledges the differences represented by members and affirms these differences for the sake of a richer common life. However, it is also clear that members must measure up to certain marks of visible unity.

The Faith and Order movement, initiated and inspired by the Anglican Bishop Brent, inherited this ambivalent vision of church unity. In some statements made by Faith and Order, differences among the churches are acknowledged as appropriate to particular contexts. More basically, however, differences are considered as accidental or condemned as divisive of an underlying unity. The fundamental impulse of Faith and Order discourse on unity has been toward overcoming or comprehending differences for the sake of conformity to long-standing marks of visible unity.

In this chapter, I will criticize the Faith and Order discourse on unity. I will argue that concluding the Community Study and culminating the Faith and Order *Baptism, Eucharist and Ministry* text at the same meeting was not accidental. The *Baptism, Eucharist and Ministry* text stands as a monument to the mode of discourse on unity called into question by the Community Study. I intend to clarify the limits of the long-standing Faith and Order discourse on unity in order to prepare the way for transgressing those limits. Specifically, I intend to create a space in which to draw a theological portrait from the local group reports of the Community Study.

"wherein we agree and . . . wherein we differ"

The Faith and Order movement, as has been noted, emerged in response to the problems of dissension and division on the mission fields. Bishop Brent and others from the Protestant Episcopal Church in the United States of America began to plan for a conference to discuss matters of faith and order immediately following the 1910 World Missionary Conference. Their activities were disrupted by World War I. The first World Conference on Faith and Order was finally convened in 1927, in Lausanne, Switzerland.

"The Call to Unity," adopted by the first World Conference and sent to the churches, reflects the initial concern for mission:

> God wills unity. Our presence in this Conference bears testimony to our desire to bend our wills to His. However we may justify the beginnings of disunion, we lament its continuance and henceforth must labour, in penitence and faith, to build up our broken walls. . . .
>
> More than half the world is waiting for the Gospel. At home and abroad sad multitudes are turning away in bewilderment from the Church because of its corporate feebleness. Our missions count that as a necessity which we are inclined to look on as a luxury. Already the mission field is impatiently revolting from the divisions of the Western Church to make bold adventure for unity in its own right. . . . We with them must gird ourselves to the task, the early beginnings of which God has so richly blessed, and labour side by side until our common goal is reached.
>
> Some of us, pioneers in this undertaking, have

grown old in our search for unity. It is to youth that we look to lift the torch on high. We men have carried it too much along through many years. The women henceforth should be accorded their share of responsibility. And so the whole Church will be enabled to do that which no section can hope to perform.[10]

This call to unity has also a call to repentance. Western churches were called to turn from imposing their classical controversies upon newly-emerging churches in other contexts. Older men were called share the responsibility with youth and women. "The Call to Unity" was an invitation to women and men, young and old, in all churches.

This vision was introduced by the Preamble to "The Call to Unity":

> We, representatives of many Christian Communions throughout the world, united in the common confession of faith in Jesus Christ the Son of God, our Lord and Saviour, believing that the Spirit of God is with us, are assembled to consider the things wherein we agree and the things wherein we differ. . . . This is a Conference summoned to consider matters of Faith and Order. It is emphatically *not* attempting to define the conditions of future reunion.[11]

This declaration was followed by a statement of purpose: "Its [the conference's] object is to register the apparent level of fundamental agreements within the Conference and the grave points of disagreements remaining; also to suggest certain lines of thought which may in the future tend to a fuller measure of agreement."[12]

The articulation of "certain lines of thought" was in effect, however, an attempt to stake out the boundaries of "one Church, holy, catholic, and apostolic." One report received by the Conference contains a list of "certain characteristics whereby it can be known of men":

> There have been, since the days of the Apostles, at least, the following:
>
> 1. The possession and acknowledgment of the Word of God as given in the Holy Scripture and interpreted by the Holy Spirit to the Church and to the individual.
>
> 2. The profession of faith in God as He is incarnate and revealed in Christ.

    3. The acceptance of Christ's commission to preach the Gospel to every creature.

    4. The observance of the Sacraments.

    5. A ministry for the pastoral office, the preaching of the Word, and the administration of the Sacraments.

    6. A fellowship in prayer, in worship, in all the means of grace, in the pursuit of holiness, and in the service of man.[13]

These "characteristics," which resemble those listed in "An Appeal to all Christian Peoples," set the agenda for Faith and Order meetings for the next fifty years.

The World Conference on Faith and Order elected a Continuation Committee. This committee was responsible for editing and disseminating the report of the conference, as well as for carrying on the work begun. Charles H. Brent was elected as chairman of the Continuation Committee. When Brent died two years later, William Temple, theologian, philosopher, then Archbishop of York and later of Canterbury,[14] was elected in his stead.

In 1930, the Continuation Committee decided to hold a second World Conference on Faith and Order no later than 1937. Worldwide economic depression inhibited preparation. In 1934, when the committee could meet again, the program for the conference was planned and the date confirmed.[15]

The Second World Conference on Faith and Order was held in Edinburgh, Scotland, in 1937, as shadows were gathering over Western countries. Economic crisis continued on both sides of the Atlantic. Hitler's rise to power in Germany portended the outbreak of another war.

William Temple delivered the opening sermon at the Second World Conference on Faith and Order. He declared:

> Let us never forget that, though the purpose of our meeting is to consider the causes of our divisions, yet what makes possible our meeting is our unity. We could not seek union if we did not already possess unity. Those who have nothing is common do not deplore their estrangement. It is because we are one in allegiance to one Lord that we seek and hope for the way of manifesting that unity in our witness to Him before the world.[16]

Temple thus called the delegates to turn from the mode of conference in Lausanne, that is, to turn from the statement of various perspectives and practices in order to clarify points of agreement and disagreement. "It is only by coming closer to Him," Temple declared, "that we can come closer to one another":

> It is not by understanding one another, but by more fully understanding Him, that we are led towards our goal. . . . Our discussion of our differences is a necessary preliminary; but it is preliminary and no more. Only when God has drawn us closer to Himself shall we be truly united together; and then our task will be, not to consummate our endeavour but to register His achievement.[17]

As economic and political crisis broke into open conflict, Temple appealed to unity created not by human will but by God.

The delegates to the Second World Conference echoed Temple as they adopted an "Affirmation of union in Allegiance to our Lord Jesus Christ":

> We are one in faith in our Lord Jesus Christ, the incarnate Word of God. We are one in allegiance to Him as Head of the Church, and as King of kings and Lord of lords . . .
> This unity does not consist in the agreement of minds or the consent of our wills. It is founded in Jesus Christ Himself, Who lived, died and rose again to bring us to the Father, and Who through the Holy Spirit dwells in His Church.[18]

At Edinburgh, the indicative of God's action thus took precedence over the imperative of human action.[19]

The "Affirmation of union in Allegiance" continued:

> Our unity is of heart and spirit. We are divided in the outward forms of our life in Christ, because we understand differently His will for His Church. We believe, however, that a deeper understanding will lead us towards a united apprehension of the truth as it is in Jesus. . . .
> We pray that everywhere, in a world divided and perplexed, men may turn to Jesus Christ our Lord, who makes us one in spite of our divisions; that He may bind in one those who by many worldly claims are set at variance; and that the world may at last find peace and unity in Him; to Whom be glory for ever.[20]

At Edinburgh, differences among the churches appear to have been viewed as accidental to an already-given unity.

Although the delegates who gathered in Edinburgh were acutely aware of the economic and political crisis in the world around them, the theological accent they articulated tended toward retreat. A delineation of theological and "non-theological" factors was at least implicit at the World Conference on Faith and Order in 1937. As the delegates discussed a proposal to join with the Life and Work movement to form an organization that could carry on the work of both, this delineation became explicit.

The first meeting of the Universal Christian Conference on Life and Work had been held in Stockholm, Sweden, in 1925. The Conference aimed "to unite the different churches in common practical work, . . . and to insist that the principles of the Gospel be applied to the solution of contemporary social and international problems."[21] Nathan Soderblom, historian of religions, Lutheran Archbishop of Uppsala, and chairman of the Conference, expressed the sentiment of those who gathered in Stockholm when he criticized a 1920 Faith and Order meeting held to plan for the Lausanne Conference. Soderblom declared:

> . . . no partiality, no word, no look, betrayed the dissension of the war, and . . . the subject of Faith and Order claimed the whole attention and different theories [were] brought about groupings quite independent of the political situation. . . . Neither big forms nor big words can repair the injuries of our epoch.[22]

The slogan of those who gathered in Stockholm was "Doctrine divides, but service unites."[23]

This slogan was challenged during discussions at the Universal Christian Conference on Life and Work. The preacher at the opening session in Stockholm proclaimed:

> We believe in the Kingdom of Heaven. We are conspirators for its establishment. . . . To set up the Kingdom of God in this complicated civilization of the twentieth century is a colossal task, a task which demands thought, skill, patience, wisdom. But, I repeat, in Christ we can do the impossible.[24]

He was chastised by another speaker who declared: "Nothing could be more mistaken or more disastrous than to suppose that we mortal men have to build up God's kingdom in the world."[25] William Adams Brown, Chairman of the Universal Christian Council for Life and Work Executive Committee and President of Union Theological Seminary in New York, later observed: "When pressed to their source the differing attitudes toward Christian duties were seen to be rooted in theological differences."[26]

The lines between Life and Work and Faith and Order were thus blurred. And, as economic and political situations worsened, it seemed to some that "the very existence of the Christian Church" was at stake.[27] Finally, in the summer of 1936, the Universal Christian Council for Life and Work and the Faith and Order Continuation Committee appointed a joint Committee of Thirty-Five "to review the work of ecumenical cooperation since the Stockholm and Lausanne conferences and to make recommendations . . . regarding the future policy, organization and work of the ecumenical movement."[28] At its meeting in 1937, the committee proposed the creation of a World Council of Churches.

This proposal was readily adopted at the second conference sponsored by the Universal Christian Council for Life and Work, held in Oxford just prior to the Second World Conference on Faith and Order.[29] In Edinburgh, however, debate concerning the proposal to create a World Council of Churches continued for days. The Conference appointed a special committee to review the proposal and bring a recommendation to the delegates. The committee recommended adoption of the proposal. However, the committee made it clear that approval of a completed design for the World Council of Churches would depend on conservation of "the distinctive character and value of each of the movements . . ."[30]

A. C. Headlam, Bishop of Gloucester, insisted to the end that his opposition to the proposal to join the Universal Christian Council for Life and Work to create World Council of Churches be recorded in the official report of the Edinburgh Conference.[31] Headlam, the chairman of two theological commissions that prepared study documents for the Second World Conference,[32] claimed to speak on behalf of other participants in the Edinburgh conference: " . . . there is a definite body of

members of the Conference who are opposed to this idea, and
many opposed to any definite connection with the Life and
Work Movement." Headlam warned: "If such a Council were
to exist, and if it passed resolutions on public affairs, it might do
a very considerable amount of harm."[33]

Headlam's remarks had a concrete referent. As early as
1934, the Universal Christian Council for Life and Work had
declared its opposition to the German Evangelical Church and
its support for the Confessing Church.[34] As late as 1937,
Headlam had publically declared that Hitler's Third Reich was
"based upon positive orthodox Christianity."[35] It was later discovered that Life and Work was viewed with suspicion in National Socialist circles, while Faith and Order was held in
higher repute insofar as it had been silent on political
situations.[36]

The World Council of Churches was officially constituted
in Amsterdam in 1948. The First Assembly expressed its vision
of unity in words that echoed Edinburgh:

> God has given to His people in Jesus Christ a unity
> which is His creation and not our achievement. We praise
> and thank Him for a mighty work of His Holy Spirit, by
> which we have been drawn together to discover that,
> notwithstanding our divisions, we are one in Jesus
> Christ. . . . we discover our unity in relation to [the
> Church's] Lord and Head.[37]

The indicative mode was once again used to affirm unity underlying diversity: "The Body of Christ *is* a unity which makes
it impossible for us either to forget each other or to be content
with agreement upon isolated parts of our belief."[38]

A heavy accent, however, fell on the "hard core of disagreement between different total ways of apprehending the
Church of Christ."[39] Traditional terms, "Catholic" and "Protestant," were redefined to designate this disagreement. Those
considered "Catholic" were most concerned about "the visible
continuity of the Church in the apostolic succession of the epis-
copate." Those considered "Protestant" emphasized the "initiative of the Word of God and the response of faith."[40] This
difference between "Catholic" and "Protestant," which cut
across ecclesial boundaries, was confessed to be "our deepest
difference" at Amsterdam.[41]

The First Assembly of the World Council of Churches at Amsterdam adopted a resolution on the "authority of the Council." This resolution made it clear that the Council did not seek "to usurp any of the functions which already belong to its constituent churches, or to control them, or to legislate for them, . . ." The resolution also made it clear that the Council would not become "a single unified church structure independent of the churches" or "a structure dominated by a centralized administrative authority."[42] In light of the confession of "our deepest difference," this resolution called for respect as well as recognition of diversity among the members of the Council.

But this resolution did not calm the fears of some member churches. The World Council Central Committee, meeting in 1950, in Toronto, therefore, adopted a statement about the purpose and nature of the World Council in relation to the member churches. In response to the fears that had arisen, "The Church, the Churches and the World Council of Churches" begins with "a series of negations." The World Council is not "Super-Church," not "to negotiate unions between Churches," not "based on any one particular conception of the Church," does not "imply that a Church treats its own conception of the Church as merely relative," does not "imply the acceptance of a specific doctrine concerning the nature of Church unity." "The whole point of the ecumenical conversations," the statement clarifies, "is precisely that all these conceptions enter into dynamic relations with each other."[43]

The Toronto Statement also sets forth "the positive assumptions" of the World Council and of membership in it. This list begins with "the common recognition that Christ is the Divine Head of the Body" and ends with this declaration: "There is no intention to impose any particular pattern of thought or life upon the Churches. . . . whatever insight has been received by one or more Churches is to be made available to all the Churches for the sake of the 'building up of the Body of Christ'."[44]

This statement stands in contrast to "The Call to Unity" and to "An Affirmation of union in Allegiance," adopted by the World Conferences on Faith and Order meeting in Lausanne and Edinburgh, respectively. "The Call to Unity" expressed the impulse to define "certain characteristics" by which church unity would be made manifest in the world. Differences among the churches were recognized in order to overcome them. "An Affirmation of union in Allegiance" expressed the impulse to define a common confession of faith, cut off from outward structures—whether ecclesial or political. Differences among the churches were viewed as accidental to an essential unity.

The question addressed by the drafters of the Toronto Statement was "how can one formulate the ecclesiological implications of a body in which so many different conceptions of the Church are represented, without using the categories or language of one particular conception of the Church."[45] In this statement, then, differences among the churches were recognized as gifts each could offer for the sake of the "building up of the Body of Christ." The marks of visible unity were not prejudged. Rather all the churches were called to "conversation, cooperation, and common witness in the world."[46]

The reports of these meetings on church unity reflect little, if any, concern for the image and role of women in the churches. Although the role of women was acknowledged and even appreciated at Lausanne, fewer women were present at Edinburgh. There and thereafter, theological discussions were in terms defined by the fathers and the sons of the fathers of the churches throughout the centuries. Women, if recognized at all, were considered to be "non-theological" factors relative to "certain characteristics" or a common confession of faith that could clarify church unity. Only the call to "conversation, cooperation, and common witness in the world" held out hope for women.

"to penetrate behind the divisions"

The Third World Conference on Faith and Order, meeting in Lund, Sweden, in 1952, began where the Second World Conference at Edinburgh ended. The question of unity was considered in light of the common confession of Jesus Christ as the Head of the Body. In "A Word to the Churches," conference participants at Lund stated:

We have seen clearly that we can make no real advance towards unity if we only compare our several conceptions of the nature of the Church and the traditions in
which they are embodied. But once again it has been
proved true that as we seek to draw closer to Christ we
come closer to one another. We need, therefore, to pene-
trate behind our divisions to a deeper and richer understanding of the mystery of the God-given union of Christ
with His Church. We need increasingly to realize that the
separate histories of our Churches find their full meaning
only if seen in the perspective of God's dealings with His
whole people.[47]

Ernst Lange later remarked: "Methodologically, this meant ad-
vancing from comparative to critical ecclesiology: ecclesiology
seen in the critical light of christology."[48]

At Lund, therefore, the delegates took the doctrine of
Christ as the starting point: "From the unity of Christ we seek
to understand the unity of the Church on earth, and from the
unity of Christ and His Body we seek a means of realizing that
unity in the actual state of our divisions on earth."[49] Other
doctrines—of the church, of ministry or the sacraments—were
considered in light of this Christological affirmation.

This christological affirmation was undergirded by study
of a "common history" of the churches. The "common history" of the churches was said to be "longer, larger and richer
than any . . . separate histories in . . . divided Churches." It was
studied in order to discover "the various levels of unity which
underlie . . . diversities and dividedness."[50] "We affirm," declared the delegates, "that throughout Christendom there is,
despite divisions, a unity already given by God in Christ. . . .
Concerning the fact of this unity and of the participation in it
of every Christian we have no doubt."[51]

At Lund, the "common history" was viewed as an interim
between the first and final comings of Christ. Accordingly, divisions among the churches were considered to be the consequences of treating interim historical forms as ultimate. And
churches were called to move beyond these "historical forms
to the full unveiling of . . . new being in the coming Lord."[52]

This eschatological note resounded at the Second Assembly of the World Council of Churches in 1954. The theme of
the gathering in Evanston, Illinois, was "Jesus Christ—Hope of

the World." Ultimate unity in Christ was affirmed in the face
of East-West tensions:

> . . . we here set our hope on our one Lord Jesus Christ,
> who comes to take control over our divided and broken
> estate and to heal it by His grace and power. At Amster-
> dam we said that we intend to stay together. He has kept
> us together. He has shown Himself again as our Hope.
> Emboldened by this Hope, we dedicate ourselves to God
> anew, that He may enable us to grow together.[53]

The focus of attention at the Evanston Assembly, as at the
World Conference on Faith and Order at Lund, was away
from divisions on earth toward unity affirmed as already
realized.

The shift from comparative ecclesiology to ecclesiology
seen in the critical light of christology was another attempt to
overcome differences. The method of comparative ecclesiology acknowledged differences and measured them in terms of
"certain characteristics" of visible church unity. Differences,
"language and thought forms coined in history," were now
judged by "the content of the Gospel," that is, by God's revelation in Christ. The "truth of God's revelation" was affirmed as
"unique and normative for all ages."[54]

Having distinguished "the content of the Gospel" from
"the language and thought forms coined in history," Faith and
Order began to study so-called "non-theological" factors. At
Lausanne, differences among the churches were viewed as differences related to doctrines of the church, ministry and the
sacraments. A report on social, cultural, and political factors
related to division and unity among the churches had been
drafted in preparation for Edinburgh.[55] Finally, at Lund, the
"bearing on the problem of unity of social, cultural, political,
racial and other so-called 'non-theological' factors" was "felt
throughout" the conference.[56]

However, social, cultural, political, racial and other "non-
theological" factors were viewed not only as finite but as sinful.
These factors were charged with creating and continuing divisions among the churches. It was clear that "the Spirit," which
always transcends social, cultural, and political and racial circumstances, "creates unity."[57]

After Lund, the Commission on Faith and Order continued to study "non-theological factors" by focusing on one such factor: Institutionalism. A commission was created to view the church from a sociological perspective. Nils Ehrenstrom, one of the commission members, reflected: "Those responsible for that decision may not have been fully aware of its implications. . . . What is at stake here is the incarnational character of the ecumenical faith."[58]

Ehrenstrom, in contrast to those who created a commission to study one among the many "non-theological" factors, affirmed that as sociology views the church in its social setting it views the incarnation, theologically speaking. Thus Ehrenstrom challenged the Faith and Order split between theological and "non-theological" in terms of Faith and Order's own christological criterion. From Ehrenstrom's point of view, the locus of christology was church life in which sociology and theology were entangled.

The locus of christology was not church life in other post-Lund Faith and Order studies. The Theological Commission on Christ and the Church issued a call to unity with reference to "a common fact, a common reality, on which the Church is built and which makes the Church to be the Church."[59] The commission's report states: "Our task is to acknowledge the unity which exists already, the unity in Christ and in the Spirit, and to draw consequences of this existing unity for the actual life of the church and for the togetherness of the denominations.[60]

The distinction between Christ and the church, which is implicit in this summary statement, is explicit elsewhere in the report. With reference to the church, the report states: "It must never seek to usurp his place or give itself out to be another Christ, but be content to be subordinated to the head as the human community of believers graciously assumed by him into unity with himself." The church, continues the report, "is the body *of Christ*. It belongs to him; he is its life; he works in it. In him the Church coheres and has its being."[61]

In this era of Faith and Order work, silence surrounds women. The christological criterion did call the emphasis on classical controversies into question and also turned attention to "non-theological" factors. But the church, the Body of Christ conditioned by social, cultural, and political circumstances, was called to subordinate itself to the Head and Lord.

The hierarchy of headship was thereby reiterated in the discussion of church unity. Men who subordinated themselves to Christ the Head were still heads relative to women. Women, as Henriette Visser't Hooft had pointed out so poignantly, were rendered headless.[62]

"all in each place"

The report on "Unity" approved by the Third Assembly of the World Council of Churches at New Delhi, in 1961, marks another era in Faith and Order history. The report stated:

> We believe that the unity which is both God's will and his gift to his Church is being made visible as all in each place who are baptized into Jesus Christ and confess him as Lord and Saviour are brought by the Holy Spirit into one fully committed fellowship holding one apostolic faith, preaching the one Gospel, breaking the one bread, joining in common prayer, and having a corporate life reaching out in witness and service to all and who at the same time are united with the whole Christian fellowship in all places and all ages in such wise that ministry and members are accepted by all, and that all can act and speak together as occasion requires for the tasks to which God calls his people.[63]

"The achievement of unity," the report declares, "will involve nothing less than a death and rebirth of many forms of church life as we have known them."[64]

The key, and most often cited, phrase in this report on "Unity" is "all in each place." This picture of unity highlights the particular places where Christians live and work. The "local situation"—"each school . . . each factory or office . . . each congregation . . . as well as between congregations"—is identified as the place where "the common life in Christ is most clearly tested."[65] In this picture, the unity given in Christ is to be made manifest not only in the church but also in the world: that "every wall of race, colour, caste, tribe, sex, class and nation" be broken down.[66]

Joseph A. Sittler delivered an address to the Third Assembly which elaborated this vision of unity. Lamenting the split between grace and nature in Western theological thought, Sittler appealed to Irenaeus and others in the Eastern theological tradition for whom the incarnation of Christ extended the gift of grace to all of nature. Sittler envisioned a renewed relationship between the power of grace and the vitalities of nature, calling for "a daring, penetrating, life-affirming christology of nature."[67]

Sittler's appeal to the Eastern theological tradition was appropriate to the Assembly where the Orthodox Churches of Russia, Bulgaria, Romania, and Poland became members of the World Council. The focus on the unity of "all in each place" was also appropriate to this occasion. From the perspective of Orthodox ecclesiology, the local community that gathers to celebrate the eucharist is the church. Indeed, the Orthodox had not become members of the World Council earlier because of their suspicion of centralized organizations or authorities.[68]

The Orthodox complicated as well as enriched the work of Faith and Order. When the Roman Catholic Church sent representatives to the Fourth World Conference on Faith and Order, held at Montreal in 1963, the complexity nearly unraveled into chaos.[69] Oliver S. Tomkins, Bishop of Bristol and Chairman of the Conference, remarked:

> The result was described by one delegate as 'a promising chaos'. The sense of vitality was at once our hope and our despair. The World Council's Faith and Order Commission now faces some searching questions about how we should proceed. But our problems arise out of the abundance of the tasks to be faced, so we thank God for them.[70]

The 'promising chaos' at Montreal was precipitated by the blooming diversity of methods as well as churches. The agenda set at Lund was not done and the vision of unity articulated at New Delhi had not been discussed. The Fourth World Conference at Montreal was an event balanced between the times.

The structure of the Fourth World Conference on Faith and Order testified to its posture. Four working sections discussed reports of commissions that had carried on work begun at Lund: "The Church and the Purpose of God;" "Scripture,

Tradition and Traditions," "The Redemptive Work of Christ
and the Ministry of the Church," "Worship and the Oneness of
Christ's Church." A fifth section discussed the report on
"Unity" drafted at New Delhi, together with the report of the
commission on "Institutionalism and Church Unity."[71] Thus,
the conference considered unity in terms of traditional theological differences among the churches and with attention to
aspects that had long been termed "non-theological."

The divergent perspectives and procedures were most
forcefully articulated by two speakers at the conference—
Ernst Kasemann and Raymond E. Brown—who delivered addresses on "Unity and Diversity in New Testament Ecclesiology." Kasemann began his address with the declaration that
"the New Testament does not present us with an *ecclesiologia
perennis*."[72] He ended with the declaration:

> No romantic postulate, dressed up as *Heilsges-
> chichte*, can relativize the sober fact that the historian
> simply cannot speak of an unbroken unity of New Testa-
> ment ecclesiology. For he perceives there the early pat-
> tern of our own situation, with its differences, dilemmas
> and antitheses, at best an early ecumenical confedera-
> tion—without a World Council of Churches.[73]

Between these declarations, Kasemann gave an account of the
"constant transformation of ecclesiology within the New
Testament."[74]

Brown, in sharp contrast, argued that "if NT ecclesiology
cannot be oversimplified in the direction of theological uni-
formity, neither can we neglect a *unity in belief* that is present
in all stages of NT thought about the Church." Brown
continued:

> . . . we must recognize that each of the NT theologians
> was conscious of belonging to the one Christian Church.
> There are common elements found in all the ecclesiolo-
> gies of the NT, and to neglect them in favor of diversity
> would be to fail to give a complete picture of the NT con-
> cept of the Church.[75]

Brown then discussed three "common elements found in all
the ecclesiologies of the NT": continuity with Israel; apostolic-
ity; baptism and the eucharist.[76]

According to one report of the Montreal conference, Kasemann's address "met with considerable opposition . . . ; some feared that, if his position was accepted generally, it would spell the end of all attempts to achieve the unity of the Church."[77] Kasemann's address was thus met inasmuch as the unity of the Bible and the unity of the Church had been mutually reinforcing in Faith and Order work. Like Brown, Faith and Order had accented the unity of the biblical message or "the content of the Gospel" and had taken this as the starting point and norm for church unity.[78] When Kasemann accented the "differences, dilemmas and antitheses" among the churches portrayed in the New Testament, the very foundations upon which Faith and Order relied for the establishment of unity were shaken.[79]

Not until the meeting of the Commission on Faith and Order at Bristol, England, in 1967, did a new direction for work toward church unity emerge. At Bristol, the commission envisioned its future work toward unity in a context wider than that of the church. Oliver S. Tomkins, who reviewed the work of Faith and Order work in the closing address at Bristol, ended with a succinct statement of this new direction: "Unity is seen as involving Man in creation and history."[80]

Anthropology was the focus of attention at the Fourth Assembly of the World Council of Churches, held at Uppsala, Sweden, in 1968. At this Assembly, Faith and Order methods were called into question:

> It seems to many, inside and outside the Church, that the struggle for Christian unity in its present form is irrelevant to the immediate crisis of our times. The Church, they say, should seek its unity through solidarity with those forces in modern life, such as the struggle for racial equality, which are drawing men more closely together, and should give up its concern with patching up its own internal disputes.[81]

Renewal of the church in the world, rather than the unity of the church, was the theme at Uppsala.

The report on "Unity" drafted at New Delhi was reaffirmed inasmuch as it served "to keep before the Council and the churches 'the obligation to manifest that unity for the sake of their Lord and for the better accomplishment of his mission in the world'."[82] The New Delhi statement was also criticized inasmuch as its focus on the unity of "all in each place" did not extend to unity "in all places" and "in all ages."

Thus the focus of attention shifted once again at Uppsala:

> We must continue to seek the unity of all Christians in a common profession of the faith in the observance of Baptism and the Eucharist, and in recognition of a ministry for the whole Church. . . . This calls the churches in all places to realize that they belong together and are called to act together. In a time when human interdependence is so evident, it is the more imperative to make visible the bonds which unite Christians in universal fellowship.[83]

Faith and Order's vision of unity now extended beyond the local church and context to comprehend the universe.

The notion of catholicity was, therefore, central to the discussions at Uppsala:

> The purpose of Christ is to bring people of all times, of all races, of all places, of all conditions, into an organic and living unity in Christ by the Holy Spirit under the universal fatherhood of God. This unity is not solely external; it has a deeper, internal dimension, which is also expressed by the term 'catholicity.' Catholicity reaches its completion when what God has already begun in history is finally disclosed and fulfilled.[84]

Catholicity was not considered to be a mark of the church in traditional terms. Catholicity was most closely connected to the mission of the church in the world.

Joseph A. Sittler had used the word "catholic" in his address at New Delhi: "Is it again possible to fashion a theology catholic enough to affirm redemption's force enfolding nature, as we have affirmed redemption's force enfolding history?"[85] By "catholic," Sittler meant a theology that would extend the boundaries of God's grace incarnate in Christ beyond the church into every nook of nature. In contrast, at Uppsala "catholicity" was a call to ecclesiological extension into all the world. Members of the World Council were called to "work for the time when a genuinely universal council may once again speak for all Christians, and lead the way into the future." The impulse toward this universal council was not division among the churches as such, but questions posed at

Bristol: "What is the function of the Church in relation to the unifying purpose of God for the world? What . . . is the relation of the Churches' quest for unity among themselves to the hope of unity of mankind?"[86] These questions were answered by an Uppsala statement: "The Church is bold to speak of itself as the sign of the coming unity of mankind."[87]

This turn from controversies among the churches to cries from every clime ignored brokenness within the church and inclined toward imperialism. The church was not "the sign of the coming unity" for all peoples and places. The statement on "Unity" drafted at New Delhi had been more promising for women, women and men of color, young women and men, members of churches in Africa, Asia, Latin America, the Pacific, and the Caribbean. It had called for the unity of "all in each place" involving "nothing less than a death and rebirth of many forms of church life."[88]

"a recognition of diversity"

The Working Committee of the Commission on Faith and Order met in Sigtuna, Sweden, immediately following the Fourth Assembly. The committee reviewed the documents drafted at Uppsala and then turned to the future work of Faith and Order. Some members of the committee were concerned about the discussion of unity at Uppsala. William A. Lazareth, American Lutheran theologian and later Director of the Commission on Faith and Order, declared:

> The quest for unity is radically called into question by the present situation. There is the trend to speak of 'planetary stewardship' based on Genesis 1. This raises the question whether there is any place left for the Church or the people of God. The question is whether unity is obtained through the Church and the means of grace. Current theological thinking speaks increasingly of God's redeeming work outside the Church; word and sacraments become obsolete. The vision of 'planetary stewardship' offers a real alternative. In the light of it the traditional concern of the Faith and Order Movement appears to be irrelevant.[89]

Lazareth then posed his key question: ". . . does salvation come

through Christ and the church or through creation?"[90] Orthodox theologians, Georges Florovsky and John Meyendorff,
joined Lazareth in expressing this concern.

In response to Lazareth, as well as Florovsky and
Meyendorff, the working committee stated:

> . . . Faith and Order's constitutional concern for the unity
> of the Church must continue to be respected. That cen-
> tral concern, however, must now be explored within a
> wider framework involving . . . interdisciplinary dialogue
> between Christian theology and the social, historical and
> natural sciences.[91]

Specifically, the committee suggested that "the radical questions posed by the new situation in which we are" demand that
"the study of the unity of the Church must be placed in the
context of the unity of mankind."[92]

The Working Committee drafted a study document on
the "Unity of Church-Unity of Mankind."[93] This document
was sent to member churches of the World Council for reflection and response. Reports from member churches were reviewed at the 1970 meeting of the Working Committee at
Cret-Berard. In light of these reports, the committee decided
that "Unity of Church-Unity of Mankind" would be the theme
of the 1971 meeting of the full Commission on Faith and
Order.[94]

At the 1971 meeting in Louvain, Belgium, John
Meyendorff delivered the opening address. Ernst Lange later
remarked that his address was "a determined effort, almost a
last-ditch attempt, to push the theme back into the old framework of the problem."[95] In Louvain, however, the commission
shifted from "doctrinal deduction" to "an inductive and inter-
disciplinary approach" to unity.[96]

This methodological shift had been adumbrated by the
studies of "non-theological factors," of "Institutionalism and
Church Unity," and, most recently, of "Spirit, Order and Organization."[97] However, the theological implications of studies
that were undertaken from a sociological perspective were not
taken seriously. Not until the Louvain meeting was there a
call for "a process of mutual questioning and answering" between sociology and theology.[98]

This call for genuine interaction between theology and

sociology, as well as disciplines such as psychology, political science, philosophy, physics, was forecast in a document drafted by a working group in preparation for the Louvain meeting. The drafters of this document called into question the Uppsala claim that the church is "the sign of the coming unity of mankind": "Have the Churches always been factors of reconciliation? Have they not themselves divided men? Has their divisiveness simply reflected the word of Jesus: 'I have not come to bring peace but a sword'?" Having posed these rhetorical questions, the drafters of this document continued: ". . . the Churches are not . . . exempt from listening to modern men and learning with them what this word of peace signifies for both Churches and mankind." The church and the world were viewed as interdependent contexts, rather than as two entities, the former being "the sign" of unity for the latter. The implied method for work toward unity was thus termed "inter-contextual."[99]

As the Commission on Faith and Order articulated this "inter-contextual" method, it also acknowledged that talk of unity includes "a recognition of diversity."[100] Heretofore, diversity had been discussed as a problem or not at all. For the first time, diversity was both recognized and respected.

The appreciation of diversity along with the articulation of an "inter-contextual" method gave rise to a new Faith and Order study. In Louvain, the commission launched a study on "Giving Account of the Hope That Is In Us." "What we have in mind," the commission stated, "is not to take the form of a Creed, a Catechism, a statement of Confession or a kind of theological handbook."[101] The study was based on three convictions:

> 1) churches and Christians have the obligation in every new age to confess afresh, in the language of that age, their faith in Christ; 2) they must strive for expressions of the Christian faith within different cultural worlds and in diversified social, political, and religious situations; 3) the divided churches might rediscover their unity by letting themselves be reconstituted by the truth of the Gospel.[102]

An invitation to participate in the study was sent to Christians throughout the world.

Responses sent to the Faith and Order Secretariat in Ge-

neva were published in four volumes.[103] Voices of women and
men from many races and ages are heard in these volumes.
Various churches, cultures, and continents are represented.
Images and invocations represent the different social, economic, and political contexts in which the accounts were written. The volumes bear witness to a vision of unity that is
discovered in the midst of manifest diversity.

In the report of the Louvain meeting, however, there is
already an intimation that the ultimate goal of this study was a
common account or confession of faith:

> What we have in common in our life together,
> prayer and teaching is in advance of what we are able to
> define together in matters of doctrine. Therefore we
> should endeavor to express what is the content of our life
> and prayer and proclamation. Thus we envisage a process
> moving towards some kind of statement which the
> Churches can make together.[104]

Two years after the Louvain meeting, when the Faith and Order Working Committee reviewed the initial reports from the
study, the central concern was: "What can be said
universally?"[105]

"as people who could not but . . ."

At the next meeting of the Commission on Faith and Order, in Accra, Ghana, in 1974, cultural rather than confessional
diversity was the focus of attention. One member of the commission, Martin Conway, later remarked:

> We were constantly made aware of each other not only as
> individuals, not only as self-critical representatives of cer-
> tain churches and Christian traditions, but still more as
> people who could not but speak out of particular and very
> different cultural heritages and outlooks.[106]

Topics for consideration at the commission meeting were chosen from responses to the "Giving Account of Hope" study,
and from "The Unity of the Church and the Unity of Mankind"
study.[107]

The following year, Faith and Order began to turn its attention to more familiar fields of study. At the Fifth Assembly of the World Council, churches were invited to consider this description of unity:

> The one Church is to be envisioned as a conciliar fellow-ship of local churches which are themselves truly united. In this conciliar fellowship, each local church possesses, in communion with others, the fulness of catholicity, wit-nesses to the same apostolic faith, and, therefore, recog-nizes the others as belonging to the same church of Christ and guided by the same spirit. . . . they are bound to-gether because they have received the same baptism and share in the same eucharist; they recognize each other's members and ministries. They are one in their common commitment to confess the Gospel of Christ by proclama-tion and service to the world.[108]

The term "conciliarity" had been used before the Nairobi As-sembly in order to integrate the New Delhi and the Uppsala statements on unity.[109] Not until Nairobi, however, was full "conciliar fellowship" connected to the requirement that churches be "united by a common understanding of the apos-tolic faith, by a common ministry, and a common Eucha-rist."[110] Not since the first World Conference on Faith and Order reiterated the Lambeth Quadrilateral of 1920 had the goal of visible unity been so definitely described.

"Conciliar fellowship," as such, was not the focus of atten-tion at the meeting of the Commission on Faith and Order in Bangalore, India, in 1978. Lukas Vischer, then Director of the Faith and Order Secretariat, explained this shift: "The need was . . . to use the idea of conciliar fellowship as a framework and to concentrate on clarifying the conditions to be fulfilled if unity is to become a reality."[111] Vischer clarified the condi-tions as he stated: "there are at least three conditions to be fulfilled: agreement in the apostolic faith; mutual recognition of baptism, eucharist and ministry; structures which make joint consultation and decision possible."[112]

Work toward "mutual recognition of baptism, eucharist and ministry" had already begun. At the Accra meeting of the Commission on Faith and Order three statements on baptism, eucharist and ministry had been agreed upon and submitted to the Central Committee of the World Council of Churches.[113] These statements were reviewed by the Fifth Assembly of the

World Council in 1975. The Fifth Assembly authorized the transmission of the statements to member churches for study and response.

In 1977, the Standing Commission on Faith and Order drafted "a reply to the replies" from the churches. The three statements were also revised.[114] Finally, at its meeting in Dresden, in 1981, the World Council Central Committee re-affirmed the authorization of the Commission on Faith and Order to transmit the revised texts to member churches with a request for their official response.[115]

The following motion, made when the Commission on Faith and Order met in Lima, Peru, in 1982, carried out this mandate:

> The Commission considers the revised text on Baptism, Eucharist and Ministry to have been brought to such a stage of maturity that it is now ready for transmission to the churches in accordance with the mandate given at the Fifth Assembly of the World Council of Churches, Nairobi 1975, and re-affirmed by the Central Committee, Dresden 1981.[116]

The motion passed. Member churches of the World Council were requested "to prepare an official response to this text at the highest appropriate level of authority" as an initial step in a longer "process of reception."[117]

The Lima text on *Baptism, Eucharist and Ministry* stands as a waymarker on the road toward visible church unity charted at Lausanne in 1927 and, before that, at Lambeth in 1920. According to the preface:

> Those who know how widely the churches have differed in doctrine and practice in baptism, eucharist and ministry, will appreciate the importance, the large measure of agreement registered here. . . . That theologians of such widely different traditions should be able to speak so harmoniously about baptism, eucharist and ministry is unprecedented in the modern ecumenical movement.[118]

These words of congratulation invite words of criticism. Neither "theologians" nor "those who know" represent the diverse membership of the World Council or its member churches. Women, and women and men of variegated colors and cultures, are invisible in this text committed to the visible unity of the church.

In the text, baptism is described as "incorporation into Christ" and as "entry into the New Covenant between God and God's people."[119] A multitude of images express the meaning of baptism: "a new birth," "a renewal by the Spirit," "an exodus from bondage . . . and a liberation into a new humanity in which barriers of division whether of sex or race or social status are transcended." Each image conveys baptism as "the sign of new life through Jesus Christ."[120]

The document also describes baptism as "a basic bond of unity"[121] among the community of Christians. It is on the basis of baptismal unity in the Body of Christ that genuine witness and service are enacted. Members thus united are called to "a common responsibility, here and now, to bear witness together to the Gospel of Christ, the Liberator of all human beings."[122]

The Lima text laments the reality that the baptismal unity of the church, and thus the witness of the church, is marred. Baptismal unity is marred insofar as churches are unable to recognize their various practices of baptism as valid. Baptismal unity is also marred, according to the text, when differences of sex, race, or social status become divisive.[123]

The various practices of baptism held as valid by the churches are then discussed. In particular, the practice of believers' baptism and the practice of infant baptism are discussed.[124] Attention is given to the divisions that derive from these various practices. And the churches are called to "mutual recognition of baptism" as "an important sign and means of expressing the baptismal unity given in Christ."[125]

Divisions *within* the churches, divisions that are racial, social, or gender-related, are merely noted. The document does not consider the ways in which these barriers continue to undermine a new creation in Christ. The document does not consider "mutual recognition" of each and every member as an indispensable sign of the unity in Christ.

This failure to call for the "mutual recognition" of each and every member is related to the document's emphasis on baptism as cleansing, pardoning, and the forgiveness of sin. The image of "the old Adam" dying beneath the baptismal waters dominates all others. This image is connected to the call to overcome differences, that is, to be united by dying to our differences. Few images are of rising out of the baptismal waters into new life; neither is there a call to celebrate differences as gifts borne by each member for the upbuilding of the Body of Christ. The implications of women, women and men of diverse colors and cultures, having "put on" Christ in baptism, are not addressed while concern for "mutual recognition" of the dominant ecclesial doctrines and orders of baptism is the focus of attention.

Accordingly, the Lima text presents a carefully crafted section on the eucharist that does not address the character of the community created by this celebration. Some significant suggestions about the community created by the eucharist are made. The eucharist is a call to all "to be in solidarity with the outcast and to become signs of the love of Christ" and it "transforms Christians into the image of Christ."[126]

The statement about the transformation of each member of the eucharistic community is most significant. It begins to break open understandings of who may or may not image Christ in, and on behalf of, the community. If the eucharist transforms all Christians into the image of Christ and if, as the text continues, "it is Christ who invites to the meal and who presides at it," women and men alike may represent Christ.[127]

The subsequent statement, however, specifies that "an ordained minister" presides at the eucharist in most churches.[128] The ordained minister is "the ambassador who represents the divine initiative."[129] The remainder of this section belabors age-old obstacles to a common celebration of the eucharist. No word regarding other obstacles is heard. This section of the text is silent about the image and role of women.

The section on ministry begins with a call to "the whole people of God."[130] The ministry of all Christians is affirmed. "Diverse and complementary gifts" are acknowledged and appreciated.[131] But these introductory statements are abbreviated; most of this section of the text is a discussion of the forms and functions of the ordained ministry. Moreover, in this section ministry is viewed according to the tradition of Apostolic succession. Ministry thus means primarily the ordained ministry; and ordained ministry is the perpetuation of the faith professed by those who are acknowledged as successors to the Apostles.

Given this understanding of ministry, it is not surprising

that the text is almost completely silent about women's ordination. There is a call "to discover the ministry which can be
provided by women as well as that which can be provided by
men."[132] But the wording of this call implies that the ministry
"provided by men" is primary while the ministry "provided by
women" is secondary. One statement directly addresses women's ordination:

> Some churches ordain both men and women, others
> ordain only men. Differences on this issue raise obstacles
> to mutual recognition of ministries. But those obstacles
> must not be regarded as substantive hindrance for further
> efforts toward mutual recognition.[133]

Even when the ordination of women is mentioned, churches
are counseled not to consider it as a "substantive" matter, important to the mutual recognition of ministry. It is clear that
mutual recognition of ministry is mutual recognition of ministry as it is "provided by men."

The statement directly addressing the ordination of women is all the more striking by contrast to another statement:

> Churches which refuse to consider candidates for
> the ordained ministry on the grounds of handicap or be-
> cause they belong, for example, to one particular race or
> sociological group should re-evaluate their practices.[134]

With regard to the ordination of women, churches are counseled not to consider it "substantive." Yet churches are counseled to "re-evaluate their practices" with reference to other
groups of people. The disparity between these two counsels is
distressing, not because women's ordination is left unresolved,
but because women's call to the ordained ministry is not seriously addressed.

The document on *Baptism, Eucharist and Ministry*
stands as a waymarker on the road to church unity charted at
Lausanne and before that at Lambeth. Measured by classical
controversies among the churches, its accomplishment is remarkable. Its failure to recognize contemporary controversies
among the churches—particularly those related to the role and
image of women—is also remarkable.

The document thus stands as a monument as well as a
waymarker. The church unity envisioned by this document

depends on an elision of difference. Its bonds of unity are tangled by constraint and conformity. The era of ecumenical exchange to which it stands is an era dominated by "people who could not but" perpetuate the "recalcitrant and sceptical frame of mind" of which the women spoke in 1948. It is an era that is effectively ended.

Voices of difference as well as brokenness have burst its bonds of unity. At the Lima meeting of the Commission on Faith and Order, Mary Tanner, Moderator of the Advisory Committee of The Community Study, spoke about the local group reports: "They describe the brokenness of community both within the Church and in the wider community which challenges our concepts of unity and all our past attempts at renewal."[135] We now turn to these reports to search for bonds of unity which celebrate rather than condemn difference.

Notes

/1/ Toward the end of the Edinburgh conference, Brent declared: "During these past days a new vision has been unfolded to us. But whenever God gives a new vision He also points to some new responsibility, and you and I, when we leave this assembly, will go away with some fresh duties to perform" (*World Missionary Conference, 1910: The History and Records of the Conference, Together with Addresses Delivered at the Evening Meetings*, 9 vols., vol. 9: *World Missionary Conference, 1910* [Edinburgh and London: Oliphant, Anderson, & Ferrier; New York, Chicago, and Toronto: Fleming H. Revell Co., n.d.], p. 330).

/2/ See Alexander C. Zabriskie, *Bishop Brent: Crusader for Christian Unity* (Philadelphia: Westminster Press, 1948).

/3/ "Joint Commission Appointed to Arrange for a World Conference on Faith and Order," in *Documents on Christian Unity*, vol. I: *1920-1924*, ed. G. K. A. Bell (London: Humphrey Milford; Oxford: Oxford University Press, 1924), p. 16.

/4/ "Report on Plan and Scope, adopted April 20, 1911," in *A Documentary History of the Faith and Order Movement 1927-1963*, ed. Lukas Vischer (St. Louis, Missouri: Bethany Press, 1963), p. 200.

/5/ Ibid.

/6/ See "An Encyclical Letter issued by the Bishops attending the third Lambeth Conference, July, 1888," in *The Six Lambeth Conferences 1867-1920*, rev. ed. with Appendix, compiled under the direction of the Most Reverend Lord Davidson of Lambeth, Archbishop of Canterbury, 1903-1928 (London: S.P.C.K., 1929), pp. 106-118.

/7/   See "An Appeal to All Christian People," Appendix, in *The Six Lambeth Conferences 1867-1920*, pp. 26-29.

/8/   Ibid., pp. 27-28.

/9/   Ibid., p. 28. These marks of visible unity were first affirmed by the House of Bishops, Protestant Episcopal Church in the U.S.A., meeting in Chicago in 1886, and then by the Lambeth Conference of 1888. Subsequently referred to as the "Chicago-Lambeth Quadrilateral" (Holy Scripture, the Creed, sacraments, ministry), these marks were first articulated by William Reed Huntington in *The Church Idea—An Essay Toward Unity* in 1870. See John E. Skoglund and J. Robert Nelson, *Fifty Years of Faith and Order: An Interpretation of the Faith and Order Movement* (New York: The Committee for the Interseminary Movement of the National Student Christian Federation, Department of Faith and Order Studies of the National Council of the Churches of Christ in the U.S.A., The Commission on Faith and Order of the World Council of Churches, 1963), p. 39.

/10/   *Faith and Order: Proceedings of the World Conference, Lausanne, August 3-21, 1927*, ed. H. N. Bates (New York: George H. Doran Co., 1927), pp. 460-461.

/11/   Ibid., p. 459.

/12/   Ibid.

/13/   Ibid., p. 464.

/14/   See William Temple, *Essays in Christian Politics and Kindred Subjects* (London: Longmans, 1933); *Nature, Man and God*. Being the Gifford Lectures Delivered in the University of Glasgow in the Academic Years 1932-1933 and 1933-1934 (London: Macmillan & Co., 1940). See also F. A. Iremonger, *William Temple, Archbishop of Canterbury: His Life and Letters* (Oxford: Oxford University Press, 1948).

/15/   See Tissington Tatlow, "The World Conference on Faith and Order," in *A History of the Ecumenical Movement 1517-1948*, ed. Ruth Rouse and Stephen Charles Neill (Philadelphia: Westminister Press, 1954), pp. 428-431. See also *Records of the Continuation Committee of the World Conference on Faith and Order, Murren, Switzerland, August 26-29, 1930, with a preliminary draft of a programme for the Second World Conference on Faith and Order*. Faith and Order pamphlet No. 63, 1st Series; *The 1934 Meeting of the Continuation Committee Held at Herstenstein, Switzerland, September 3-6*. Faith and Order pamphlet No. 71, 1st Series. Archives, Library of the Ecumenical Centre, Geneva, Switzerland.

/16/   *The Second World Conference on Faith and Order, Edinburgh, August 3-18, 1937*, ed. Leonard Hodgson (New York: Macmillan Co., 1938), p. 21.

/17/   Ibid., pp. 22-23.

/18/   Ibid., p. 275.

/19/   Continental theology, most especially the theology of Karl Barth, set the tone at the Second World Conference on Faith and Order. In 1935, Barth had addressed the human tendency to attempt "righteousness by works": "*God will not be mocked. . . .* We can 'have an unenlightened zeal for God' throughout our lives . . . but behind this stands the immovable fact . . . that God will not be deceived, that we . . . are discovered to be those who refuse him faith in order to be able to believe in ourselves and trust ourselves that much better. Behind all this stands the fact that this means judgment on all our works by which we think we can justify ourselves, and above all on the works of our faith by which we think we can justify ourselves" ("Gospel and Law" in *Community, State and Church: Three Essays by Karl Barth*, with an Introduction by Will Herberg [New York: Doubleday & Co., Anchor Books, 1960], pp. 92-93 [Originally published as *Evangelium und Gesetz*, No. XXXII in the series *Theologische Existenz heute* by Chr. Kaiser Verlag in Munchen, 1935]). Barth's sharp, even scornful, criticism of the current tendency to identify the Kingdom of God with some social or political or ecclesial order established by human hands spoke to the sense of crisis that swirled below the surface of the conference.

/20/ *The Second World Conference on Faith and Order, Edinburgh, August 3-18, 1937*, pp. 275-276.

/21/ Excerpt from the minutes of a preparatory meeting held in Zurich in 1923. Cited by Charles S. Macfarland, *Steps Toward the World Council: Origins of the Ecumenical Movement as Expressed in the Universal Christian Council for Life and Work* (New York, London, and Edinburgh: Fleming H. Revell Co., 1938), p. 84.

/22/ Nathan Soderblom, *Christian Fellowship or The United Life and Work of Christendom* (New York, Chicago, London, and Edinburgh: Fleming H. Revell Co., 1923), pp. 170, 171. Cf. *Report of the Preliminary Meeting at Geneva, Switzerland, August 12-20, 1920*. Faith and Order pamphlet No. 33, 1st Series. Archives, The Library of the Ecumenical Centre, Geneva, Switzerland. For a summary of this preliminary meeting see Tatlow, "The World Conference on Faith and Order," *A History of the Ecumenical Movement 1517-1948*, pp. 417-420.

/23/ Quoted in a letter sent by Nathan Soderblom and Henry A. Atkinson, General Secretary of the Life and Work Executive Committee, to Robert H. Gardiner, Secretary of the Faith and Order Continuation Committee. The letter is cited by Macfarland, *Steps Toward the World Council*, p. 110.

/24/ The preacher was the Rt. Reverend Theodore Woods, Anglican Bishop of Winchester. Quoted in *The Stockholm Conference 1925: The Official Report of the Universal Christian Conference on Life and Work held in Stockholm, 19-30 August 1925*, ed. G. K. A. Bell (Oxford: Oxford University Press; London: Humphrey Milford, 1926), pp. 38, 45.

/25/ The speaker was the Rt. Reverend Ludwig Ihmels, Lutheran Bishop of Saxony, who went on to declare: "We can do nothing, we have nothing, we are nothing." Ibid., p. 76.

/26/ William Adams Brown, *Toward a United Church: Three Decades of Ecumenical Christianity* (New York: Charles Schribner's Sons, 1946), p. 91.

The Universal Christian Conference on Life and Work emerged out of the Social Gospel movement in the United States and in Europe. Shailer Mathews stated the central and common conviction: "By the Kingdom of God Jesus meant *an ideal* (though progressively approximated) *social order. . . .* an ideal society is not beyond human attainment but is the natural possibility for man's social capacities and powers" (*The Social Teaching of Jesus: An Essay in Christian Sociology* [New York: Macmillan Co., 1915], pp. 54, 77 [Originally published in 1897]). See Charles Howard Hopkins, *The Rise of the Social Gospel in American Protestantism, 1865-1915* (New Haven: Yale University Press, 1940). Cf. W. A. Visser't Hooft, *The Background of the Social Gospel in America* (Haarlem: H. D. Tjeenk Willink, 1928). The central and common conviction of the Social Gospel movement was being called into question by theologians of the Lutheran and Reformed traditions.

/27/ In an "Explanation to the Churches'" J. H. Oldham concluded his reflections on the theme of the second world conference on Life and Work with this statement. The theme of the conference, held in Oxford, was "Church, Community and State." Cited by W. A. Visser't Hooft, *The Genesis and Formation of the World Council of Churches* (Geneva: World Council of Churches, 1982), p. 32.

/28/ W. A. Visser't Hooft, *The Genesis and Formation of the World Council of Churches*, p. 39.

/29/ J. H. Oldham, *The Oxford Conference: Official Report* (Chicago and New York: Willett Clark & Co., 1937), p. 267.

/30/ *The Second World Conference on Faith and Order, Edinburgh, August 3-18, 1937*, p. 186.

/31/ After the Report of the Committee of Thirty-Five, including the paragraph on the organization of the World Council of Churches, had been adopted, Headlam stated: "I want to move the addition of the words 'some members of the Conference desire to record their opposition to the formation of such a council'. . . . I want to be perfectly clear. If you do not allow my words to be added I shall move the rejection of the paragraph, and if the paragraph stands I shall refuse to assent to the Report, and by our standing orders it can only be adopted if accepted *nemine contradicente.*" Ibid., pp. 184-185.

/32/ See *The Doctrine of Grace*, ed. W. T. Whitley, with an Introduction by the Archbishop of York (London: S.C.M. Press, 1932); *The Ministry and the Sacraments*. Report of the Theological Commission appointed by the Continuation Committee of the Faith and Order Movement under the Chairmanship of the Rt. Rev. A. C. Headlam, ed. R. Dunkerley (London: S.C.M. Press, 1937). "In point of fact," according to Tatlow, "he did far more than chair . . . , having the major responsibility for selecting and inviting scholars from a number of Churches and countries, who both wrote and exchanged documents and met to discuss the points of theology before them," (Tatlow, "The World Conference on Faith and Order," p. 417).

/33/ *The Second World Conference on Faith and Order, Edinburgh, August 3-18, 1937*, p. 151.

/34/ In 1933, the evangelical provincial churches in Germany were unified to constitute the German Evangelical Church. The "Faith Movement of German Christians," founded at the behest of the National Socialist party, had campaigned vigorously for this unification. Ludwig Muller, Hitler's special advisor on Protestant church affairs and leader of the "German Christians," carried out the task of unification and was appointed Reichsbischof. The Confessing Church, based upon a confession of faith in the supremacy of the scripture over prevailing ideological or political conviction, was created a year later. Sometimes called the Confessing Synod of the German Evangelical Church, in distinction from the National Synod, the Confessing Church claimed to be the true church in Germany. See Peter Matheson, ed. *The Third Reich and the Christian Churches* (Grand Rapids: Wm. B. Eerdmans, 1981). *See* also Klaus Scholder, *The Churches and the Third Reich*, Vol 2: *The Years of Disillusionment: 1934, Barmen and Rome* (Philadelphia: Fortress Press, 1988).

/35/ "W. A. Visser't Hooft, *The Genesis and Formation of the World Council of Churches*, p. 47.

/36/ Armin Boyens, in *Kirchenkampf und Okumene, 1933-1939*, documented the collaboration of Bishop A. C. Headlam with Bishop Theodor Heckel, head of the Department of Foreign Office of the German Evangelical Church, who was closely related to the Foreign Office of the Third Reich. On September 10, 1938, Headlam, Bishop of Gloucester, sent a letter to Heckel: "My dear Bishop . . . I am just back from the Faith and Order meeting in Switzerland. As you may have expected, we were not successful in preventing the World Council, but considerable efforts were made to take care that in its constitution the rights of Faith and Order were preserved. I know, many people have misgivings about the whole thing, but the people who have engineered it have been much too clever for us. Believe me yours sincerely A. C. Gloucester" (Cited by Boyens, *Kirchenkampf und Okumene, 1933-1939: Darstellung und Dokumentation* [Munich: Chr. Kaiser Verlag, 1969], p. 246). I note this exchange and the entire affair not as an intimation that Faith and Order had Facist sympathies, but as a case study of the consequences of the theological/ "non-theological" split in its thinking.

/37/ *Man's Disorder and God's Design*, 5 vols., vol. 5: *The First Assembly of the World Council of Churches, held at Amsterdam, August 22nd to September 4th, 1948. The Official Report*, ed. W. A. Visser't Hooft. The Amsterdam Assembly Series (New York: Harper & Bros. Publishers, 1948), p. 51.

/38/ Ibid., p. 55. Emphasis theirs.

/39/ Ibid., p. 52.

/40/ Ibid.

/41/ Ibid., p. 51.

/42/ Ibid., p. 127.

/43/ "The Church, the Churches and the World Council of Churches: The Ecclesiological Significance of the World Council of Churches," in *A Documentary History of the Faith and Order Move-*

ment, 1927-1963, ed. Lukas Vischer (St. Louis, Missouri: Bethany Press, 1963), pp. 169-171. Cf. *Minutes and Reports of the Third Meeting of the Central Committee of the World Council of Churches, Toronto (Canada), July 9-15, 1950* (Geneva: World Council of Churches, 1950).

/44/   Ibid., pp. 171, 176.

/45/   Ibid., pp. 168-169.

/46/   Ibid., p. 171.

/47/   *The Third World Conference on Faith and Order, held at Lund, August 15th to 28th, 1952*, ed. Oliver S. Tomkins (London: S.C.M. Press, 1953), p. 15. Emphasis theirs.

/48/   Ernst Lange, *And Yet It Moves: Dream and Reality of the Ecumenical Movement*, trans. Edwin Robertson (Geneva: World Council of Churches, 1978), p. 40 [Originally published under the title *Die okumenische Utopie oder Was bewegt die okumenische Bewegung?*, Stuttgart, 1978].

/49/   *The Third World Conference on Faith and Order, held at Lund, August 15th to 28th, 1952*, p. 18.

/50/   Ibid., p. 27.

/51/   Ibid., p. 33.

/52/   Ibid., p. 20.

/53/   *The Evanston Report: The Second Assembly of the World Council of Churches, 1954*, ed. W. A. Visser't Hooft (London: S.C.M. Press, 1955), p. 91.

/54/   *The Third World Conference on Faith and Order, held at Lund, August 15th to 28th, 1952*, p. 61.

/55/   See *The Non-Theological Factors in the Making and Unmaking of Church Union*. Prepared by the Commission on the Church's Unity in Life and Worship for the World Conference on Faith and Order, Edinburgh, 1937. Drafted by Willard Learoyd Sperry. Faith and Order pamphlet No. 84, 1st series (New York and London: Harper & Bros., Publishers, 1937).

/56/   *The Third World Conference on Faith and Order, held at Lund, August 15th to 28th, 1952*, pp. 12-13. See C. H. Dodd, G. R. Cragg, Jacques Ellul, *Social and Cultural Factors in Church Divisions*, with a Preface by Oliver Tomkins and the Report of a Conference held at the Ecumenical Institute at Bossey in November, 1951 (New York: World Council of Churches, 1952). See also C. H. Dodd, "A Letter Concerning Unavowed Motives in Ecumenical Discussions," *The Ecumenical Review* 2 (Autumn 1949):52-56.

    The Constitution of the Faith and Order Commission was amended at Lund. Among the amendments was a paragraph on another function of Faith and Order: "To study questions of faith, order and worship with the relevant social, cultural, political, racial and other factors in their bearing on the unity of the Church," (*The Third World Conference on Faith and Order, held at Lund, August 15th to 28th, 1952*, p. 360).

/57/   Ibid., p. 257.

/58/   *Institutionalism and Church Unity*. A Symposium Prepared by the Study Committee on Institutionalism, Commission on Faith and Order. World Council of Churches, ed. Nils Ehrenstrom and Walter G. Muelder (New York: Association Press, 1963), p. 24. Cf. "The Report of the Study Commission on Institutionalism," in *Faith and Order Findings*. The Final Report of the Theological Commissions to the Fourth World Conference on Faith and Order, Montreal 1963, ed. Paul Minear (Minneapolis: Augsburg Publishing House, 1963), pp. 1-31.

/59/ *One Lord One Baptism*. "Report on The Divine Trinity and the Unity of the Church" and "Report on the Meaning of Baptism" by the Theological Commission on Christ and the Church. Faith and Order Paper No. 29 (London: S.C.M. Press, 1960), p. 8.

/60/ Ibid., p. 9.

/61/ Ibid., p. 60.

/62/ "I hope that you have understood," declared Henriette Visser't Hooft, "I am only against decapitation . . . ." ("Aus den Briefwechsel mit Karl Barth 1934" in Gundrun Kaper, Henriette Visser't Hooft, u.a. *Eva wo bist du? Frauen in internationalen Organisation der Okumene: Eine Dokumentation* [Gelnhausen, Berlin, Stein Mfr.: Burckhardthaus-Laetare Verlag, 1981], p. 19). My translation.

/63/ *The New Delhi Report. The Third Assembly of the World Council of Churches, 1961*, ed. W. A. Visser't Hooft (New York: Association Press, 1962), p. 116.

/64/ Ibid., p. 117.

/65/ Ibid., p. 118.

/66/ Ibid., p. 119.

/67/ Joseph A. Sittler, "Called to Unity," *The Ecumenical Review* 14 (January 1962):183.

/68/ See "The Moscow Patriarchate and the First Assembly of the World Council of Churches," *The Ecumenical Review* 1 (Winter 1949):188-195. See also L. Zander, "The Ecumenical Movement and the Orthodox Church," *The Ecumenical Review* 1 (Spring 1949):267-276; *The Orthodox Church in the Ecumenical Movement: Documents and Statements 1902-1975*, ed. Constantin G. Patelos (Geneva: World Council of Churches, 1978). For fuller discussion of Orthodox ecclesiology see Timothy Ware, *The Orthodox Church* (Harmondsworth, Middlesex, England: Penguin Books, 1963); Sergius Bulgakov, *The Orthodox Church*, ed. Donald A. Lowrie, trans. Elizabeth S. Cram (London: Centenary Press, 1935) [Originally published in Paris, 1935]; John Meyendorff, *The Orthodox Church: Its Past and Its Role in the World Today*, trans. John Chapin (New York: Pantheon Books, 1962) [Originally published under the title *L'Eglise Orthodoxe: hier et aujourd'hui*, Paris, 1960].

/69/ In 1919, a Faith and Order deputation was sent to invite the Pope to participate in a World Conference on Faith and Order. Pope Benedict XV declined the invitation (See Tatlow, "The World Conference on Faith and Order," pp. 415-416). The Second Vatican Council inaugurated a new era in ecumenical relations. In 1960, Pope John XXIII established a Secretariat for Promoting Christian Unity. The

Second Vatican Council asked the Secretariat, headed by Augustin Cardinal Bea, to draft a "Decree on Ecumenism" (See "Unitatis Redintegratio" in *The Documents of Vatican II*, a New and Definitive Translation, with Commentaries and Notes by Catholic, Protestant and Orthodox Authorities, ed. Walter M. Abbot, S.J., trans. Joseph Gallagher [New York: Herder and Herder; Association Press, 1966], pp. 341-366). The Roman Catholic Church has not become a member of the World Council of Churches. However, because the Commission on Faith and Order retained the right to appoint members from churches that are not members of the council, there have been Roman Catholic members of the Commission on Faith and Order since 1968 (See *The Uppsala Report 1968: Official Report of the Fourth Assembly of the World Council of Churches, Uppsala, July 4-20, 1968*, ed. Norman Goodall [Geneva: World Council of Churches, 1968], p. 223). Roman Catholic representatives were received by the Commission on Faith and Order already in 1963.

/70/   Oliver S. Tomkins, Foreword to *The Fourth World Conference on Faith and Order, Montreal 1963*, ed. P. C. Rodger and L. Vischer. Faith and Order Paper No. 42 (London: S.C.M. Press, 1964).

/71/   Ibid., pp. 41-90.

/72/   Ernst Kasemann, "Unity and Diversity in New Testament Ecclesiology," *Novum Testamentum* 6 (1963):290. Also published as "Einheit und Vielfalt in der neutestamentlichen lehre von der Kirche," *Exegetische Versuche und Besinnungen 2*, Gottingen, 1964.

/73/   Ibid., p. 295.

/74/   Ibid., p. 293.

/75/   Raymond E. Brown, S.S. "The Unity and Diversity in New Testament Ecclesiology," *Novum Testamentum* 6 (1963):302-303. Also published as "Einheit und Verschiedenheit in der neutestamentlichen Ekklesiologie," *Okumenische Rundschau* 13, 1964.

/76/   Ibid., pp. 303-307.

/77/   Ellen Flesseman-van Leer, Introduction to *The Bible: Its Authority and Interpretation in the Ecumenical Movement*, ed. Ellen Flesseman-van Leer. Faith and Order Paper No. 99 (Geneva: World Council of Churches, 1983), p. 4.

/78/   See Suzanne de Dietrich, "The Bible, a Force of Unity," *The Ecumenical Review* 1 (1949):410-416; Wolfgang Schweitzer, "The Bible and the Church's Message to the World," *The Ecumenical Review* 2 (1950):123-132; *Biblical Authority for Today*, ed. A. Richardson and W. Schweitzer (London: S.C.M. Press, 1951).

/79/   Kasemann, "Unity and Diversity in New Testament Ecclesiology," *Novum Testamentum* 6 (1963):295.

/80/   *New Directions in Faith and Order, Bristol, 1967: Reports-Minutes-Documents*. Faith and Order Paper No. 50 (Geneva: World Council of Churches, 1968), p. 163.

/81/   *The Uppsala Report 1968*, p. 12.

/82/   Ibid., p. 223.

/83/   Ibid., p. 17.

/84/   Ibid., p. 13. The notion of "catholicity" had been introduced to

Faith and Order discussions at the Fourth World Conference on Faith and Order in Montreal, 1963. See Lukas Vischer, Vitaly Borovoy, Claude Welch, "The Meaning of Catholicity," *The Ecumenical Review* 16 (October 1963):24-42.

/85/ Sittler, "Called to Unity," p. 182.

/86/ *New Directions in Faith and Order, Bristol, 1967*, pp. 131-132.

/87/ *The Uppsala Report 1968*, p. 17. Cf. "Lumen Gentium," in *The Documents of Vatican II*, pp. 14-101.

/88/ *The New Delhi Report*, p. 117.

/89/ *Minutes of the Meeting of the Commission and Working Committee 1968, Uppsala and Sigtuna*. Faith and Order Paper No. 53 (Geneva: World Council of Churches, 1968), p. 18.

/90/ Ibid.

/91/ Ibid., p. 21.

/92/ Ibid., p. 20.

/93/ See "The Draft Study of 1969 on the Theme 'Unity of Church-Unity of Mankind'," in *Unity in Today's World: The Faith and Order Studies on "Unity of the Church-Unity of Humankind,"* ed. Geiko Muller-Fahrenholz. Faith and Order Paper No. 88 (Geneva: World Council of Churches, 1978), pp. 28-51. Cf. *What Unity Implies: Six Essays After Uppsala*. World Council Studies No. 7 (Geneva: World Council of Churches, 1969); *No Man is Alien: Essays on the Unity of Mankind*, ed. J. Robert Nelson (Leiden: E.J. Brill, 1971).

/94/ See *Minutes of the Meeting of the Working Committee 1970, Cret-Berard*. Faith and Order Paper No. 57 (Geneva: World Council of Churches, 1970).

/95/ Ernst Lange, *And Yet It Moves*, p. 88. Cf. John Meyendorff, "Unity of Church-Unity of Mankind," *The Ecumenical Review* 24 (January 1972):30-46.

/96/ *Faith and Order, Louvain, 1971: Study Reports and Documents*. Faith and Order Paper No. 59 (Geneva: World Council of Churches, 1971), pp. 117, 198.

/97/ For reference to the study on "Spirit, Order and Organization," see *Minutes of the Meeting of the Commission and Working Committee, 1964, Aarhus, Denmark*. Faith and Order Paper No. 44 (Geneva: World Council of Churches, 1965), pp. 40-41, 58-59.

/98/ *Faith and Order, Louvain, 1971*, p. 125.

/99/ Ibid., pp. 186-187.

/100/ "The Draft Study of 1969 on the Theme 'Unity of Church-Unity of Mankind'," p. 40.

/101/ *Faith and Order, Louvain, 1971*, p. 215.

/102/ *Uniting in Hope, Accra 1974: Reports and Documents from the Meeting of the Faith and Order Commission, 23 July-5 August 1974, University of Ghana, Legon*. Faith and Order Paper No. 72 (Geneva: World Council of Churches, 1975), p. 25.

/103/ See "Giving Account of Hope and Salvation," *Study Encounter*, no. 2 (1975); "Giving Account of Hope in these Testing Times," *Study Encounter*, nos. 1-2, (1976); *Giving Account of the Hope Today*. Faith and Order Paper No. 81 (Geneva: World Council of Churches,

1977); *Giving Account of the Hope Together*. Faith and Order Paper No. 86 (Geneva: World Council of Churches, 1978).

/104/   *Faith and Order, Louvain, 1971*, p. 215.

/105/   *Minutes of the Meeting of the Working Committee, 1973, Zagorsk (U.S.S.R.)*. Faith and Order Paper No. 66 (Geneva: World Council of Churches, 1973), p. 39.

/106/   *Uniting in Hope, Accra 1974*, p. 2.

/107/   Ibid., pp. 25-47, 90-94. See *Accra 1974: Meeting of the Commission on Faith and Order. Minutes and Documents*. Faith and Order Paper No. 71 (Geneva: World Council of Churches, 1974).

/108/   *Uppsala to Nairobi, 1968-1975: Report of the Central Committee to the Fifth Assembly of the World Council of Churches*, ed. David Enderton Johnson (New York: Friendship Press; London: S.P.C.K., 1975), p. 79.

/109/   See *Faith and Order, Louvain, 1971*, pp. 225-229.

/110/   "What Unity Requires" in *Breaking Barriers, Nairobi, 1975: The Official Report of the Fifth Assembly of the World Council of Churches, Nairobi, 23 November-10 December, 1975*, ed. David M. Paton (London: S.P.C.K.; Grand Rapids: Wm. B Eerdmans for the World Council of Churches, 1976), p. 61.

/111/   *Sharing in One Hope: Reports and Documents from the Meeting of the Faith and Order Commission, 15-30 August 1978, Ecumenical Christian Centre, Bangalore, India*. Faith and Order Paper No. 92 (Geneva: World Council of Churches, n.d.), p. xi.

/112/   Ibid., p. 30.

/113/   See *One Baptism, One Eucharist and a Mutually Recognized Ministry: Three Agreed Statements*. Faith and Order Paper No. 73 (Geneva: World Council of Churches, 1975).

/114/   See *Towards an Ecumenical Consensus on Baptism, the Eucharist and the Ministry: A Reply to the Replies of the Churches*. Faith and Order Paper No. 84 (Geneva: World Council of Churches, 1977).

/115/   See *World Council of Churches Central Committee, Minutes of the Thirty-Third Meeting, Dresden, German Democratic Republic, 16-26 August 1981* (Geneva: World Council of Churches, 1981).

/116/   *Towards Visible Unity: Commission on Faith and Order, Lima, 1982*, vol. I: *Minutes and Addresses*, ed. Michael Kinnamon. Faith and Order Paper No. 112 (Geneva: World Council of Churches, 1982), p. 83.

/117/   *Baptism, Eucharist and Ministry*. Faith and Order Paper No. 111 (Geneva: World Council of Churches, 1982), p. x.

/118/   Ibid., p. ix.

/119/   Ibid., par. 1, p. 2.

/120/   Ibid., par. 2, p. 2.

/121/   Ibid., par. 6, p. 3.

/122/   Ibid., par. 10, p. 4.

/123/   Ibid., "Commentary," par. 6, p. 3.

/124/   Ibid., pars. 11-13, p. 4.

/125/   Ibid., par. 15, p. 6.

/126/   Ibid., pars. 24, 26, p. 14.
/127/   Ibid., par. 29, p. 16.
/128/   Ibid.
/129/   Ibid.
/130/   Ibid., pars. 1-6, pp. 20-21.
/131/   Ibid., par. 5, p. 20.
/132/   Ibid., par. 18, p. 24.
/133/   Ibid., par. 54, p. 32.
/134/   Ibid., par. 50, p. 32.
/135/   "The Community Study and the unity of the church and renewal of human community," in *Towards Visible Unity: Commission
on Faith and Order, Lima, 1982*, vol. II: *Study Papers and Reports*,
ed. Michael Kinnamon. Faith and Order Paper No. 113 (Geneva:
World Council of Churches, 1982), p. 156.

CHAPTER IV

"THIS IS MY BODY": A THEOLOGICAL PORTRAIT OF WOMEN AND MEN

In the preceding chapter, I articulated my critique of Faith and Order discourse on unity. Faith and Order discourse on unity has either considered difference as accidental or condemned it as divisive, and so the variegated voices raised in the context of the Community Study could not be heard and honored. I clarified the limits of the Faith and Order discourse in light of the conclusion of the Community of Women and Men in the Church Study. That the conclusion of the Community Study and the culmination of the *Baptism, Eucharist and Ministry* study coincided, became highly significant. *Baptism, Eucharist, and Ministry*, considered unprecedented in the ecumenical movement and basic to visible church unity, bears witness to the resurgence of a vision of unity that requires conformity and thus constraint.

I criticized the limits of this discourse on unity to prepare the way for transgressing those limits.[1] I therefore treated examples of Faith and Order discourse as historical events, viewing their content in context, rather than considering their content as expressions of formal structures given to be universal. I intended to carve from the circumstance of limitation a space in which to draw from the local group reports of the Community Study a theological portrait. I also intended to create a space in which another vision of unity may emerge, a vision that recognizes and receives difference as integral to the fullness of life together.

In this chapter, therefore, I present voices heard in the local group reports of the Community Study. My attempt to hear what these voices say is also my wrestling with the questions: Where is change possible? In what ways can change be

manifest? I do not clarify my method at the outset but work
at, and at times beyond, the limits of my clarity. Only thus am
I able to hear voices that are different from the dominant
voices, and voices that are not-the-same-as my own.[2]

I wish, however, to acknowledge some of the assumptions
that are at work with me. I assume that my work cannot altogether reflect what was written in the local group reports. The
way I hear, and the way in which I represent, are conditioned
by my own language and life. I also assume that these reports
are not altogether representative of their originating cultural
or ecclesial contexts. Each report is a singular piece as well as
a response to the same study book.

I further assume that my representational limitations,
and those of the reports, help rather than hinder the afore-
mentioned transgression of limits. The limits of Faith and Order discourse, given to be universal, required conformity and
thus constraint. Representational limitations basic to the community reports and my perception of them, are conditioned by
the writers' contexts as well as my own. They are offered as
confessions, as a portrait of women and men in churches. Such
confession opens the possibility of change, particularly of my
perception of others and thus of myself.[3]

This is a theological portrait of women and men in
churches. The Community of Women and Men in the Church
Study was founded in the conviction that all the people of God
are called to engage in theological conversation. Women and
men were invited to reflect together on traditional theological
teachings in light of their own experience. I read the reports
as theological texts, transgressing the long-pervasive distinction between theological and "non-theological."

In the vision of unity emerging from the Community
Study, different experiences and perspectives are acknowledged and appreciated. I highlight these differences in this
chapter. I therefore arrange responses written in the reports
with reference to what they have in common.[4] I refer, that is,
to the Community of Women and Men in the Church Study
booklet as I draw this portrait. In the first section, I look at the
character of the groups who sent reports. I then listen to responses to personal and cultural questions, to questions about
scripture and tradition, and to questions about church structures.[5] These responses are reflections on past as well as pres-

ent circumstances. In the final section I listen to what the groups said about change and a newly-created community of women and men.

Throughout this chapter, I portray the widest possible range of responses to the same questions. I do this so the diversity of voices may be heard. As I draw this portrait, I am impressed by the impossibility of articulating a consonant or logically coherent answer to any question. Difference, dissonance, even division, predominate within as well as among groups, cultures, and ecclesial contexts.

This chapter anticipates my theological vision of unity, presented in the last chapter. As noted in the introduction, my vision of unity is informed by my understandings of relinquishment and conversation. In this chapter, therefore, I seek to draw the reader with me into conversation with variegated voices rather than to determine comparisons or draw conclusions. I hope to draw the reader with me toward that moment in conversation when each and every one is changed, toward that instant of loosing in which bonds that celebrate difference may be created.[6]

"not . . . the whole picture"

Groups that gathered were constituted by members whose affiliations with one another were diverse. There were groups based in local parishes or congregations, within denominations, and across denominations and communions. There were groups whose members were students or teachers or clergy or clergy wives or deaconesses or church administrators. There were groups that had long gathered for study and groups that came together for the first time.

As examples: In Barbados, women involved in community-based Home and Family Education Programs studied with women and men involved in local churches. The group that met in Groningen, The Netherlands, to discuss questions posed by the Community of Women and Men in the Church Study had met every six weeks since 1960 to discuss "a selected theme from the field of culture and religion." They first came together because of "a feeling of estrangement with regard to Church structures and traditional teachings." Women

and men who worked on the national staff of the Lutheran
Church of America met in their New York offices. Ten
Anglican clergy wives studied in a group organized by the
Bristol (England) Council of Churches. Women who are leaders in churches belonging to the Sudan Council of Churches,
women involved in ecumenical organizations such as the Korean Church Women United, the Women's Inter-Church
Council of Canada, and the World Union of Catholic Women's
Organizations, also met. Anglican, Methodist, and Reformed
students of The Federation of Cambridge (England) Theological Colleges studied together. Women gathered in local settings such as a Greek Orthodox parish in Beirut, a Waldensian
congregation in Uruguay, a Baptist congregation in Burundi,
and an Evangelical Lutheran parish in Thuringen, the Federal
Republic of Germany.

Groups were influenced by diverse cultural contexts in
which they gathered. A group on the Isle of Man wrote:

> Man's society is more equable and less tense than that of
> the United Kingdom in general. While it shares in West-
> ern attitudes completely, its geographical isolation creates
> a time lag. Because the Island offers less incentives to wo-
> men to find a career outside the home, tensions are less
> developed.

Members of an Orthodox group in Paris reflected on the way
in which two distinct cultural traditions—Russian Orthodox
and western, secular—were intermingled in their context. A
group in Geneva was constituted by women from Asian, North
American, European, and African cultural contexts. Most of
them were in Geneva because of their husbands' work. According to their report:

> [They] had come to the group feeling that they had an
> individual problem and had never reflected on the eco-
> nomic, cultural, or theological roots and dimensions of
> what they were experiencing. They began to discover the
> complexity and the universality of the problems women
> face.

Likewise, many women in Latin America had heretofore participated in "traditional religious meetings" and had not re-

flected on "their role of complete passivity within a society dominated by 'machismo'."

The groups expressed various points of view on the Community of Women and Men in the Church Study. One Presbyterian group in the United States warned: ". . . if the course is continued in its present format and adopted as a Presbyterian approved curriculum, it will do more harm than good toward the unity of men and women in the church." Another Presbyterian group in the United States thought that the Community Study was "very threatening to both male and female members of the group." This group also noted: "The men especially seemed to feel that the goal was to push feminism. Some women seemed to gain 0ome new confidence and feeling of worth."

The point of view expressed by women in the group organized by the National Federation of Kyodan Women's Societies was akin to that of the Presbyterian men in the United States. These women noted the tardiness of their response to the Study and remarked:

> This was not only because we were very busy with our own programs, but also we thought the theme was motivated by an over-emphasis on 'human rights' and 'discrimination' and we were not interested in just going along with the trend of the times.

This group of ten women included several pastors.

"Some questions were irritating in their simplicity and lack of applicability," according to a parish-based Presbyterian group in New Zealand. This group stated: "We . . . found them at times too simple, too general, too vague or too enormous." The group concluded "that people in other countries may have found them mind-boggling."

A group of Greek Orthodox women meeting in Ras Beirut found the study "challenging and interesting." These women also found that "its approach to some points is not in line with our traditional approach to the issues that we still believe in and live up to till now." Echoing the Kyodan women, they concluded: "The focus of praying in our Church is on learning the Lord's rights. This is our main concern rather than seeking women's rights."

The Executive Committee of the Orthodox Church in

America said the study was "irrelevant to the climate of Orthodox Christian parishes across the nation." By this, the Executive Committee did not mean that the study of women and
men in the church as such was "irrelevant." Rather, the way
in which the Community Study was formulated was "irrelevant." The Executive Committee formulated its own study
book, "Women and Men in the Church."[7]

The Executive Committee of the Orthodox Church in
America also hosted a Woman's Day for discussion of women
and men in the church. The committee later reported:

> . . . The Study on the Community of Women and Men in
> the Church has created great interest in the Orthodox
> Church in America. It must be reported that Orthodox
> Christians often are 'on the other side of the fence' in con-
> clusions drawn when discussing women's issues. Ortho-
> dox Christians in general radically refuse feminist
> philosophy and theology. Nevertheless, creating an Or-
> thodox response to a feminist position is all-important, and
> the Orthodox Church in America is accepting this task
> and responsibility with fervor.

An Orthodox group in Finland also affirmed that "women
questions" were important but stated that the questions in the
Community Study booklet had "a basically Protestant background and an emphasis on the Ordination of Women."[8]

Groups studied together for various periods of time. A
Special Committee appointed by the Church of Scotland studied for several years. "In the process," the Special Committee
reported, "the Committee itself has become a community of
men and women, who through worship, study and discussion
have reached a level of openness and commitment for which
they are profoundly grateful." A group in Australia, with
members from Anglican, Roman Catholic, and Uniting (Congregational, Methodist, Presbyterian) churches, met for many
months. The group reported:

> From time to time the group paused to look at its life and
> to express celebrations and frustrations. It became obvi-
> ous that participants had different expectations of the
> group. Sometimes members were accused of not being
> open and honest enough. There were times of anger and
> hurt as well as laughter and celebration.

This group often structured its meetings around an evening meal. According to the group, these meals "in some ways became the most important aspect of the time we spent together. . . . The bonding which grew from these times is perhaps what kept us together."

A group sponsored by the Caribbean Council of Churches met in the Jamaican Centre once every week. The constituency of the group changed as frequently. The group's reporter remarked that, "the exchange of ideas" was enriched by the coming and going of participants.

In the Anglican Diocese of Waikato, New Zealand, the Adult Council sponsored a Study Day. During the day, women and men discussed the questions posed by the Community Study in various groups. The reporter of this Study Day noted: "Women felt a noticeable difference between groups which had male participation and those without men." "The women," continued the reporter, "felt able to talk more freely and personally in the absence of men." A Nigerian group of Methodists, Anglicans, and Baptists reported a similar dynamic:

> In the Baptist Church, women do not keep silence in the Church, or rather, our democratic belief welcomes women's contributions and not their total subordination. But home and traditional demands usually creep into the Church. The men speaking in the Church's general meeting are the husbands of these women and the fear of opposing them may not make them want to share and contribute.

These women, the Nigerian group remarked, "have to be appealed to over and over again before one of them will 'bell the cat'."

An ecumenical group meeting in Copenhagen lamented: "Unfortunately no men participated. The whole debate on women's role in the society and the church is unfortunately considered to be of interest for women only." "There was at times a male component," the Jamaican group reported, "but always outnumbered by the women." The reporter who read all the United States group reports observed:

> Women were the majority of participants and provided the most support. Perhaps this is as it should be (or at

least as it should be expected to be) for the Study questions hold out the possibility of a new place for women in the church which threatens many men.

"For the most part," concluded this reporter, "this was a 'women's study'."[9]

The Women's Committee of the Ecumenical Council of Finland wrote:

> Approximately 800 copies of the Study were sent out. The Women's Committee has been informed of the work of 20 discussion groups. 8 groups have sent in written reports of their work to the Committee. When the program was sent out, it was emphasized that the use of it was not tied to reporting in writing, although reports were encouraged. The comparatively small amount of reports signifies that they do not give the whole picture of how largely and significantly this study has influenced the discussions of different groups in our country.

Likewise, the reports received in Geneva and those refracted here are but remnants of the voices at once distinguished and dispersed by this study process.

"differences are . . . determined"

"When we have the courage to be ourselves," declared Dutch women in an ecumenical group, "we just are women":

> We should not try to fix the difference between man and woman; there are no typical male and female qualities . . . . We felt the same hesitation to define with some certainty what feminine experience might be. Women may have more attention for small-scale things; women may be more practically than theoretically-minded; they may talk from their own experience rather than from an objective point of view . . . but these differences cannot be pointed out clearly . . . Women should accent their being a woman, but no general definition can be made as to what this being a woman exactly means.

"The 'inherent' nature in women," remarked a women's group in The Gambia, "is a better description of the moulding processes that women have undergone." A group of women and men from various Asian contexts who met in Bangalore, India, stated "that, except for biological differences, all other differences are culturally, socially, and economically determined."[10]

Male and female characteristics are "created," according to the report of the Church of Sweden: "We think that the main basis of these characteristics is not the once for all given nature of man and woman but the different social roles of women and men." The report clarifies: "Formally and legally, the equality of men and women in Sweden has developed far." It was then acknowledged: "The largest obstacles for equality in Sweden are informal and ideological. It is necessary to overcome attitudes of the sex roles that are mirrors of an old fashioned social view, situation and structure."

Women are caught in the crisis that accompanies social and cultural change. Women from the Waldensian Church of Uruguay wrote:

> The Uruguayan woman has sought to go out of the home to study with total freedom, choosing the jobs or professions she has desired. The question which is posed at present is 'What has she gained from it?' Conflicts have grown between her responsibilities within and outside of the home.

Women from various churches in Sudan wrote: "Nowadays, especially in towns, women who are educated go to work outside their homes. . . . As the woman is expected to do both well, housework and work outside, she feels hard pressed." Women and men from Argentina wrote:

> Being a country with fundamentally a latin culture, the situation of a woman is difficult. . . . *In the moral aspect* a woman is judged far more severely than a man although both are responsible for the same deed. *In the professional aspect* an exceptionally intelligent woman is recognized and appreciated but, against this, the fact of being a man, even though incapable, brings him greater praise and better prospects in his profession. More is expected of a woman just because she is in fact a woman. To this specific problem can be added the inherent difficulty of a housewife who cannot count on much useful help from her husband.

Women in Copenhagen wrote about "a conflict of conscience" in the woman: "She has to invest all her effort to be up to date in her job, and she feels she ought to be the perfect housewife, an image which our culture puts in front of her."

Men are also caught in the crisis of change. According to one report, the Cuban *Family Code* states that "the work of the home is not the exclusive and excluding responsibility of women." The report continues:

> But there is still much machismo which makes men (not to say also some women) believe that those who share the traditional tasks of the home (washing, cooking, cleaning, etc.) are necessarily effeminate or homosexual or in most cases 'men with weak characters who allow themselves to be ruled by their wives'.

Women in the Netherlands declared: "Men have no choice. If we want a society of equal dignity, we have to create room for men so they can choose as well.

The statements of guilt, generated in the midst of the crisis, came from women. One woman from Norway wrote:

> My responsibilities within and outside the home are conflicting: I feel I am neither a good professional worker nor a good mother and housewife. My husband does not experience the conflict the same way I do, and sometimes I feel this to be unjust: *He* is considered to be a very good father because he takes more part in child-care than what is usual in the average family . . . and *he* is very successful in his career. . . . It is he who then is the kind and helping person, while I am the one who constantly demands of him that he share in the household duties and in caring for the children in order for me to have some time on my own. Truly not a pleasant part to play!

Women from six parishes of the Church of England wrote:

> . . . are today in an intermediate, ambivalent situation in which women generally do not know what is their role, to be primarily housewives, a state increasingly belittled and despised, or to be out at work. Women who go out to work tend to feel guilty about doing so, while those who remain at home tend to feel guilty about not going out to work.

"Today's changing attitudes create difficulties;" these women declared, "at one moment the wife is expected to fulfil her traditional role, but not at the next, so she does not know where she stands."

Church of England clergywives expressed the confusion as well as the conflict of change:

> . . . how do most women [in this group] describe them-
> selves on say, a passport: retired? O.A.P.? housewife? The
> latter was most commonly used, and following discussion
> around this it was suggested that the term 'housewife'
> presented no threat. In any group the 'dregs' have to go
> through somebody. . . . There is no applause for cleaning,
> scrubbing, standing at the kitchen sink, but if a woman
> hated doing this then that would indeed be slavery. . . .
> There is a great deal talked about being 'tied to the
> kitchen sink,' but many women have no great intellectual
> prowess anyway!

These women then commented: "But for those who want to use their intellect, the handicaps are still enormous for women with families."

". . . in the traditional African system," one woman wrote, "both men and women are free to seek a fulfillment of their lives both as individuals and as members of the community":

> . . . it is an indictment on the Euro-Christian world that
> African Church women have no place of significance in
> the Church and women of European oriented education
> seem very irrelevant to the life of the community. And
> worse still, that women declare they cannot command fol-
> lowership, neither from men nor women. Furthermore,
> it is painful to the essence of African womanhood whose
> female ancestors were very dynamically involved in every
> aspect of human life, that she now defines herself in terms
> of irrelevance and impotence.[11]

One woman from India remarked: "We had the joint family, but for many socioeconomic reasons this has been destroyed":

> Two decades ago it seemed a step in the right direction
> away from male domination and traditional values which
> hampered the development of the individual and the wo-
> man in particular. But today we realize that merely aping
> the west will not do. The western concept of a nuclear
> family has only dehumanized people.[12]

A group from Trinidad pondered their "proximity to the United States and the influence that is felt through this location" as they talked about tensions related to female and male roles.

The groups that gathered in Norway were "too dependent on a western individualizing pattern of thoughts," according to the Norwegian Theological Commission that read those local reports. In an ecumenical group in Australia, the women "had a less clear sense of self." "The servant role, denial and emptying of self," said these women, "had led to nothingness. 'I am nobody'." One man in this Australian group challenged the women, noting "a need to revalue the contemplative, passive side of our natures as being a general problem in the West common to both men and women." Discussion of the western notion of equality made it "more difficult" to define new images and roles for study groups in the Church of Finland. The Church of Finland reported: "The action models of men have been the measure of equality. The aim has been to reach 'the likeness of men' or 'the rights of men' . . . instead of finding new models for acting like human beings."

Members of the Orthodox Church who met in Paris, Lebanon, Finland, and the United States also called the western notion of equality between women and men into question. According to the report of the Orthodox Church in America:

> . . . while Jesus is generally the model and pattern of all human perfection, and while Mary is the person who has accomplished divine perfection most fully, Jesus is still specifically a man, and Mary specifically a woman. This means not only that we contemplate the model of human perfection in a male form, and its perfect realization in a female form; it means as well that there is a sense in which Jesus is also the perfect example for men, as the Virgin Mary is for women. . . . It is claimed that Jesus realizes the general Christian virtues in a particularly masculine form, while Mary actualizes them in a particularly feminine form. The sexual distinctions and images of Jesus and Mary endure everlastingly.

Thus, from the Orthodox point of view, men and women are different and their respective "eternal archetypes" are Jesus and Mary[13].

Orthodox in Paris also affirm that women and men, uni-

fied in human being, are created "in the IMAGE OF GOD."
The "fertile tension of Unity and Difference," they wrote, is at
the heart of Orthodox anthropology.[14] This anthropology is
grounded theologically in the trinitarian God, in whose image
women and men are created.[15]

"The family is . . . a creaturely reflection of the Holy Trinity itself," affirmed members of the Orthodox Church in
America. They thus declared:

> The 'liberation' of women, and their massive entry into
> 'public life,' has led to a radical alteration of family life
> and, in many cases, to its ideological rejection and factual
> decomposition. This is the most critical issue for Orthodox
> Christians since, in the Orthodox view, the family is not
> simply the 'traditional form' of human community, but it
> is the basic and essential form of human being and life as
> created by God in his own image and likeness.

An Orthodox bishop in Lebanon declared:

> It seems to me that the great powers have an interest in
> involving woman in production so that the consumption
> of the family would increase and thereby increase their
> plundering of the smaller countries. Therefore, we must
> not imitate the current women's liberation in the West
> because if they emancipated woman in America this
> would increase their own wealth, but it would only de-
> grade woman in our countries. It follows that the Western
> model in woman's liberation is beneficial to the West but
> not to us. We must seek our own special model for wo-
> man's liberation.

The bishop concluded: "I don't have a formula now. I tell you
frankly I don't know how to go about it, but we must emanci-
pate woman here in order to strengthen and liberate the Third
World.[16]

Many groups noted the way in which roles ascribed to
women and men in churches reflect current sociocultural
roles. The Norwegian Theological Commission surveyed local
group reports from Norway and stated:

> Women are engaged in jobs like caring for children, being
> members of social committees (serving at tables), carrying
> out secretarial duties in committees, relief work in the
> congregation—in short, jobs similar to those ranging

within the traditional role of women in the home. Men most often carry duties as leaders, are active speakers etc..—tasks that are of higher prestige and esteem than the traditional female occupations.

A group wrote from New Zealand:

Within most church structures, women have, at least in theory, the opportunity to participate on equal terms with men. However, in practice women are poorly represented at all levels of decision-making while they have almost sole responsibility for such duties as childminding, cleaning and providing food and drink.

Participants in the Latin American Regional Consultation commented:

Situated within a society wherein the woman is marginalized and subjected, our churches have marginalized her in their own structures, assigning tasks that accompany the roles traditionally seen as feminine (cleaning and arranging the church, cooking the meals, teaching Sunday School, etc.). These structures, based on a male-centered ideology, close the space for a new relationship of liberty and full companionship, in order to perpetuate the societal roles for the man and for the woman.[17]

At the Middle Eastern Council of Churches Consultation, a woman remarked:

In our church we have a pastoral committee and a women's committee. The women's committee takes care of the bazaars and the church flowers. We are not prohibited from the pastoral committees, but mostly women are related to church schools and church social projects such as houses for the deaf, dumb and aged and retarded.[18]

She concluded: "The jobs that women hold in the church relate to the cultural expectations and traditions."[19]

"As everywhere else, so in Madagascar, the women are the most active in the church, they visit the sick and represent the congregation; to them, these visits are very important because in our culture we have ancestor worship." This Malagasy group went on to say:

. . . before the French influence, women had significant

places in the society and in the Protestant churches. . . .
now, Malagasy people still suffer from the French coloni-
zation. During that time there was an attempt to erase
our culture and replace it with French, white, Western
culture. In the church this is still a problem. If there is
any sector where tradition is difficult, it is in the church.
In our country where socialism is being built and where
instead of a head of household (male) we are going to now
have, for instance the joint leadership of the spouses and
the parental authority, the church seems still to be far
from these concepts.[20]

"In Jamaica, as in most Caribbean lands, women predominate
in the family and outnumber men in other socializing institu-
tions, namely the School and the Church." However, the
Jamaican report also remarks: "In spite of their numerical su-
periority, women continue—by and large—to do the 'donkey
work' and to vote the few available men into office." "In
Cuba," according to the report of the Cuba Ecumenical Council, "85% of the participants are women. In the leadership of
ecclesiastical structures, 100% are men."

"The present structure of the church, and the tradition
on which it is based, hinder women from assuming leadership
roles," stated women and men who were in a workshop at the
Asian Consultation. "The ordination of women," these women
and men went on to say, "would help to restructure the existing patterns of ministry as well as improve the percentage
ratio and strength of women in various church organizations."[21] A group of women from a village in India asked:
"When the Church allows women to share the Gospel with
their neighbors and preach on the streets, why doesn't the
Church allow the women to speak within the four walls of the
Church?"[22]

"The ordination of women is still a 'hot potatoe' in the
Lutheran Church of Finland":

We feel there is a need for female ministers. There are
questions that are better handled by a woman than by a
man. We believe women's approach to be personal, warm
and creating security. Female pastors are needed also for
equality and balance. . . . The most important aspect is
that also a woman can fulfill her vocation as an ordained
minister.[23]

Women who are members of the Church of England wrote: "Sadly, throughout the ages the Church in its leadership has often shown a 'double think.' 'This is what we say; this is what we do'." These women then declared: "The situation is perpetuated by the official statement on the ordination of women: No theological reasons against it, but not at this moment."[24] "Women are still impure, taboo!" women from Belgium clarified. They continued: "This is particularly true for the Catholics where distance between the priest . . . and women is justified by means of . . . the sacralization of celibacy."[25] According to the report of the Orthodox Church in America: ". . . Orthodox Christian women felt the Orthodox Church *should hold firmly against* ordination of women to the priesthood." Greek Orthodox women in Beirut wrote: "The woman is as awake to the needs of the community as is the man in general, if not more; thus she has equal capacity for leadership. But she often tries to work discreetly and insists on that, if she is really living her Christian Orthodox faith."[26]

According to the report of the Women's Inter-Church Council of Canada: "Most mainline churches ordain women." This report continues:

> However, there are groups in different denominations (e.g. Presbyterian and Anglican) that are against the ordination of women and are trying to reverse that decision. . . . It is doubtful if there is real equality of access to women structurally within the church. . . . Our structures allow women to be involved as ministers, but individual attitudes are blocking this. There are very few female role models in ministry and those women who do achieve leadership often act out of the male model and are co-opted. There is very little assistance and support for women in transition.

The Theological Commission of the Church of Norway was uncertain whether or not the ordination of women was an "evangelical necessity": "If this would be a necessary consequence of the Gospel, the question of female ministers . . . must be considered as something that might lead to a division in the Church."[27]

According to the report of the African Regional Consultation: "The problem or question of women's ordination exists

mainly in the established churches. It is not much of a problem in the indigenous churches." The report clarifies:

> When the missionaries came, they were mostly men. . . .
> when women tried to enter church structures, they were
> questioned. The role of African priests is a case in point.
> This tradition of woman as a spiritual leader got left out of
> the church. Now it is coming back somewhat in some of
> the indigenous churches.[28]

"In the evangelical Churches women have always been pastors," according to a report from Barbados.

"Ordained women mostly go into institutional or hospital
work," wrote a woman who is ordained in the Presbyterian
Church of Ghana. She declared:

> There is only one ordained woman pastor in charge of a
> parish in a fishing village. She is AME Zion. We always
> hear the reaction that women 'are not ready', or that the
> parish 'is not ready yet' for women pastors. I say, let the
> women try. Women ought to be allowed to fail.

A woman who is ordained in an African Reformed Church
wrote: "My feeling about women, based on my parish experience, is that we are good at handling extreme, even extraordinary, human situations, but we are often docile in effecting
change in the normal life situation in church and society.[29]
Korean women cried out:

> No woman can stand on the pulpit. No woman pray at
> Sunday worship service. No woman preach sermon on
> Sunday morning Service. No woman minister, not even a
> elder. . . . Bible tells us help the outsiders. We feel we are
> also outsiders from men's world. Men must treat women
> as themselves. . . . Even those who are involved in human
> right movement do not understand women's right. They
> do not see women's suffering. Aren't we all belong to out-
> siders of power structures of church?

Australian women and men wrote:

> Although society is structured in accordance with . . . male
> and female role expectations, the reality is changing and
> therefore women and men experience conflict. Instead of
> recognizing this, the church tends to reinforce old roles of

male/female, work/home, dominance/submission, and inhibit the working of new models.

Presbyterian women wrote from Beirut: "We have noted that
the Church itself is still reluctant in looking at women as equal
to men. It is amazing how men cling to the ancient law and its
concept of women. They forget that in Christ we are a new
creation."

"The status quo has been maintained within the Church
by appeal to tradition, certain prejudices about womenhood
and particularly to the words of the scriptures," states the Report of the Asian Consultation.[30] The Latin American Regional Report states: "The traditional teaching done from the
Bible tends to marginalize women, by saying that the Bible
presents women as inferior to men."[31] "The Genesis account
is what Nigerians . . . use as an evidence of inferiority of woman to man," wrote a group from that country. This Nigerian
group added: "In a Primary School, a boy and a girl had a quar-
rel and the boy said 'Come here, if you dare, I will prove to you
today that I have 9 rib-bones while you have just seven'."

"We admit that in the church there exist, or at least sur-
vive, retarding tendencies influenced by superficial understanding of some biblical passages, like for instance Genesis 2,
3 or even I Corinthians 7," wrote a Evangelical Church of
Czech Brethren group. These Czech Brethren continued:

> We discern, however, that the Scriptures are not uniform
> even in this matter. It is possible to pursue in them an
> inner struggle for the situation of woman. For instance,
> already in Genesis 2:24 inside the patriarchal society quite
> a contradictory element breaks through.[32]

Swiss Reformed women wrote:

> Amidst the numerable biblical texts that refer to men and
> women, there is much diversity. Numerous passages
> evoke equality, reciprocity, responsibilities assumed in
> common. Others, on the contrary, insist on the differ-
> ences between men and women and on the subordination
> of woman to her husband.[33]

Participants in the African Regional Consultation agreed that
"there is ample evidence in the Bible of the downgrading of
women." However, they affirmed that "over against this is

Acts 2 and the repetition of the prophesy of Joel where there is no discrimination in those who receive the Holy Spirit."[34]

Women in the Waldensian Church of Uruguay "considered the importance of the historical social context of the epoch in which the Bible was written":

> . . . then we were able to encounter biblical passages which reinstate women in face of the concepts and ideas of the time in which it was written. We were then able to see women considered on the same level as men before God.

". . . the discrimination against women is not divine revelation but from the culture of the peoples and life of the Church within given cultures," wrote a Lutheran group from the German Democratic Republic. A Scottish group declared: *"The Scriptures* are there. They cannot be changed, but has it not always been accepted that there is a continuing process of understanding, interpretation and revelation of their meaning?" The Theological Commission of the Church of Norway cautioned against an " 'unchangeable Christianity' where the concrete applications of the gospels would be given once and for all":

> For the gospel . . . all the time meets new people in new situations. The testimony of the very Bible shows this. The four gospels got their distinctive characters according to the situation of the different congregations. And when the centre of the Biblical message is to be proclaimed, the word of the death and resurrection of Jesus, even that finds different expressions.

"We are convinced," continued the Norwegian Theological Commission, "that a right proclamation of the gospel will lead to still increasing freedom and equality for women."

"Within our church," wrote Finnish Lutherans, "the Bible has long been studied only from a male perspective":

> The status of women in quite different from what we have been made to believe. Each one of us has her own interpretation of the Bible. This is connected to personal characteristics, nature and . . . knowledge. It is natural that women interpret the Bible in a different way from men.

Lutheran women from Indonesia wrote:

> We discussed much concerning the status and roles of wo-
> men in church and society through the Biblical outlook. It
> was always compared with our tradition, as the traditions
> of Israel and ours are similar, the patriarchal society with
> women playing a subordinate role. We realized that the
> Biblical message we got was quite often misinterpreted
> and quoted with bias.

"Our conclusion," wrote these women, "was that we need
more women theologians, and women should participate fully
and actively in theology."

Members of the World Union of Catholic Women's Organizations observed:

> St. Paul's statement in I Cor. 11 appears to be often inter-
> preted as anti-woman; a closer look at the passage illus-
> trates that women did, in fact, pray and prophesy, and
> that the question of head covering was a minor detail ca-
> tering to the accepted social and religious custom of the
> period in which St. Paul was writing. I Cor. 14 is simply
> another example of how culture and custom influence the
> expression of the message. . . . There are many instances
> of Paul praising the work of the women in the various
> churches; so the picture of down-trodden, male-domi-
> nated women is hardly appropriate.

A group of Protestant women in Geneva recognized that for
Paul to consider it "natural" for women to "pray and 'prophesy'" was "extraordinary" in his time and place and thus revised their "anti-pauline prejudices."[35] One woman who
delivered an address at the Asian Regional Consultation
remarked:

> . . . it is interesting that behind St. Paul's concern about
> the scandal of going bare-headed, he recognizes the part-
> nership of women in some of the actual functions of the
> Church, like praying and prophesying.

"Thus," she stated, "even in the conservative Pauline era, we
recognize a new role of women emerging."[36]

Korean women wrote: "Most churches like to quote I
Cor. 11 and 14 for women." However, these women declared:

... Gal. 3:28 tells us we are as equal as men. It is really a
declaration of women's rights. Because of this verse we
can forgive Paul for what he has done to women throughout Christian tradition. Paul is not the only one to blame
for women's dehumanization. All the men who were in
responsible positions of the Christian tradition are to
blame. They interpreted the Bible for their own good.

A Lutheran group in the United States read Galatians 3:28, as
well as biblical stories in which "women were treated as
human beings." The group reported: "A 60 year old widow ...
breathed a sigh of great relief. 'Why that means that I am just
as good as anyone'."[37]

"It was on an issue of language that we came to grief,"
wrote a woman from Australia, "and it was really the fact that
we came to grief that was our salvation. In being able to touch
each other at the point of our pain we reached a deeper level
of trust and acceptance." "Language ... is vitally involved in
the cry of women," another Australian woman clarified. She
went on to say:

> Whilst few men say they believe in God as a male being,
> yet they find it difficult to think of God in other than male
> terms. Women are disappointed when men will not sup-
> port them in the language struggle.

Greek Orthodox women from Ras Beirut wrote: "We cannot
understand the necessity for raising the issue about the identity of God. Christ came in history as a man and taught us to
pray: 'Our Father who art in Heaven'."

"The true meeting with God takes place beyond all
images and all words, in the silence that is not mute," according to an Orthodox group from France. The group then eluci-
dated its affirmation:

> This 'apophasticism' permeating Orthodox belief avoids
> the trap of a unilaterally masculine image of God. Ortho-
> dox iconography never represents God the Father. The
> divine paternity would not be represented by a sexual
> image.

"The Heavenly Father," the group concluded, "should not be
imagined as a bearded patriarch."[38]

"God is neither man nor woman," declared the Theological Commission of the Church of Norway. The commission further stated:

> He is the 'Wholly Other' that no one can see or understand. . . . No roles, titles or comparisons with human lives (or earthly thing whatsoever) can be exhaustive in describing God. Therefore, it is wrong to think of God as a man. Likewise, the kind of feminist theology that wants to call God a mother instead of a father, and describe him in female rather than in male categories, shows in our opinion that it has misunderstood the intentions of the Biblical imagery. It is remarkable that God, when asked about his name in the Old Testament, answers: 'I am who I am' (Exod. 3, 14).

Members of the Church of Sweden stated:

> . . . we find it important to point to female symbols in our way to speak about God. . . . At the same time we want to point out the risk to get caught in female terminology. To call God "Mother" does not take us very far. It is a matter of not fixing the conception of God, neither to male nor to female expressions.

"More emphasis to be placed on the spiritual nature of God—neither male nor female but the essence of all the finest qualities found in finite quantities in male/female, father/mother, sister/brother," declared a Jamaican group. This group then explained: "Finite images limit God's magnitude."

"Women and men correctly relate to God as Father because He revealed Himself as Father," said one member of a group in the United States. Members of the Orthodox Church in America confirmed: "We would never think of questioning that God was the Father, and could never conceive of God as Mother. Christ named God the Father; if we believe in Christ, we cannot compromise."[39]

"In general, there should be no normative . . . image of God," wrote the group in Groningen, The Netherlands. According to this group: "If people, including people of the Bible, have a certain image of God, this expresses something of themselves and their own experiences." At the African Regional Consultation, a group declared:

> . . . the images that come to mind on the mention of God

. . . are dependent upon the person's background. In Doula in the Camerouns, for example, when God is mentioned, what comes to mind is not a physical image of a man or a woman, but the *sense of the omnipotent, the supreme, the super natural.* In the Akan tradition, God is always spoken of as 'He' in Ga language, the name for God is sometimes Akaa Maa Nyogmo—Father Mother God.[40]

"The image of God confined in one's mind," the group reiterated, "depends on one's cultural background."[41]

"The father image is sometimes hard to understand," pointed out a Lutheran group from the United States. The group then clarified:

> . . . some children, particularly in families without a father or which a father has deserted, do not know what 'father' means. It is important to define God in a parent image, not just to think of God as being remote, but rather as a loving God. We would probably continue to call God the father because Jesus used this term.

Another Lutheran group from the United States wrote: "We accept God as being male and find it difficult to say that God is female. We see God as being: caring, nurturing, and compassionate."

"God has to be liberated from having been made to the image of man," declared a Lutheran group in the German Democratic Republic. Women from Korea reflected:

> We used to imagine God with male imagery. We were taught to call God father. We need to change man-made language. Now we understand we can imagine God with female imagery. Reading Isaiah 49:14-18 we were so amazed to find these words in the Bible. Nobody has ever told us to imagine God as a loving mother. Thinking of God who has graven my name on the palm of God's hands makes us feel so much closer to God, just like to our own mother. It makes it easier for us to understand God. We have our own children. We love them very much. I can forgive them again and again. I do not want them to suffer. I only want them to be happy. How wonderful to think of God as a mother. How come we have never paid any attention to the Bible verses about a hen caring for her chickens? When we had read the same verses before, it had never struck us that God could be a mother. Now we know so many verses about God's image as a loving

mother. When we were reading these verses we cried,
'Amen, Halleluja!'[42]

Women who are members of the Church of England wrote:

> The greatest significance and outcome of our discussions
> was . . . the new insight they gave to at least some of us
> into the nature of God Him/Herself. One member, for
> whom the concept of the Godhead including feminine
> qualities was quite revolutionary, said how much this had
> affected her prayer life and her whole relationship to God,
> not least in the sphere of confession. She now found that
> she had to be more honest in her confessions, just as a
> child willingly shares all its peccadillos with its earthly
> mother, whereas it approaches its father in a more digni-
> fied way and owns up only to its more serious
> misbehaviour.

"When I first heard 'she' used in relation to God," a woman
from Australia confessed, "I felt that this was irreverent." She
continued:

> Then I realized that this was really a reflection of my feel-
> ings about myself. When I truly believed that I was made
> in the image of God, I had no more problems with God as
> 'she'.

"It was a salvation experience," she exclaimed.

Women in an ecumenical group in Copenhagen wrote:

> The Bible often uses female metaphors when its speaks
> about God: the breast-feeding mother, the hen which
> gathers its chickens. 'Soft values' like love, mercy, care,
> forgiveness, are valuable, bringing forth the female side of
> God. We should, however, be well aware identifying 'soft
> values' with the female. First because the patriarchal so-
> ciety has made the division between 'male, strong values'
> and 'soft, female values', secondly: If it is 'soft' to love, to
> care, to forgive, how can men then be convinced that
> these values are *human* values? . . . we found it extremely
> difficult to say positively how we ought to express female
> aspects in God with words which are not influenced by
> 'male understanding'.

"It is *impossible*," said Swiss women, "to describe God as being
at the same time masculine and feminine for in our culture

most of the words that refer to man are positive and those that refer to woman are negative."

According to the African Regional report: "Since human beings have physical limitations, it is inevitable that in order to grasp the concept of God, He/She has to be anthropomorphised."[43] "In spite of the fact that the words 'God' and the third person pronoun (he/she) in the Finnish language are neither masculine nor feminine," wrote Finnish Lutherans, "the image of God as father is so strong that God is naturally seen as a male." "God is indubitably male, as are most of 'his' priests and ministers, and the dominant culture of the church is a patriarchal culture," charged an Australian woman.

"Jesus spoke of God as our Father—but what appears to be significant here in the image of father is the relational aspect, not the person of the father as man," wrote a Lutheran group in the Federal Republic of Germany. The group went on to suggest: "The patriarchal structure is carried in the father-image, therefore that of the mother is not chosen. Perhaps God can come to be spoke of as father or/and mother to us: thus the relational aspect can be kept without sexist linguistic usage."[44] French women wrote: ". . . to understand and feel God's love we need human images . . . and while the concept of a loving father still dominates our vision of God, there is evidence in the recent reflections of WUCWO [World Union of Catholic Women's Organizations] of a new openness to God as Mother."

According to the report from the Church of Sweden: "Much of the so-called liberal theology faces a special problem here, as it has had a tendency to stress the human aspect in the Christian language." "By withdrawing from the deeper thoughts on Trinity," the report explains, "the liberal theology has more and more concentrated on the image of God as Father which has become the overall metaphor of God. . . . the human aspect won and the image of Father prevailed." The Special Committee appointed by the Church of Scotland "found in the doctrine of the Trinity an image of God as community." From the perspective of this committee, to imagine the Trinity as community "avoided attributing gender to the Godhead and related the work of God to creation, redemption and the new community of the Church." A group on the Isle of Man suggested: "As the Trinity absorbed the generation

gap, so it could bridge the sex one. Yet merely to raise the
question of sex in the Godhead is to open our eyes to the fact
that God's nature contains every quality, male and female."

"If we continue the present practice of using only male
words and images for God, this becomes a kind of idolatry, fix-
ing God in a male box," declared an Australian woman. She
suggested:

> We need to broaden our terms to include, if we can, our
> whole experience of God, sometimes using female expres-
> sions, sometimes male ones, and sometimes expressions
> not restricted by sex. The use of a variety of terms might
> help us not fall into idolatry of any one aspect of God, save
> us from excluding any one group from being fully part of
> the Christian community, and free us to respond more
> spontaneously to whatever way God comes to us.

". . . referring to change"

"The church converted would be one in which we live
the beginning of . . . human reunion in God," envisioned Latin
American women and men. It would be a church, they continued, "in which . . . there is no discrimination between men and
women, neither oppressed nor oppressor, but persons living
the liberty of the gospel as signs of the children of God." Discrimination "refers to the discernment of differences," declared women and men in the Lutheran Church of America.
"But," they went on, "the word has come to mean distinguish-
ing people from each other not as individuals but in terms of
categories. Thus, it moves easily into the realm of prejudice
and stereotypes." "Our vision of the ideal community of men
and women in the church," wrote another group in the Lutheran Church of America, "was based upon the ethical awareness that every human being is to be treated with equal
respect, regard, rights and integrity simply by virtue of being a
person." "One's sex," stated this group, "is incidental and cannot figure into one's equal regard for another."

". . . tragically, the injustices within our communities of
equality usually lead us to minimize the vivid differences between person and person, woman and man, recognition of

which alone can satisfy the creative balance and unison of the throb of life itself," wrote Presbyterian group from New Zealand. An Orthodox group in Paris wrote:

> In a world that aspires to make individuals more and more uniform and that tolerates differences less and less, the church reveals a community in which names, functions, statuses are different—without this difference being subjection—a community called to express the unity of God in three Persons in which, without inferiority or superiority, only the Father is creator, only the Son is incarnated, only the Spirit is outpoured. The ecclesiastical community renders to the woman all her dignity. It is not necessary to identify her with man, to imitate, but on the contrary, it is for herself, in its original particularity, that she is welcomed and loved by the church.[45]

"The remedy to the current 'sick emotional climate' of the Church," according to a group of Finnish Lutherans, "is the realization of the importance of respect for one another and honouring of the value of diversity."

"Real unity," wrote one Finnish woman, "cannot be built on lies or hiding realities." She clarified:

> Through centuries have women tried to build unity as mediators. In practice it has often meant avoiding conflicts, hiding the truth and so gaining peace at any price. We could strive towards unity with courage which is not based in avoiding conflicts and hiding the truth, but in the new chance that reconciliation creates.

"Women have never learned to fight with one another openly, to carry out conflict, and then to stand together in solidarity again," said a group of Swiss Reformed women.[46] Women from Belgium wrote:

> Tensions and internal conflicts form part of the reality that churches have to face in order to be alive. Churches are to offer neither certainty nor security. Life, according to Jesus Christ, is full of joy today, of insecurity as for tomorrow, the only certitude being hope.[47]

According to these women, in order to move toward the fuller participation of women in the church, it is necessary "to accept the conflicts instead of effacing them."

A group of Australian women and men reported: "Again and again there was expressed a feeling of being 'let down' by the church." This group went on to say:

> No one expects the church to be perfect, yet by its hierarchical structures, patriarchal teachings, exclusiveness and outmoded attitudes towards relationships the church is guilty of limiting concepts of wholeness, affirmations of self and being a community of women and men. . . . So we ask, is the church beyond redemption? Is patriarchy one of Christianity's essential dynamics? . . . Most of us wanted to affirm that 'we are the church'. But we are short of models as to what a Community of Women and Men in the church might look like.

A group of women and men in New Zealand concluded: ". . . although we may change structures and provide opportunities for women and men to share together the life of the Church, it may take a much more basic change." One man in this group emphasized: ". . . I am not referring to 'progress', I am referring to change."[48]

Notes

/1/   In using the word "transgression" I follow Michel Foucault in his essay "What Is Enlightenment?" Foucault wrote: "Criticism indeed consists of analyzing and reflecting upon limits. But if the Kantian question was that of knowing what limits knowledge has to renounce transgressing, it seems to me that the critical question today has to be turned back into a positive one: in what is given to us as universal, necessary, obligatory, what place is occupied by whatever is singular, contingent, and the product of arbitrary constraints? The point, in brief, is to transform the critique conducted in the form of necessary limitation into a practical critique that takes the form of a possible transgression" ("What Is Enlightenment?" in *The Foucault Reader*, ed. Paul Rabinow [New York: Pantheon Books, 1984], p. 45). Of course, the word, transgression carries moral and religious connotations. To transgress is to go beyond limits or boundaries; it is also to break laws or commandments that bind a community together. Transgression is acutely appropriate at this juncture in my dissertation. Transgression prepares the way for new creation, creation of a community whose bonds are not based on conformity or constraint.
/2/   "Logicians . . . demand that the main terms of the discussion be 'clarified'. And to 'clarify' the terms of a discussion does not mean to study the additional and as yet unknown properties of the domain in

question which one needs to make them fully understood, it means to fill them with *existing* notions from the entirely different domain of logic and common sense, preferably observational ideas, until they sound common themselves, and to take care that the process of filling obeys the accepted laws of logic. The discussion is permitted to proceed only *after* its initial steps have been modified in this manner. So the course of an investigation is deflected into the narrow channels of things already understood and the possibility of fundamental conceptual discovery (or of fundamental conceptual change) is considerably reduced. Fundamental conceptual change . . . presupposes new world views and new languages capable of expressing them" (Paul Feyerabend, *Against Method: Outline of an anarchistic theory of knowledge* [London: Verso, 1978], p. 256. Emphasis his).

/3/ "Since the Middle Ages at least, Western societies have established the confession as one of the main rituals we rely on for the production of truth . . . One confesses—or is forced to confess. . . . The obligation to confess is now . . . so deeply ingrained in us, that we no longer perceive it as the effect of a power that constrains us; . . . The confession is a ritual of discourse in which the speaking subject is also the subject of the statement; it is also a ritual that unfolds within a power relationship, for one does not confess without the presence (or virtual presence) of a partner who is not simply the interlocutor but the authority who requires the confession, prescribes and appreciates it, and intervenes in order to judge, punish, forgive, console, and reconcile; a ritual in which the truth is corroborated by the obstacles and resistances it has had to surmount in order to be formulated; and finally, a ritual in which the expression alone, independently of its external consequences, produces intrinsic modifications in the person who articulates it: it exonerates, redeems, and purifies him; it unburdens him of his wrongs, liberates him, and promises him salvation" (Michel Foucault, *The History of Sexuality*, vol. I: *An Introduction*, trans. Robert Hurley [New York: Random House, Vintage Books, 1980], pp. 58, 59, 60, 61-62).

I find Foucault's perceptions of "confession" compelling. Confession has often been the enactment of power relationships, particularly of compulsive and coercive relationships. Unlike Foucault, I also "confess" when I speak of my sense of limitation. "Confession" discloses my predisposition and point of view, which are perforce limited. Confession does not deliver me from my limits or the conditions of my existence. I thus use the word "confession" in a way akin to H. Richard Niebuhr. In his classic text on revelation, Niebuhr wrote: "As we begin with revelation only because we are forced to do so by our limited standpoint in history and faith so we can proceed only by stating in simple, confessional form what has happened to us in our community, how we came to believe, how we reason about things and what we see from our point of view" (*The Meaning of Revelation* [New York: Macmillan Co., 1941], p. 29). However, unlike Niebuhr, I am convinced that a confession of one's limited point of view can be a prelude to the transgression of those limits. In this sense, confession is a moment in the critical task of which Foucault wrote: ". . . this critique . . . will separate out, from the contingency that has made us what we are, the possibility of no longer being, doing, or thinking what we are, do, or think" ("What Is Enlightenment?" p. 46).

/4/   Local groups were advised: "The questions should not limit you, but be a common starting point in our international, ecumenical search for community" (*Study on the Community of Women and Men in the Church* [Geneva: World Council of Churches, 1978], p. 15).

/5/   Cf. p. 77 above.

/6/   I put into the text only what is necessary to continue the conversation. While my commentary is confined to footnotes, I am fully engaged in the conversation. My voice is present as I make choices about the articulation and arrangement of other voices. I confine my commentary to footnotes in order to prevent my predisposition to reduce or resolve difference, dissonance, and division.

   The local group reports remain unpublished. I quote them as they were written, hoping to heighten the readers' awareness that English was a foreign language for many local group members, and that their contexts were quite diverse. The reports are fastened in three binders and may be found on shelves in the Archives, Library of the Ecumenical Centre, Geneva, Switzerland, and in my personal files.

/7/   See *Women and Men in the Church* (Syosset, New York: Department of Religious Education, Orthodox Church in America, 1980).

/8/   Women are not ordained to the priesthood of the Orthodox Church. See Thomas Hopko, ed., *Women and the Priesthood* (Crestwood, New York: St. Vladimir's Seminary Press, 1983). See especially Thomas Hopko, "On the Male Character of Christian Priesthood," pp. 97-134.

/9/   The Community of Women and Men in the Church Study was not conceived as a "women's study." See pp. 74-76 above. Cf. pp. 29-31 above.

/10/   *The Community of Women and Men in the Church: Report of the Asian Consultation at the United Theological College, Bangalore on 11-15 August 1978* (Bangalore: Printers India, 1978), p. 87.

   According to Michelle Zimbalist Rosaldo, Margaret Mead was among the first to emphasis the fact "that what Westerners take to be the 'natural' endowments of men and women are hardly necessary, natural, or universal" ("Women, Culture, and Society: A Theoretical Overview," in *Women, Culture, and Society*, ed. Rosaldo and Lamphere [Stanford, California: Stanford University Press, 1974], p. 18). Another pioneer, Simone de Beauvoir, stated: "Woman is determined not by her hormones or by mysterious instincts, but by the manner in which her body and her relation to the world are modified through the action of others than herself. The abyss that separates the adolescent boy and girl has been deliberately opened out between them since earliest childhood; later on, woman could not be other than what she *was made*, and that past was bound to shadow her for life. If

we appreciate its influence, we see clearly that her destiny is not pre-
determined for all eternity" (*The Second Sex*, trans. and ed. H. M.
Parshley [New York: Alfred A. Knopf, 1953], p. 725. Emphasis hers).
For a recent analysis and critique of ways in which biological theories
have shaped gender roles see Anne Fausto-Sterling, *Myths of Gender:
Biological Theories About Women and Men* (New York: Basic Books,
1985).

/11/ *Report of the All-Africa Regional Consultation on Community
of Women and Men in the Church Study, Ibadan, Nigeria, 15-19 September 1980* (Nairobi: An All-Africa Conference of Churches Publication, 1981), p. ix.

/12/ *Report of the Asian Consultation*, p. 91.

/13/ "In Orthodox Christian theology, masculinity and femininity
are viewed as gifts from God to be used in personal expression; they
are not cultural impositions. Jesus Christ did not come to destroy the
natural, God-willed distinction between the sexes which He created
for perfect goodness and order" (Deborah Belonick, *Feminism in
Christianity: An Orthodox Christian Response* [Syosset, New York:
Department of Religious Education, Orthodox Church in America,
1983], p. 35). From an Orthodox point of view, the difference between women and men is stereotypic and ontological. Orthodox pro-
fess to know the universally appropriate and valid way of being
women and men. In this dissertation, I am calling for recognition and
respect in relation to differences among as well as between women
and men. However, unlike the Orthodox, I do not assume that these
differences are stereotypic or ontological. Indeed, I highlight differences in order to break open stereotypes and thus break down boundaries that have endured among and between women and men so long
that they seem to be eternal.

/14/ My translation of "la tension feconde de l'unite et de la
difference."

/15/ "God is one and God is three: the Holy Trinity is a mystery of
unity in diversity, and of diversity in unity. Father, Son, and Spirit are
'one in essence' . . . yet each is distinguished from the other two by
personal characteristics. 'The divine is indivisible in its divisions', for
the persons are 'united yet not confused, distinct yet not divided';
'both the distinction and the union alike are paradoxical'" (Timothy
Ware, *The Orthodox Church* [Harmondsworth, Middlesex, England:
Penguin Books, 1963], p. 219). Deborah Belonick discusses the Orthodox understanding of the Trinity in the context of her response to
feminist theologians. See "The Spirit of the Female Priesthood," in
Women and the Priesthood, pp. 157-165.

/16/ *Report of the Middle Eastern Council of Churches Consultation on the Community of Women and Men in the Church, Beirut,Lebanon, 22nd-26th January, 1980* (Geneva: World Council of
Churches, 1981), p. 8.

/17/ My translation of "Situadas dentro de una sociedad donde se
margina y se somete a la mujer, nuestras iglesias la han marginado de
sus propias estructuras, asignandole tareas que se compaginan con los

papeles que tradicionalmente han sido vistos como femeninos (la limpieza y arreglo del templo, la confeccion de comidas, la ensenanza en la escuela dominical, etc.). Estas estructuras basadas en una ideologia masculinizante cierran el espacio para una nueva relacion de libertad y de companerismo pleno al perpetuar los roles que la sociedad le da al hombre y a la mujer" (*Communidad de Mujeres y Hombres en la Iglesia: Encuentro latinamericano de mujeres, 15-18 marzo de 1981* [San Jose, Costa Rica: Sebila, 1981], pp. 26-27).

/18/ *Report of the Middle Eastern Council of Churches Consultation*, p. 81.

/19/ Ibid.

/20/ *Report of All-Africa Regional Consultation*, pp. 4-5.

/21/ Report of the Asia Consultation, p. 88.

/22/ Latin Americans spoke about the marginalization of women within the churches. Middle Easterners spoke about the ministry of women outside the churches among the marginalized. Women's place, or lack of place, in established ecclesial orders is clarified by this contrast between the presence of women's voices "on the streets" and the absence of women's voices "within the four walls of the Church."

/23/ For an account and analysis of the status of women in the ministry of the Church of Sweden, which also sheds light on the situation in Finland, see Brita Stendahl, *The Force of Tradition: A Case Study of Women Priests in Sweden*, with an Appendix by Constance F. Parvey (Philadelphia: Fortress Press, 1985). See also n. 85, pp. 46-47 above.

/24/ Women may be ordained to the priesthood of the Anglican Church in New Zealand, Australia, Canada, and of the Protestant Episcopal Church in the United States. The Church of England, however, does not ordain women to the priesthood. For an illustration of the Anglican argument against the priesthood of women see E. L. Mascall, "Women and the Priesthood of the Church," in *Why Not?: Priesthood and the Ministry of Women*, ed. Michael Bruce and G. E. Duffield (Appleford: Marcham Manor Press, 1972). Cf. pp. 86-87 above.

/25/ Women may not be ordained to the priesthood of the Roman Catholic Church. For discussion of the ordination of women within the Roman Catholic Church see Ida Raming, *The Exclusion of Women From the Priesthood: Divine Law or Sex Discrimination?*, trans. Norman R. Adams (Metuchen, New Jersey: The Scarecrow Press, 1976); *Women Priests: A Catholic Commentary on the Vatican Declaration*, ed. Leonard Swidler and Arlene Swidler (New York: Paulist Press, 1977); *Women and Catholic Priesthood: An Expanded Vision*. Proceedings of the Detroit Ordination Conference, ed. Anne Marie Gardiner, S.S.N.D (New York, Paramus, Toronto: Paulist Press, 1976); *Women and Priesthood: Future Directions*. A Call to Dialogue from the Faculty of the Catholic Theological Union at Chicago, ed. Carroll Stuhlmueller (Collegeville, Minn.: Liturgical Press, 1978).

/26/ As noted above, women are not ordained to the priesthood of the Orthodox Church. See Thomas Hopko, ed., *Women and the Priesthood*. Women in the Orthodox Church, unlike women in Roman Catholic and Protestant traditions, have not called for ordination to the priesthood. Orthodox women have, however, called for the renewal of the order of the deaconess. See Kyriaki Karidoyanes Fitz-Gerald, "The Characteristics and Nature of the Order of the Deaconess," in *Women and the Priesthood*, pp. 75-95. See also Deborah Belonick, "The Spirit of the Female Priesthood," in *Women and the Priesthood*, pp. 157-165. Cf. *Orthodox Women: Their Role and Participation in the Orthodox Church, Agapia, Romania, September, 1976* (Geneva: World Council of Churches, 1977).

/27/ Cf. pp. 31, 53, 81-82, 92, 152-153 above.

/28/ *Report of All-Africa Regional Consultation*, pp. 48, 41.

/29/ Ibid., p. 42.

/30/ *Report of the Asian Consultation*, p. 96.

/31/ My translation of "La lectura tradicional que se hace de la Biblia tiende a marginar a la mujer, al decir que la Biblia presenta a la mujer como inferior al varon" (*Communidad de Mujeres y Hombres en la Iglesia: Encuentro latinoamericano de mujeres*, p. 22).

/32/ Gen. 2:24 (RSV): "Therefore a man leaves his father and his mother and cleaves to his wife, and they become one flesh." Gen. 3 is the story of the temptation of Adam and Eve and of their expulsion from the Garden of Eden. In I Cor. 7, Paul wrote concerning marriage.

/33/ My translation of "Parmi les textes bibliques tres nombreux se rapportant a l'homme et a la femme, il en est de tres divers. De nombreux passages evoquent l'egalite, la reciprocite, les responsabilites assumees en commun. D'autres, par contre, insistent sur les differences entre l'homme et la femme, et sur la subordination de cette derniere a son mari."

/34/ *Report of All-Africa Regional Consultation*, p. 35. The verse in Acts 2 to which reference is made is verse 17: "And in the last days it shall be, God declares, that I will pour out my Spirit upon all flesh, and your sons and your daughters shall prophesy . . ." (RSV). Cf. Joel 2:28.

/35/ My translation from this longer remark: "Mais l'essential demeure que Paul considere common naturel, allant de soi, que la femme prie et 'prophetise,' pensee extraordinaire quand on se rappelle ce que etait le culte a la synagogue. Les participantes ont montre un vif interet par leurs questions, leurs reactions, leurs interventions. Ce jour-la, elles ont eu l'occasion de reviser leurs prjuges anti-pauliniens."

/36/ *Report of the Asian Consultation*, p. 39. It is remarkable that these women, unlike Henriette Visser't Hooft, were willing to pardon Paul's prejudices. Cf. Henriette Visser't Hooft's commentary on the same Pauline passage, p. 25 above.

/37/ Gal. 3:28 (RSV): "There is neither Jew nor Greek, there is neither slave nor free, there is neither male nor female; for you are all one in Christ Jesus."

/38/ My translation of "La veritable rencontre avec Dieu a lieu au-dela de toute image et de toute parole, dans le silence qui n'est pas mutisme. Cet 'apophastisme' permet au croyant orthodoxe d'eviter les pieges d'une imagerie de Dieu unilateralement masculine. L'iconographie orthodoxe ne represente jamais Dieu le Pere. La paternite divine ne saurait etre representee par une image sexee. Le Pere celeste ne doit pas etre imagine comme un patriarche barbu." For a succinct statement of the "apophatic" character of Orthodox theology see Thomas Hopko, "On the Male Character of Christian Priesthood," pp. 128-130. For a fuller discussion see Vladimir Lossky, *The Mystical Theology of the Eastern Church* (London, 1957); *Orthodox Theology: An Introduction* (New York, 1978).

/39/ "Apophaticism in theology is not the same as total ignorance. It is not the claim that we know nothing whatsoever of God. . . . It is rather a way—the traditional Orthodox Christian way—of knowing God. . . . It is the affirmation that divine reality is always infinitely more than and infinitely other than whatever can be known and claimed about it. It is the affirmation that the inner being of the Father and the Son and the Holy Spirit remains eternally and essentially beyond what creatures can experience and know" (Thomas Hopko, "On the Male Character of Christian Priesthood," p. 129).

/40/ *Report of the All-African Regional Consultation*, p. 37.

/41/ Ibid.

/42/ Isaiah 49:14-18 (RSV) begins: "But Zion said, 'The Lord has forsaken me, my Lord has forgotten me.' 'Can a woman forget her sucking child, that she should have no compassion on the son of her womb? Even these may forget, yet I will not forget you'."

/43/ *Report of All-Africa Regional Consultation*, p. 37.

/44/ My translation of "Jesus hat von Gott als von unseren Vater gesprochen—wichtig scheint hier aber doch im Bild des Vaters der Beziehungsaspekt zu sein, nicht aber die Person des Vaters als Mann. Im Vaterbild kommen die patriarchalen Strukturen zum Tragen, darum ist nicht das der Mutter gewählt. Vielleicht kann aber auch Gott ist uns wie Vater oder/und Mutter gesagt werden: der Beziehungsaspekt ohne sexistisch Sprachgebrauch erhalten."

/45/ My translation of "Dans un monde qui vise de plus en plus a uniformiser les individus et qui tolere de moins en moins les differences, l'Eglise leur revele une communaute ou les appels, les fonctions, les status sont differents—sans que cette difference de sujetion—une communaute appelee a exprimer l'unite du Dieu en trois Personnes ou, sans inferiorite ni superiorite, seul le Pere est source, seul le Fils s'incarne, seul l'Esprit est repandu (effuse). La communaute ecclesiale rend a la femme sa totale dignite. Point n'est besoin de s'identifier a l'homme, de l'imiter, mais au contraire, c'est pour elle-meme, dans son originalite particuliere, qu'elle est accueillie et aimee par l'Eglise."

/46/ My translation of "Die Frauen haben nie gelernt, offen miteinander zu kampfen, Konflikte auszutragen, und dann doch wieder solidarisch zusammenzustehen."

/47/ My translation of "Les tensions et les conflits internes font partie des realites auxquelles les eglises doivent faire face pour etre vivantes. Les eglises n'ont pas a donner la certitude ni la securite. La vie, selon JC, est pleine de joies aujourd'hui, d'insecurite et d'insecurite quant a demain, la seule certitude etant l'esperance."

/48/ ". . . I wanted to write this . . . neither as an indictment nor as an apology, and I have taken care not to pass judgment. Today's public no longer forgives an author for failing, after the action he describes, to give his verdict; indeed, in the very course of the drama he is told to take sides, to declare himself for Alceste or Philinte, for Hamlet or Ophelia, for Faust or Marguerite, for Adam or Jehovah. I do not claim, of course, that neutrality (I was about to say: indecision) is a sure sign of a great mind; but I do believe that many great minds have been disinclined to . . . conclude—and that to state a problem properly is not to suppose it solved in advance. . . . Be that as it may, I have tried to prove nothing, but to paint my picture well and light it properly" (Andre Gide, *The Immoralist*, trans. Richard Howard [New York: Random House, Vintage Books, 1970], pp. xiii, xiv, xv [Originally published under the title *L'Immoraliste*, Paris, 1921]).

Like Gide, I have "taken care not to pass judgments" or "to . . . conclude," but have attempted "to paint my picture well and light it properly." Unlike Gide, however, I have *not* "tried to prove nothing." I have drawn this portrait to express my theological conviction that diversity is not a problem to be solved. In this chapter, I have viewed diversity christologically, as the living contexts in which God calls members of Christ's Body to be engaged.

CHAPTER V

". . . BROKEN FOR YOU"

The conversation has faded into the final footnote. No critical word dispelled the complexities, contradictions, and conflicts that deepened during the conversation. No conclusion was drawn at the end of the chapter.

Today's public is no more forgiving than the public in Gide's day. Today's academic public may be even less forgiving. It is certainly incumbent upon the writer of a doctoral dissertation "to give [her] verdict" or "to take sides" or "to declare [herself]" for some one or the other.[1]

But to do so at this point in this dissertation would be to fall prey to and thus perpetuate precisely that mode of thought from which I set out, seeking a new way of life and thought. Throughout this text, I have articulated my voice as it is woven together with other voices. I have not attempted an unadulterated account of either subject or object. If I now declare myself "for some one or the other," I would distinguish self and other, subject and object, the same and not-the-same-as, ascribing to the former a positive and to the latter a negative value.[2] My vision of unity would thus yield to rather than transgress the requirement of conformity. I have committed myself to transgression in hope of transformation, i.e., in hope of bonds of unity created in celebration not constraint of difference.

The difficulty at this point in this dissertation is that the creation of such bonds of unity cannot be the work of my head or hands alone. If I clarified newly-created bonds, I would extend my particular voice and vision to universal proportion. So I have attempted to clear a space into which all may enter. I have attempted to hear voices that are unique and different from my own and from one another. But transformation can come only as all are engaged. For no one can fully represent another, and everyone will be changed by such engagement. Therefore, at this point in this dissertation, as at the beginning, I can only confess that which has informed my perception. Specifically, I confess three temptations I encountered as I wrote in search of a new way of life and thought.[3] I will then choose to let go and listen as each and everyone engages in conversation.

I first confess the temptation to reduction: to diminish and degrade, to constrain or compel, to limit persons or phenomena. Two illustrations of the temptation to limit are important in this dissertation.

In working on the first three chapters, I discovered the way in which one group established limits in relation to another group. For example, Faith and Order established limits to discourse on unity, particularly with its distinction between theological and so-called "non-theological." The effect of establishing these limits was exclusion: in this case the exclusion of women from Faith and Order discourse on unity. I exposed the effect of establishing these limits, thus opening the possibility for trespassing them. This move was the transition from one chapter to the next.

Second, as I wrote the fourth chapter, I mistook the limits of my perception for the limits of others' perception. As I read and attempted to represent the voices raised in the local group reports, I assessed what others saw and the way they saw in terms of what and the way in which I saw. I discovered, to my dismay, that there are limits to what I can see. I discovered, to my delight, that as I confessed my perceptual limits, the perceptions of others enhanced my own.

My temptation to reduction, to establish or enforce limits in relation to persons or groups or phenomena, emerges from my fear to recognize complexities and conflicts. Personal and corporate identity is often defended by casting out what is complex and conflictual onto others. By recognizing complexities and conflicts represented in others, I may recall those I have cast out from myself. To recall my own complexities and conflicts threatens my identity and may lead me to another temptation.

I therefore confess a second temptation, the temptation to resolution: to answer a question or solve a problem. The temptation to resolution is a deeper dimension of the tempta-

tion to reduction. Reduction is the establishment or enforce-
ment of limits with regard to complexities and conflicts;
resolution seeks to disentangle or dissolve complexities and
conflicts.[4]

Situations in life are often spoken about in terms of
"problem" and "solution." I *can* look upon life situations as
problems to be solved. Indeed, "if the work has been well
done the result will then appear inevitable." Precisely this
predestinarian sense betrays the way in which the words
"problem" and "solution" seduce me to inadequate and false
habits of thought. Viewing life as a problem for which solutions must be found is, as Dorothy Sayers noted, "fast becoming a deadly danger."[5]

I encountered that "deadly danger" which attends the
habit of problem/solution thinking as I wrote this dissertation.
I was tempted to set up a problem in the first three chapters
and then present its solution. Instead, I attempted to convey
the complex and often conflictual life and thought of women in
the World Council, of Faith and Order, and of women and
men in local groups of the Community Study.

As I resisted the problem/solution habit of thought, so I
did not merely describe the drama about which I have written.
I played a plotting role. The narrative yields to my perspective and commitment, as well as to my limitation and location.
I attempted to write a "plot of revelation" rather than a "narrative of resolution."[6]

I have attempted to write a "plot of revelation" to enact
my commitment to hear from within complex and even conflictual life circumstances voices that have been silent. In
terms of resolution, nothing changes from the beginning of the
first chapter to the end of the fourth chapter. Very fundamentally, however, my perception begins to change as I risk recognition of my own limitation and of what is not-the-same-as
myself. I change as I am drawn outside my own terms of reference. Recognition is thus transposed as revelation. Such revelation indeed is *not* concealment; it occurs as complexities and
conflicts are received so that everyone may be engaged.

My temptation to resolution, to set out a problem and its
solution, emerges from a deeper root of my fear. If I risk recognition of complexities and conflicts represented in others, I
risk being changed. The certainty to which I would cling, that

life problems are "capable of a single, necessary, and categorical solution," is called into question. Insofar as my identity is determined and defended by casting out what defies certainty, I feel my identity threatened. Such threat may lead me to the temptation of retreat.

I therefore confess the third temptation, that of retreat: withdrawal to a private, safe or secluded place. Retreat may be passive or active. I may also step back from that which threatens, or move back to a former posture. Retreat points to a still deeper dimension of the first and the second temptations. The possibility of retreat illumines the presupposition of these two temptations. It sheds light on the self that is creator and creature of thinking that casts out complexities and conflicts. The self which reduces or resolves what is other, whether within or without, also chooses concealment rather than risking revelation.

I encounter the temptation to retreat most profoundly at this point in my dissertation. Having attempted to recognize difference and dissonance, complexities and conflicts, I am tempted to withdraw and write simply from my own point of view, from within my own context. I am tempted to construct a platform on which I can stand to make judgments about what has been presented. I would evidence myself as utterly "unencumbered," as "empty" of prejudice and predisposition.[7]

As at the outset, so at this point, I attempt to enunciate my embeddedness and encumbrance. I tried to identify and indeed intensify my own particular constitution, so I could recognize the particularity of others. Clarity about myself was a caution against confusion of myself and others.[8]

Does self-identity lead to retreat of another sort—retreat into a personal or corporate "relaxed pluralism of privacies"?[9] It does, if I recall only selected stories from narratives of constitution: personal and corporate stories of exemplary events and effects. It does not, if I also recall "dangerous memories": personal and corporate stories of suffering inflicted as well as undergone.[10] Such stories call me from privatistic or pretentious retreat. Stories of suffering inflicted call forth criticism of myself and my context. What I would eschew I see embodied within myself and my context.

The deepest dimension of my fear is thus revealed. My

location in the world, as well as my identity, is threatened.
When I recall internal as well as external complexities and conflicts, I may discover that I can belong to no *one* context, certainly to no *one* community. That discovery tempts me to
privatistic or pretentious retreat. Yet, if I risk revealing that I
myself am also the other, I may return to others; I may discover that I belong to others in the midst of brokenness.[11]

To risk revelation rather than retreat takes me to the
threshold of conversation. I can never predict what will happen in conversation that gives and receives graciously, if not
without guard. But I can point to three moments in conversation that may move toward the transformation about which I
have written.

The first moment in conversation is recognition. In the
moment when I encounter others, I may be taken across the
threshold. My initial impulse is to objectify them or to assume
affinity with them. When I objectify them, I oppose myself to
others; when I assume affinity with them, I obscure them. In
both instances, my perception of others, as well as of my self in
relation to them, sets the terms for our encounter. If I recognize others as they present themselves, I respect them as utterly unique creatures and creators.

This is also the moment in which I am recognized. I may
already have risked self revelation. But my uniqueness is confirmed only as I meet and am met by others.

The recognition of uniqueness is not unambiguous. I may
not understand or be understandable to others. Indeed, I may
come into conflict with others. This risk is unavoidable, insofar
as I do not outright oppose or obscure my uniqueness, others'
uniqueness, or our difference from one another.

I came to know the moment of recognition among Orthodox. When I met the Orthodox, I countered their thoughts
about the image and role of women. I later tried to understand the Orthodox point of view by stepping within their ecclesial context. I found Orthodox ecclesiology congenial, even
compelling.[12] But with these initial steps, I fell prey first to the
impulse to oppose, and then to the impulse to obscure others.

I am now clear that my perspective is different from that
of the Orthodox. I am also clear about the ways in which I am
attracted to their life and thought. I thus recognize them as
different from me, even as I respect their unique perceptions.

In short, my critique of the Orthodox is also my confession of closeness to them.[13]

Indeed, in reading an Orthodox theologian, I began to identify a second moment in conversation, namely, relinquishment.[14] Relinquishment is not simply the subordination or subjugation or surrender of one to another.[15] It is a moment of offering; I offer the griefs as well as the gifts I bear to others as we are engaged in conversation. Such offering is not sacrificial; the gifts and griefs I offer are not consumed but contributed to the upbuilding of common life. In the moment of relinquishment, I choose to participate with others, rather than to make predictions about a new creation.

At this point in my dissertation, I choose relinquishment. I have already articulated my perceptions and priorities. In particular, I have made clear my perception that the Community of Women and Men in the Church Study was beset behind and before by Faith and Order discourse on unity. This discourse did not acknowledge the variegated voices or allow them to speak. I have made clear my priority for these silenced voices as I cleared a space for them to speak. Rather than withdrawing or stepping back from the conversation to make personal judgments, I now choose to let go of my perceptions and priorities. I set them loose, following my deepest commitment that all may participate in the newly-emerging creation.

Relinquishment is the prelude to a third moment in conversation. Having let go our grasp, having offered what we bear, we are able to receive. We do not receive the gifts and griefs we bore. We receive the selves we offered, enhanced by our engagement with others.

Our identities, personal and corporate, are thereby transformed. We are not who we were. We are not able to identify ourselves alone; who we are is constituted by each and every one with whom we have engaged in conversation. We are still unique and different from one another. We may still be unable to understand and come into conflict with one another. But we now belong together in our brokenness—as breath and bones in a body.

I articulated no blueprint for the blessed community at the beginning, nor will I at this ending. Instead, I invite a new beginning. Bonds of unity, able to celebrate difference, may be created only as we continue to engage in conversation.

Notes

/1/   Andre Gide, *The Immoralist*, trans. Richard Howard (New York: Random House, Vintage Books, 1970), p. xiii.

/2/   I attempt to "[negotiate] difference and sameness, marginality and inclusion in a constant dialogue . . ." This "constant transition that does not crystallize into any 'state' . . . [dissolves] alternative, polarized, either/or possibilities into infinite potentiality" (Rachel Blau DuPlessis, *Writing beyond the Ending: Narrative Strategies of Twentieth-Century Women Writers* [Bloomington: Indiana University Press, 1985], pp. 43, 150).

Methodologically, if I made distinctions between self and other, subject and object, the same and not-the-same-as, I would consider content over context or context over content. To choose either mode of consideration would be to enact a methodological reduction. I assume that significance can be illumined only as content and context are considered in the integrity of their inseparability.

/3/   For clarification of my use of the word "confession" see n. 3, pp. 157-158 above.

/4/   Much twentieth-century theology is written in the form of either question and answer or problem and solution. Paul Tillich, in his *Systematic Theology* for example, set out questions which he then answered. Tillich assumed his answers to be ultimate, that is, unconditional. Tillich's project thus entailed a further assumption: that the content of his answers—the eternal truth of the Christian message—was contextually interchangeable. See Paul Tillich, *Systematic Theology*, 3 vols. (Chicago: University of Chicago Press, 1951-1963).

In a similar manner, much North American feminist theology has implicitly if not explicitly attempted to articulate solutions to "the problem" named by Betty Friedan. From Friedan's point of view, "the unknown heart of woman's problem" was an identity crisis rooted in the lack of public images for women. As a result, women were relegated for their life-meaning to the private sphere. Many feminist theologians worked with the assumption that the public-private split they knew in white, middle-class, male-structured society was "the problem" for all women. More recently feminist theologians have recognized that Friedan and her followers worked within one particular context. See Betty Friedan, *The Feminine Mystique* (New York: W. W. Norton & Co., 1963).

/5/   Dorothy L. Sayers, *The Mind of the Maker* (Westport, Connecticut: Greenwood Press, Publishers, 1976), p. 194 [Originally published in New York, l941]. Sayers reflected on the words "problem" and "solution" in her essay "Problem Picture." Knowing human beings are most satisfied when their experience is presented in terms of a prob-

lem that can be solved by a "predictable, final, complete and sole possible answer," Sayers believed it a "deadly danger" to use these words
indiscriminately (Ibid., p. 190). Renowned as a writer of detective stories and a scholar of medieval literature, Sayers assumed that the
human longing for satisfying solutions to named problems accounted
for the popularity of the former rather than the latter genre. The
creator of the charming Lord Peter Wimsey, Sayers was not concerned that her readers were satisfied by this gentleman sleuth. Sayers was concerned about her readers' inability to distinguish the
"detective problem" and the "life-problem" (Ibid., p. 194).

Sayers spoke about four characteristics differentiating a "detective problem" from a "life-problem." A detective problem is always
soluble, completely soluble, soluble in the same terms in which it is
set, and finally soluble—"when it is solved, there is an end of it" (Ibid.,
pp. 204-205). Thence the satisfaction. Human desire is directed toward a problem that is plotted precisely in order to puzzle and per-
plex and then prepare us to "cease upon the midnight with no pain"
(Ibid., p. 205).

But Sayers reminded her readers that "the beautiful finality
with which the curtain rings down on the close of the investigation
conceals" as much as it reveals. That is, "no part of the 'problem' has
been 'solved' *except that part which was presented in problematic
terms*" (Ibid., p. 189. Emphasis hers). "Here," Sayers went on to say,
"is one of the most striking differences between the detective problem and the work of the creative imagination. The detective problem
is deliberately set in such a manner that it can be solved without stepping outside its terms of reference" (Ibid., p. 202). Indeed, the structure, and so the satisfaction, of detective stories depend upon an
"initial arbitrary rule" that "is to exclude from the terms of the problem everything that the solution cannot solve" (Ibid., p. 210). Only if
certain circumstances and claims, details, differences, and discrepan-
cies, particular people and perspectives, places and phenomena, are
included and others are not can a problem be "capable of a single,
necessary, and categorical solution, which must be wholly right, while
all others are wholly wrong" (Ibid., p. 191). Such revelation, i.e., for
the sake of such solution, indeed *is* concealment.

/6/ Seymour Chatman, *Story and Discourse: Narrative Structure in
Fiction and Film* (Ithaca and London: Cornell University Press, 1978),
p. 48. Chatman characterizes a "narrative of resolution" as one in
which "there is a sense of problem-solving, of things being worked
out in some way, of a kind of ratiocinative or emotional teleology."
The "basic question" in such a narrative is "What will happen?" This
question is neither answered nor addressed in a "plot of revelation."
"Early on" in a plot of revelation, says Chatman, "we gather that
things will stay pretty much the same. It is not that events are resolved (happily or tragically), but rather that a state of affairs is
revealed."

/7/ Robert N. Bellah, Richard Madsen, William M. Sullivan, Ann
Swidler, and Steven M. Tipton speak of the "unencumbered" or

"empty" self in *Habits of the Heart: Individualism and Commitment in American Life* (Berkeley: University of California Press, 1985). They speak about this self in terms of "the notion of pure, undetermined choice, free of tradition, obligation, or commitment." Bellah et al. also speak about "a self that is not empty," about "a constituted self" who "makes sense in terms of . . . what we would call, in the fullest sense of the word, community" (Ibid., pp. 152-153). "Community," in this sense, "attempts to be an inclusive whole, celebrating the interdependence of public and private life and of the different callings of all. . . ." A "lifestyle enclave," in contrast, is "segmental" and celebrates "the narcissism of similarity." "The different, those with other lifestyles, are not necessarily despised. They may be willingly tolerated. But they are irrelevant or even invisible in terms of one's own lifestyle enclave" (Ibid., p. 72).

/8/   Theological work changed in the nineteenth-century, when history was "no longer merely one aspect of a way of looking at things" but "the foundation of all thinking" and "the medium for . . . self-reflection." But the question that reverberated was: "How can we pass beyond the diversity with which history presents us to norms for our faith and for our judgments about life?" Twentieth-century theologians, thus raised to historical consciousness, viewed religious and moral diversity as a question or a problem for which a solution must be found (Ernst Troeltsch, *The Absoluteness of Christianity and the History of Religions*, trans. David Reid, with an Introduction by James Luther Adams [Richmond, Virginia: John Knox Press, 1971], pp. 47, 61) [Originally published under the title *Die Absolutheit des Christentums und die Religionsgeschichte: Vortrag gehalten auf der Versammlung der Freunde der Christlichen Welt zu Muhlacker am 3. Oktober 1901. Erweitert und mit einem vorwort versehen*, Tubingen, 1929].

I work with the assumption that diversity is not a problem but is both the reality of life, and the raw stuff of life's new possibilities. Cf. n. 2, p. 194 above; n. 4, p. 196 above; n. 5, pp. 196-197 above.

/9/   David Tracy, *The Analogical Imagination: Christian Theology and the Culture of Pluralism* (New York: Crossroad, 1981), p. 451.

/10/   Bellah et al., *Habits of the Heart*, p. 153.

"Dangerous memories" are integral to life-bearing communities: "Communities, in the sense in which we are using the term, have a history . . . and for this reason we can speak of a real community as a 'community of memory,' one that does not forget its past. In order not to forget that past, a community is involved in retelling its story, its constitutive narrative, and in so doing, it offers examples of the men and women who have embodied and exemplified the meaning of the community. . . . A genuine community of memory will also tell painful stories of shared suffering that sometimes creates deeper identities than success. . . .   And if the community is completely honest, it will remember stories not only of suffering received but of suffering inflicted—dangerous memories, for they call the community to alter ancient evils." Cf. Johann Baptist Metz, *Faith in History and Society:*

Toward a Practical Fundamental Theology (New York: Seabury Press, 1980), pp. 66-67. For a discussion of Metz' understanding of dangerous memory as critique of universal pretensions in society and church see Sharon D. Welch, *Communities of Resistance and Solidarity: A Feminist Theology of Liberation* (Maryknoll, New York: Orbis Books, 1985), pp. 36-39.

/11/ I distinguish between a broken body and a body broken. A broken body is fragmented, unable to act. A body broken recalls the words of Jesus: "This is my body which is [broken] for you" (I Cor. 11:24). In the following chapter of his crisis-laden Corinthian correspondence, Paul presents the image of the Body of Christ. The Body of Christ, like the body of Jesus, is a body broken: a body that chooses to offer its life in diverse, even disparate ways.

/12/ See n. 68, p. 134 above.

/13/ See n. 3, p. 157-158 above.

/14/ As I read Nadejda Gorodetzky's *The Humiliated Christ in Modern Russian Thought*, I first saw that the context for theological reflection on relinquishment is not the event of crucifixion but God's act of creation (London: S.P.C.K.; New York: Macmillan Co., 1938).

/15/ Relinquishment, as it is sometimes used, connotes passivity, e.g., the understanding of "Gelassenheit" among those Anabaptists referred to as the "Stillen im Lande" (See *Mennonite Encyclopedia*, s.v. "Gelassenheit," by Robert Friedmann [Scottdale, Pennsylvania: Mennonite Publishing House; Newton, Kansas: Mennonite Publication Office; Hillsboro, Kansas: Mennonite Brethren Publishing House, 1956], pp. 448-449).

Relinquishment, as it is sometimes used, connotes self-emptying or self-abandonment, e.g., some interpretations of the *kenosis* passage in Paul's Epistle to the Philippians (For examples see Harvey Cox, *Religion in the Secular City: Toward a Postmodern Theology* [New York: Simon and Schuster, 1984], pp. 143-144).

Relinquishment, as it is sometimes used, connotes yieldedness or obedience to God's will or to the Gospel's demand, e.g., the understanding of "Gelassenheit" among those Anabaptists referred to as the "Spiritual Reformers" and the understanding of some contemporary social ethicists (See *Mennonite Encyclopedia*, s.v. "Gelassenheit." See also Marie Augusta Neal, S.N.D. deN., *A Socio-Theology of Letting Go: The Role of the First World Church Facing Third World Peoples* [New York, Ramsey, Toronto: Paulist Press, 1977], esp. pp. 103-111).

The word, used in these ways and carrying these connotations, suggests some person or community juxtaposed to something external, i.e., to the world, others, God's will, or the Gospel's demand. Relinquishment, used in these ways, *is* the subordination or subjugation or surrender of one to another.

My use of the word is grounded in an understanding of Jesus' self-offering in life and particularly on the cross as "a real *letting go* of the self," a "loss of identity *in the satanic terms of possession and identity*" (Arthur C. McGill, *Suffering: A Test of Theological Method* [Philadelphia: Westminster Press, 1982], p. 95. Emphasis his). The crucifixion, as McGill interpreted the event, exposed satanic power, i.e., "the whole pretense of dominative power" and of "self-enclosed security" (Ibid., pp. 96, 98). McGill went on to contrast satanic power, force and domination, with "true power," service and self-giving (Ibid., pp. 99-100).

My use of the word is even more fundamentally grounded in an understanding of compassion that "knows not the demands of ego, of possessiveness, or even of justice," that "protects and nourishes but does not possess and control" (Phyllis Trible, *God and the Rhetoric of Sexuality* [Philadelphia: Fortress Press, 1978], p. 33).

Phyllis Trible presents this understanding of compassion as she presents the "Journey of a Metaphor." The Hebrew root, *rhm*, is present in the words "womb" and "[God's] compassion." It is a metaphor that journeys from concrete to abstract, from the wombs of women to the compassion of God. The journey begins with the biblical story of the two women who both claim a child is their own. Having heard claim and counterclaim, the king who is the judge in this case decides to divide the child in two, giving half to one woman and half to the other woman. The mother reveals herself when she chooses to relinquish her claim to the child for the sake of the child's life (Ibid., pp. 31-33; Cf. I Kings 3:16-28). Thus, as the journey continues, God's compassion is revealed as God relinquishes possessive or punitive claim for the sake of life.

BIBLIOGRAPHY

Aagaard, Anna Marie. "Unscientific Postscript." *Gladly We Rebel!* *Risk* 7:1 (1971):59-63.

Accra 1974: Meeting of the Commission of Faith and Order. Minutes and Documents. Faith and Order Paper, no. 71. Geneva: World Council of Churches, 1974.

"Affirmation of Faith." In *Words to the Churches: Voices of the Sisters. Risk* 10:2 (1974):32.

Anthony, Susan B. II. *Out of the Kitchen and into the War: Women's Role in the Nation's Drama.* New York: Stephen Day, 1943.

"Appeal to All Christian People." In *The Sixth Lambeth Conferences 1867-1920.* Rev. ed. with Appendix, pp. 26-29. Compiled under the direction of the Most Reverend Lord Davidson of Lambeth, Archbishop of Canterbury, 1903-1928. London: S.P.C.K, 1929

Baptism, Eucharist and Ministry. Faith and Order Paper, no. 111. Geneva: World Council of Churches, 1982.

Barot, Madeleine. "Considerations on the Need for a Theology of the Place of Women in the Church." *The Ecumenical Review* 7 (January 1955):151-160.

—. "What *Do* These Women Want?" In *Faith and Faithfulness: Essays on Contemporary Ecumenical Thought. A Tribute to Philip A. Potter*, pp.76-83. Edited by Pauline Webb. Geneva: World Council of Churches, 1984.

Barth, Karl. *Church Dogmatics*, III/1-4. Edited by G. W. Bromiley and T. F. Torrance. Edinburgh: T. & T. Clark, 1958-1961. Originally published under the title *Kirchliche Dogmatik*, III/1-4. Zollikon, Zurich: Evangelischer Verlag A.G., 1948.

—. "Gospel and Law." In *Community, State and Church: Three Essays by Karl Barth*, pp.71-100. Introduction by Will Herberg. New York: Doubleday & Co., Anchor Books, 1960. Originally published under the title *Evangelium und Gesetz*. Theologische Existenz heute, no. 32. Munich: Kaiser Verlag, 1935.

—. *Protestant Theology in the Nineteenth Century: Its Background and History.* Valley Forge, PA: Judson Press, 1973. Originally published under the title *Die protestantische Theologie im 19. Jahrhundert.* Zollikon, Zurich: Evangelischer Verlag A.G., 1956.

Beaver, Robert Pierce. *All Loves Excelling: American Protestant Wo-men in World Mission*. Grand Rapids: Wm. B. Eerdmans, 1968.

Bellah, Robert N.; Madsen, Richard; Sullivan, William M.; Swidler, Ann; and Tipton, Steven M. *Habits of the Heart: Individualism and Commitment in American Life*. Berkeley: University of California Press, 1985.

Belonick, Deborah. *Feminism in Christianity: An Orthodox Christian Response*. Syossett, NY: Department of Religious Education, Orthodox Church in America, 1983.

—. "The Spirit of the Female Priesthood." In *Women and the Priesthood*, pp. 157-165. Edited by Thomas Hopko. Crestwood, NY: St. Vladimir's Press, 1983.

Bennett, John C. "Capitalism and Communism at Amsterdam." *Christian Century* 65 (15 December 1948):1362-64.

Berstein, Hilda. *For Their Triumphs and for Their Tears: Conditions and Resistance of Women in Apartheid South Africa*. Rev. ed. London: International Defense and Aid Fund for South Africa, 1978.

Biblical Authority for Today. Edited by A. Richardson and W. Scheitzer. London: S.C.M. Press, 1951.

Bliss, Kathleen. *The Service and Status of Women in the Churches*. London: S.C.M. Press, 1952.

Boegner, Marc. *The Long Road to Unity: Memories and Anticipations*. Translated by Rene Hague. Introduction by W. A. Visser't Hooft. London: Collins, 1970. Originally published under the title *L'exigence oecumenique: Souvenirs et perspectives*. Paris: Editions Albin Michel, 1968.

Bourguigon, Erika and Contributors. *A World of Women: Anthropological Studies of Women in the Societies of the World*. New York: Praeger Publishers, 1980.

Bowman, Rufus D. *The Church of the Brethren and War*. Elgin, IL: Brethren Publishing House, 1944.

Boyens, Armin. *Kirchenkampf und Okumene, 1933-1939: Darstellung und Dokumentation*. Munich: Chr. Kaiser Verlag, 1969.

Brash, Alan. *Amsterdam 1948: Being a Report on the First Assembly of the World Council of Churches, August 22-September 4, 1948*. Christchurch & Dunedin, New Zealand: Presbyterian Bookroom, 1948.

Breaking Barriers, Nairobi 1975: The Official Report of the Fifth Assembly of the World Council of Churches, Nairobi, 23 November-10 December, 1975. Edited by David M. Paton. London: S.P.C.K, 1976; Grand Rapids: Wm. B. Eerdmans for the World Council of Churches, 1976.

Brethren Encyclopedia. S.v. "*Gemeinde, Gemeinschaft*," by Vernard M. Eller.

Brown, Raymond E. "The Unity and Diversity in New Testment Ecclesiology." *Novum Testamentum* 6 (1963):298-308.

Brown, William Adams. *Toward a United Church: Three Decades of Ecumenical Christianity.* New York: Charles Schribner's Sons, 1946.

Brunner, Emil. *Dogmatics.* Vol. 2: *The Christian Doctrine of Creation and Redemption.* Translated by Olive Wyon. London: Lutterworth Press, 1952. Originally published under the title *Dogmatik.* Vol. 2: *Die christliche Lehre von Schopfung und Erlosung.* Zurich: Zwingli-Verlag, 1952.

Bulgakov, Sergius. *The Orthodox Church.* Edited by Donald A. Lowrie. Translated by Elizabeth S. Cram. London: Centenary Press, 1935. Originally published in Paris, 1935.

Calkins, Gladys Gilkey. *Follow Those Women: Church Women in the Ecumenical Movement. A History of the Development of United Work Among Women of the Protestant Churches in the United States.* New York: National Council of Churches of Christ in the U.S.A., 1961.

Central Committee of the World Council of Churches, Minutes and Reports of the Twentieth Meeting, Heraklion, Crete (Greece), August 15th-26th, 1967. Geneva: World Council of Churches, 1967.

Central Committee of the World Council of Churches, Minutes and Reports of the Twenty-Third Meeting, University of Kent at Canterbury, Canterbury (GB), August 12th-22nd, 1969. Geneva: World Council of Churches, 1969.

Chakko, Sarah. "Reflections on Recent Travels in Europe and North America." *The Ecumenical Review* 3 (January 1951):148-49.

Chatman, Seymour. *Story and Discourse: Narrative Structure in Fiction and Film.* Ithaca and London: Cornell University Press, 1978.

Choose Life-Work for Peace, and International Workshop, Nassau, Bahamas. Geneva: World Council of Churches, 1981.

Christian Newsletter (London). Nos. 1-341 (1939-1949)."Church, the Churches and the World Council of Churches: The Ecclesiological Significance of the World Council of Churches." In *A Documentary History of the Faith and Order Movement, 1927-1963*, pp. 167-176. Edited by Lukas Vischer. St. Louis: Bethany Press, 1963.

Communidad de Mujeres y Hombres en la Iglesia: Encuentro latinamericano de mujeres, 15-18 marzo de 1981. San Jose, Costa Rica: Sebila, 1981.

Community of Women and Men in the Church: A Proposal for Study Groups. Geneva: World Council of Churches, 1975. Also published in *The Ecumenical Review* 27 (October 1975):386-393.

Community of Women and Men in the Church: Report of the Asian Consultation Held at the United Theological College, Bangalore, on 11-15 August 1978. Bangalore: Printers India, 1978.

"Community of Women and Men in the Church: The Sheffield Recommendations." In *The Community of Women and Men in the Church: The Sheffield Report*, pp.83-90. Edited Constance F. Parvey. Geneva: World Council of Churches, 1983.

Community of Women and Men in the Church: The Sheffield Report. Edited by Constance F. Parvey. Geneva: World Council of Churches, 1983.

Concerning the Ordination of Women. Geneva: World Council of Churches, 1964.

"Conspectus of Studies and Programme." Appendix VIII to *Accra, 1974: Meeting of the Commission on Faith and Order. Minutes and Documents*, Faith and Order Paper, no. 71. Geneva: World Council of Churches, 1974.

Consultation of European Christian Women, Brussels, 29 January to 4 February 1978. Geneva: World Council of Churches, 1978.

Cox, Harvey. *Religion in the Secular City: Toward a Postmodern Theology*. New York: Simon and Schuster, 1984.

Crabtree, Davida Foy. "Women's Liberation and the Church." *Gladly We Rebel! Risk* 7:1 (1971):12-20.

Crawford, Janet, and Kinnamon, Michael, eds. *In God's Image: Reflections on Identity, Human Wholeness and the Authority of Scripture*. Geneva: World Council of Churches, 1983.

Cruz, Leila Shaheen da. Interview. In *Words to the Churches: Voices of the Sisters. Risk* 10:2 (1974):36-37.

D'Aubigne, Jeanne Merle, and Mouchon, Violette. *God's Underground*. Translated by William and Patricia Nottingham. St. Louis: Bethany Press, 1970. Originally published under the title *Le clandestine de Dieu*. Paris: Fayard, 1968.

Daly, Mary. *Beyond God the Father: Toward a Philosophy of Women's Liberation*. Boston: Beacon Press, 1973.

—. *The Church and the Second Sex*. New York: Harper & Row Publishers, 1968.

—. *Gyn/Ecology: The MetaEthics of Radical Feminism*. Boston: Beacon Press, 1978.

De Beauvior, Simone. *The Second Sex*. Translated and edited by H. M. Parshley. New York: Alfred A. Knopf, 1953. Originally published in two volumes under the title *Le deuxieme sexe: I* and *Les faits et les mythes: II. L'experience vecue*. Paris: Librairie Gallimard, 1949.

De Dietrich, Suzanne. "The Bible, a Force of Unity." *The Ecumenical Review* 1 (1949):41-416.

—. *Free Men: Mediations on the Bible Today*. Translated by Olive Wyon. Philadelphia: The Westminster Press, n.d. Originally published in London: S.C.M. Press, 1961.

Dietrich, Gabriele. "Liberating Women: A Comparative Survey." *Gladly We Rebel! Risk* 7:1 (1971):44-57.

Doctrine of Grace. Edited by W. T. Whitley. Introduction by the Archbishop of York. London: S.C.M. Press, 1932.

Dodd, C. H. "A Letter Concerning Unavowed Motives in Ecumenical Discussions." *The Ecumenical Review* 2 (Autumn 1949):52-56.

Dodd, C. H.; Cragg, G. R.; and Ellul, Jacques. *Social and Cultural Factors in Church Divisions.* Preface by Oliver Tomkins and with the report of a conference held at the Ecumenical Institute at Bossey in November, 1951. New York: World Council of Churches, 1952.

Doely, Sarah Bentley, ed. *Women's Liberation and the Church.* New York: Association Press, 1970.

"Draft Study of 1969 on the Theme 'Unity of Church-Unity of Mankind.' " In *Unity in Today's World: The Faith and Order Studies on "Unity of the Church-Unity of Humankind,"* pp. 28-51. Edited by Geiko Muller-Fahrenholz. Faith and Order Paper, no. 88. Geneva: World Council of Churches, 1978.

Dreyfus, Hubert L., and Rabinow, Paul. *Michel Foucault: Beyond Structuralism and Hermeneutics.* 2nd ed. Chicago: University of Chicago Press, 1983.

Dulles, John Foster. "The Christian in a Changing World." In *Man's Disorder and God's Design.* 5 vols. The Amsterdam Assembly Series. Vol. 4: *The Church and International Disorder*, pp. 73-114. New York: Harper & Bros., Publishers, 1948.

DuPlessis, Rachel Blau. *Writing beyond the Ending: Narrative Strategies of Twentieth-Century Women Writers.* Bloomington: Indiana University Press, 1985.

Durnbaugh, Donald F. *The Believers' Church: The History and Character of Radical Protestantism.* New York: Macmillan Co., 1968.

—. *The Brethren in Colonial America: A Source Book on the Transplantation and Development of the Church of the Brethren in the Eighteenth Century.* Elgin, IL: Brethren Press, 1967.

—. *European Origins of the Brethren: A Source Book on the Beginnings of the Church of the Brethren in the Early Eighteenth Century.* Elgin, IL: Brethren Press, 1958.

Ecumenical Perspectives on Baptism, Eucharist and Ministry. Edited by Max Thurian. Faith and Order Paper, no. 116. Geneva: World Council of Churches, 1983.

Eisenstein, Hester. *Contemporary Feminist Thought.* Boston: G. K. Hall & Co., 1983.

Eller, Vernard M. "Beliefs." In *The Church of the Brethren Past and Present*, pp. 39-51. Edited by Donald F. Durnbaugh. Elgin, IL: Brethren Press, 1970.

"Encyclical Letter Issued by the Bishops Attending the Third Lambeth Conference, July, 1888." In *The Sixth Lambeth Conferences 1867-1920*. Rev. ed.with Appendix, pp. 106-118. Compiled under the direction of the Most Reverend Lord Davidson of Lambeth, Archbishop of Canterbury, 1903-1928. London: S.P.C.K., 1929.

Ermarth, Margaret Sittler. *Adam's Fractured Rib: Observations on Women in the Church*. Philadelphia: Fortress Press, 1970.

"European Response." In *The Community of Women and Men in the Church: The Sheffield Report*, pp.99-101. Edited by Constance F. Parvey. Geneva: World Council of Churches, 1983,

Evanston Report: The Second Assembly of the World Council of Churches, 1954. Edited by W. A. Visser't Hooft. London: S.C.M. Press, 1955.

Faith and Order, Louvain, 1971: Study Reports and Documents. Faith and Order Paper, no. 59. Geneva: World Council of Churches, 1971.

Faith and Order: Proceedings of the World Conference, Lausanne, August 3-21, 1927. Edited by H. N. Bate. New York: George H. Doran Co., 1927.

Fausto-Sterling, Anne. *Myths of Gender: Biological Theories about Women and Men*. New York: Basic Books, 1985.

Fey, Harold E. "Amsterdam Strikes Middle Way in Discussing Economic Order." *Christian Century* 65 (22 September 1948):980.

Feyerabend, Paul. *Against Method: Outline of an Anarchistic Theory of Knowledge*. London: Verso, 1978.

First Six Years, 1948-1954: A Report of the Central Committee of the World Council of Churches on the Activities of the Departments and Secretariats of the Council. Geneva: World Council of Churches, 1954.

FitzGerald, Kyriaki Karidoyanes. "The Characteristics and Nature of the Order of the Deaconess." In *Women and the Priesthood*, pp. 75-95. Edited by Thomas Hopko. Crestwood, NY: St. Vladimir's Press, 1983.

Flesseman-van Leer, Ellen. Introduction to *The Bible: Its Authority and Interpretation in the Ecumenical Movement*. Edited by Ellen Flesseman-van Leer. Faith and Order Paper, no. 99. Geneva: World Council of Churches, 1983.

Foucault, Michel. *The Archeology of Knowledge and The Discourse on Language*. Translated by A. M. Sheridan Smith and Rupert Swyer. New York: Pantheon, 1972. Originally published under the titles *L'Archeologie du savoir* and *L'ordre du discours*. Paris: Editions Gallimard, 1969 and 1971 respectively.

—. *Discipline and Punish: The Birth of the Prison*. Translated by Alan Sheridan. New York: Vintage Press, 1979. Originally published under the title *Surveiller et punir: Naissance de la prison*. Paris: Editions Gallmard, 1975.

—. *The History of Sexuality*. Vol. 1: *An Introduction*. Translated by Robert Hurley. New York: Vintage Books, 1980. Originally published under the title *La volonte de savior*. Paris: Editions Gallimard, 1976.

—. *Language, Counter-Memory, Practice: Selected Essays and Interviews*. Edited by Donald F. Bouchard. Translated by Donald F. Bouchard and Sherry Simon. Ithaca: Cornell University Press, 1977.

—. *Madness and Civilization. A History of Insanity in the Age of Reason*. Translated by Richard Howard. New York: Vintage Books, 1973. Originally published under the title *Histoire de la Folie*. Paris: Librairie Plon, 1961.

—. *Power/Knowledge: Selected Interviews and Other Writings, 1972-1977*. Edited by Colin Gordon. Translated by Colin Gordon, Leo Marshall, John Mepham, and Kate S. Oper. New York: Pantheon Books, 1977.

—. "What Is Enlightenment?" In *The Foucault Reader*, pp. 32-50. Edited by Paul Rabinow. New York: Pantheon Books, 1984.

Fourth World Conference on Faith and Order, Montreal, 1963. Edited by P. C. Rodger and L. Vischer. Faith and Order Paper, no. 42. London: S.C.M. Press, 1964.

Friedan, Betty. *The Feminine Mystique*. New York: W. W. Norton & Co., 1963.

Gaines, David A. *The World Council of Churches: A Study of Its Background and History*. Peterborough, NH: Richard R. Smith, 1966.

Gathered for Life: Offical Report, VI Assembly, World Council of Churches, Vancouver, Canada, 24 July-10 August 1983. Edited by David Gill. Geneva: World Council of Churches, 1983; Grand Rapids: Wm. B. Eerdmans, 1983.

Gathering to Share Our Hope: Report on the National Consultation U.S. Section of the World Council of Churches Study of the Community of Women and Men in the Churches, Stony Point, New York, March 25-26, 1981. New York: National Council of Churches, 1981.

Gide, Andre. *The Immoralist*. Translated by Richard Howard. New York: Random House and Vintage Books, 1970. Originally published under the title *L'Immoraliste*. Paris: Mercure de France, 1921.

"Giving Account of Hope and Salvation." *Study Encounter* 2 (1975). "Giving Account of Hope in These Testing Times." *Study Encounter* 1-2 (1976).

Giving Account of the Hope Today. Faith and Order Paper, no. 81. Geneva: World Council of Churches, 1977.

Giving Account of the Hope Together. Faith and Order Paper, no. 86. Geneva: World Council of Churches, 1978.

Goldstein, Valerie Saiving. "The Human Situation: The Feminine View." *Journal of Religion* 40 (April 1960):100-112.

Gorodetzky, Nadejda. *The Humiliated Christ in Modern Russian Thought.* London: S.P.C.K., 1938; New York: Macmillan Co., 1938.

Greenwald, Maurine Weiner. *Women, War and Work: The Impact of World War I on Women Workers in the U.S.* Westport, CT: Greenwood Press, 1980.

Half the World's People: A Report of a Consultation of Church Women Executives, Glion, Switzerland. Geneva: World Council of Churches, 1978.

Herklots, H. G. G. *Amsterdam 1948: An Account of the First Assembly of the WCC.* London: S.C.M. Press, 1948.

Herzel, Susannah. *A Voice for Women: The Women's Department of the World Council of Churches.* Geneva: World Council of Churches, 1981.

Hill, Patricia R. *The World Their Household: The American Woman's Foreign Mission Movement and Cultural Transformation, 1870-1920.* Ann Arbor, Michigan: University of Michigan Press, 1985.

Honey, Maureen. *Creating Rosie the Riveter: Class, Gender, and Propaganda during World War II.* Amherst, Massachusetts: University of Massachusetts Press, 1984.

Hopkins, Charles Howard. *The Rise of the Social Gospel in American Protestantism, 1865-1915.* New Haven: Yale University Press, 1940.

Hopko, Thomas. "On the Male Character of Christian Priesthood." In *Women and the Priesthood*, pp. 97-134. Edited by Thomas Hopko. Crestwood, NY: St. Vladimir's Press, 1983.

Hopko, Thomas, ed. *Women and the Priesthood.* Crestwood, NY: St. Vladimir's Press, 1983.

Hromadka, Joseph L. "Christian Responsibility in Our Divided World." In *Man's Disorder and God's Design.* 5 vols. The Amsterdam Assembly Series. Vol. 4: *The Church and International Disorder.* New York: Harper & Bros., Publishers, 1948.

Institutionalism and Church Polity. A symposium prepared by the Study Committee on Institutionalism, Commission on Faith and Order, World Council of Churches. Edited by Nils Ehrenstrom and Walter G. Muelder. New York: Association Press, 1963.

Iremonger, F. A. *William Temple, Archbishop of Canterbury: His Life and Letters.* Oxford: Oxford University Press, 1948.

Janeway, Elizabeth. *Man's World, Woman's Place: A Study in Social Mythology.* New York: William Morrow & Co., 1971.

Joint Commission Appointed to Arrange for a World Conference on Faith and Order." In *Documents on Christian Unity.* Vol. 1: *1920-1924.* Edited by G. K. A. Bell. London: Humphrey Milford, 1924; Oxford, Oxford University Press, 1924.

Jones, Jacqueline. *Labor of Love, Labor of Sorrow: Black Women, Work and the Family from Slavery to the Present.* New York: Basic Books, 1985.

"Justice and Freedom in New Community." In *The Community of Women and Men in the Church: The Sheffield Report*, pp. 145-154. Edited by Constance F. Parvey. Geneva: World Council of Churches, 1983.

Kaledin, Eugenia. *Mothers and More: American Women in the 1950s.* Boston: Twayne Publishers, 1984.

Kasemann, Ernst. "Unity and Diversity in New Testament Ecclesiology." *Novum Testamentum* 6 (1963):290-297.

Keller, Adolf. *Karl Barth and Christian Unity: The Influence of the Barthian Movement upon the Churches of the World.* Translated by Manfred Manrodt. Revised by A. J. MacDonald. Introduction by Luther A. Weigle. New York: The Macmillan Company, 1933.

"Laila Khaled Answers Some Questions." *Gladly We Rebel! Risk* 7:12 (1971):38-43.

Lange, Ernst. *And Yet It Moves: Dream and Reality of the Ecumenical Movement.* Translated by Edwin Robertson. Geneva: World Council of Churches, 1978. Originally published under the title *Die okumenische Utopie oder Was bewegt die okumenische Bewegung.* Stuttgart: 1978.

"Letter from Sheffield." In *The Community of Women and Men in the Church: The Sheffield Report*, pp. 91-93. Edited Constance F. Parvey. Geneva: World Council of Churches, 1983.

Littell, Franklin H. *The Anabaptist View of the Church.* 2nd ed., rev. and enl. Boston: Starr King Press, 1958.

Lossky, Vladimir. *The Mystical Theology of the Eastern Church.* London: 1957.

—. *Orthodox Theology: An Introduction.* New York: 1978.

"Lumen Gentium." In *The Documents of Vatican II.* A New and Definitive Translation, with Commentaries and Notes by Catholic, Protestant and Orthodox Authorities, pp. 14-101. Edited by Walter M. Abbot. Translated by Joseph Gallagher. New York: Herder and Herder and Association Press, 1966.

Macfarland, Charles S. *Steps toward the World Council: Origins of the Ecumenical Movement as Expressed in the Universal Christian Council for Life and Work.* New York, London, and Edinburgh: Fleming H. Revell Co., 1938.

Machel, Josina. "Revolutionary Women." *Gladly We Rebel! Risk* 7:1 (1971):21-23.

Mandela, Nelson. *The Struggle Is My Life*. London: International Defense and Aid Fund for South Africa, 1978.

Man's Disorder and God's Design. 5 vols. The Amsterdam Assembly Series. Vol. 5: *The First Assembly of the World Council of Churches, Held at Amsterdam, August 22nd to September 4th, 1948. The Offical Report*. Edited by W. A. Visser't Hooft. New York: Harper & Bros, Publishers, 1948.

Mascall, E. L. "Women and the Priesthood in the Church." In *Why Not?: Priesthood and the Ministry of Women*. Edited by Michael Bruce and G. E. Duffield. Appleford: Marcham Manor Press, 1972.

Matheson, Peter, ed. *The Third Reich and the Christian Churches*. Grand Rapids: Wm. B. Eerdmans, 1981.

Mathews, Shailer. *The Social Teaching of Jesus: An Essay in Christian Sociology*. New York: Macmillan Co., 1915. Originally published in 1897.

McGill, Arthur C. *Suffering: A Test of Theological Method*. Philadelphia: Westminster Press, 1982.

Mead, Margaret. *Male and Female: A Study of the Sexes in a Change World*. New York: William Morrow & Co., 1967. Originally published in 1949.

Men and Women in Church and Society: A Statement Commended to the Churches by the Central Committee of the World Council of Churches. Geneva: World Council of Churches, 1956.

Mennonite Encyclopedia. S.v. "Gelassenheit," by Robert Friedmann.

Metz, Johann Baptist. *Faith in History and Society: Toward a Practical Fundamental Theology*. New York: Seabury Press, 1980.

Meyendorff, John. *The Orthodox Church: Its Past and Its Role in the World Today*. Translated by John Chapin. New York: Pantheon Books, 1962. Originally published under the title *L'Eglise Orthodoxe: Hier et aujourd'hui*. Paris: 1960.

—. "Unity of Church-Unity of Mankind." *The Ecumenical Review* 24 (January 1972):30-46.

Meyer, Sibylle, and Schulze, Eva. "Trummer-Frauen." *Emma: Das Magazin von Frauen fur Frauen*, May 1985, pp. 30-34.

Mid-Stream: An Ecumenical Journal 21 (July 1982).

Miller, Jean Baker. *Toward a New Psychology of Women*. Boston: Beacon Press, 1976.

Millett, Kate. *Sexual Politics*. New York: Doubleday & Co., 1970.

Ministry and the Sacraments. Report of the Theological Commission appointed by the Continuation Committee of the Faith and Order Movement under the chairmanship of the Rt. Rev. A. C. Headlam. Edited by R. Dunkerley. London: S.C.M. Press, 1937.

Minutes and Reports of the Second Meeting of the Central Committee of the World Council of Churches, Held at Chichester (England), July 9-15, 1949. Geneva: World Council of Churches, 1949.

Minutes and Reports of the Tenth Meeting of the Central Committee of the World Council of Churches, Yale Divinity School, New Haven (Connecticut, U.S.A.), July 30-August 7, 1957. Geneva: World Council of Churches, 1957.

Minutes and Reports of the Third Meeting of the Central Committee of the World Council of Churches, Toronto (Canada), July 9-15, 1950. Geneva: World Council of Churches, 1950.

Minutes and Reports of the Thirteenth Meeting of the Central Committee of the World Council of Churches, St. Andrews (Scotland), August 16-24, 1960. Geneva: World Council of Churches, 1960.

Minutes and Reports of the Twelfth Meeting of the Central Committee of the World Council of Churches, Rhoades, (Greece), August 19-27, 1959. Geneva: World Council of Churches. 1959.

"Minutes of the 1963 Assembly of the Church of Finland." In *Adam's Fractured Rib: Observations on Women in the Church.* By Margaret Sittler Ermarth. Philadelphia: Fortress Press, 1968.

Minutes of the Meeting of the Commission and Working Committee 1968, Uppsala and Sigtuna. Faith and Order Paper, no. 53. Geneva: World Council of Churches, 1968.

Minutes of the Meeting of the Working Committee 1970, Cret-Berard. Faith and Order Paper, no. 57. Geneva: World Council of Churches, 1970.

Minutes of the Meeting of the Working Committee, 1973, Zagorsk (U.S.S.R.). Faith and Order Paper, no. 66. Geneva: World Council of Churches, 1973.

Mitchell, Juliet. *Psychoanalysis and Feminism.* New York: Pantheon Books, 1974.

Moltmann-Wendel, Elisabeth. *Liberty, Equality, Sisterhood.* Translated by Ruth C. Gritsch. Philadelphia: Fortress Press, 1978. Originally published under the title *Freiheit, Gleichheit, Schwesterlickeit.* Munich: Chr. Kaiser Verlag, 1977.

Morton, Nelle. *The Journey Is Home.* Boston: Beacon Press, 1985.

—. "Towards a Whole Theology." In *Sexism in the 1970s: Discrimination Against Women. A Report of a World Council of Churches Consultation, West Berlin, 1974,* pp.56-65. Geneva: World Council of Churches, 1975.

—. "Women's Liberation and the Church." *Tempo,* 1 October 1970.

"Moscow Patriarchate and the First Assembly of the World Council of Churches." *The Ecumenical Review* 1 (Winter 1949):188-195.

Nairobi to Vancouver, 1975-1983: Report of the Central Committee to the Sixth Assembly of the World Council of Churches. Geneva: World Council of Churches, 1983.

Neal, Marie Augusta. *A Socio-Theology of Letting Go: The Role of the First World Church Facing Third World Peoples.* New York, Ramsey, Toronto: Paulist Press, 1977.

New Delhi Report: The Third Assembly of the World Council of Churches, 1961. Edited by W. A. Visser't Hooft. New York: Association Press, 1962.

New Directions in Faith and Order, Bristol, 1967: Reports-Minutes-Documents. Faith and Order Paper, no. 50. Geneva: World Council of Churches, 1968.

Niebuhr, H. Richard. *The Meaning of Revelation.* New York: Macmillan Co., 1941.

No Man is Alien: Essays on the Unity of Mankind. Edited by J. Robert Nelson. Leiden: E. J. Brill, 1971.

Non-Theological Factors in the Making and Unmaking of Church Union. Prepared by the Commission on the Church's Unity in Life and Worship for the World Conference on Faith and Order, Edinburgh, 1937. Drafted by Willard Learoyd Sperry. Faith and Order Pamphlet, no. 84, 1st series. New York and London: Harper & Bros., Publishers, 1937.

"Notes on *Ministry, Mariology and Biblical Hermeneutics* Consultation, sponsored by the Community of Women and Men in the Church Study, June 26-29, 1978, Foyer John Knox, Geneva, Switzerland." Unpublished document in the personal files of Melanie A. May, Lombard, IL.

Oldham, J. H. *The Oxford Conference: Official Report.* Chicago and New York: Willett Clark & Co., 1937.

One Baptism, One Eucharist and a Mutually Recognized Ministry: Three Agreed Statements. Faith and Order Paper, no. 73. Geneva: World Council of Churches, 1975.

One Lord One Baptism. "Report on the Divine Trinity and the Unity of the Churches" and "Report on the Meaning of Baptism" by the Theological Commission on Christ and the Church. Faith and Order Paper, no. 29. London: S.C.M. Press, 1960.

Ordination of Women in Ecumenical Perspective: Workbook for the Church's Future. Edited by Constance F. Parvey. Faith and Order Paper, no. 105. Geneva: World Council of Churches, 1980.

Orthodox Church in the Ecumenical Movement: Documents and Statements 1902-1975. Edited by Constantin G. Patelos. Geneva: World Council of Churches, 1978.

Orthodox Women, Their Role and Participation in the Orthodox Church: Report on the Consultation of Orthodox Women, Agapia, Roumania, September, 1976. Geneva: World Council of Churches, 1977.

Ortner, Sherry. "Is Female to Male as Nature Is to Culture?" In *Women, Culture, and Society*, pp. 67-87. Edited by Michelle Zimbalist Rosaldo and Lousie Lamphere. Stanford: Stanford University Press, 1974.

Parvey, Constance F. "The Community of Women and Men in the Ecumenical Movement: Held Together in Hope and Sustained by God's Promise—A Personal Reflection." In *The Community of Women and Men in the Church: The Sheffield Report*, pp. 156-183. Edited by Constance F. Parvey. Geneva: World Council of Churches, 1983.

—. "The Journey from the Sheffield International Consultation to Dresden: Plenary Report on the Sheffield International Consultation, The Community of Women and Men in the Church Study." World Council of Churches Central Committee, meeting in Dresden, German Democratic Republic, August 1981. Unpublished document in the personal files of Melanie A. May, Lombard, IL.

—. "Journey of a Dream: Beginning Again." In *Report of Regional Consultation on Community of Men and Women in the Church Study*, pp.6-13. Nairobi, Kenya: All-Africa Conference of Churches Production, n.d.

—. "Reflections on the Questions Asked at the Task Force Meeting of August 5, 1980." Geneva, 7 August 1980. Unpublished memorandum in the personal files of Melanie A. May, Lombard, IL.

Potter, Philip. "A Chance to Change." In *The Community of Women and Men in the Church: The Sheffield Report*, pp. 23-28. Edited by Constance F. Parvey. Geneva: World Council of Churches, 1983.

—. "The Community of Women and Men in the Church." *Mid-Stream: An Ecumenical Journal* 21 (July 1982):279-284.

Preface to "The Community of Women and Men in the Church: The Sheffield Recommendations." As presented to the World Council of Churches Central Committee, meeting in Dresden, German Democratic Republic, August, 1981. Unpublished document in the personal files of Melanie A. May, Lombard, IL.

Raming, Ida. *The Exclusion of Women from the Priesthood: Divine Law or Sex Discrimination*. Translated by Norman R. Adams. Metuchen, NJ: Scarecrow Press, 1976.

Renewal of the Church: Report of a Consultation of the World Council of Churches, Yale Divinity School, New Haven, Connecticut, U.S.A., July 15-20, 1957. Geneva: World Council of Churches, 1957.

Report of Conference on Women, Human Rights and Mission, Venice, Italy. Geneva: World Council of Churches, 1979.

"Report of Minutes of the Working Committee, Meeting 1-3 September 1953." A statement drafted 11 March 1954 in preparation for the Second Assembly of the World Council of Churches. Unpublished document in the Archives, Library of the Ecumenical Centre, Geneva, Switzerland.

Report of the All-Africa Regional Consultation on Community of Women and Men in the Church Study, Ibadan, Nigeria, 15-19 September 1980. Nairobi: All-Africa Conference of Churches Publication, 1981.

Report of the Consulation Held at "Uplands," High Wycombe, Bucks, England, July 27-August 2, 1960, on "Towards Responsible Cooperation between Men and Women, Our Christian Responsibility." Geneva: World Council of Churches, 1960.

Report of the Consulation on "Relationships of Men and Women at Work," Held at the College Protestant Romand at Founex, Switzerland, 1964. Geneva: World Council of Churches, 1965.

Report of the Consultation Held at Cite Universitaire ,Paris, France, July 25-30th, 1963, on "Marriage and Family Life." Geneva: World Council of Churches, 1963.

Report of the Consultation Held at St. Cergue, Switzerland, 1967, on "International and Inter-Church Counseling and Family Education." Geneva: World Council of Churches, 1967.

Report of the Consultation Held at Women's Christian College, Madras, India, November 13-17, 1961, on "Changing Patterns of Men-Women Relationships in Asia." Geneva: World Council of Churches, 1961.

Report of the Consultation Held at the College Protestant Romand at Founex, Switzerland, July 6-10, 1964, on "Sexual Ethics Today." Geneva: World Council of Churches, 1964.

Report of the Consultation Held by the Department on the Co-operation of Men and Women in Church and Society, at Herrenalb. Germany, 15th-19th July, 1956. Geneva: World Council of Churches, 1956.

Report of the Consultation on Obstacles to the Cooperation of Men and Women in Working Life and Public Service: Implications for the Work of the Department, Held at Odense, Denmark, August 8-12, 1958. Geneva: World Council of Churches, 1958.

Report of the Consultation on the Christian Approach to Women's Questions: Freedom of Marriage-Freedom of Work, Held at the John Knox House, Geneva, Switzerland, March 27-30, 1958. Geneva: World Council of Churches, 1958.

Report of the Middle Eastern Council of Churches Consultation on the Community of Women and Men in the Church, Beruit, Lebanon, 22nd-26th January, 1980. Geneva: World Council of Churches, 1981.

Report of the Preliminary Meeting at Geneva, Switzerland, August 12-20, 1920. Faith and Order Pamphlet, no. 33, 1st series. Located in the Archives, the Library of the Ecumenical Centre, Geneva, Switzerland.

"Report of the Study Commission on Institutionalsim." In *Faith and Order Findings*. The final report of the Theological Commissions to the Fourth World Conference on Faith and Order, Montreal 1963, pp. 1-31. Edited by Paul Minear. Minneapolis: Augsburg Publishing House, 1963.

Report on Middle East Consultation on Women in Church and Society, Cairo, Egypt. Geneva: World Council of Churches, 1978.

"Report on Plan and Scope, Adopted April 20, 1911." In *A Documentary History of the Faith and Order Movement 1927-1963*, Edited by Lukas Vischer. St. Louis: Bethany Press, 1963.

Report on Two Consultations in Africa: Ibadan, Nigeria, 4th to 10th January, 1958, Nkongsamba, Cameroons, 21st to 23rd February, 1958. Geneva: World Council of Churches, 1958.

Report on the Consultation on Developing Relations of Men, Women and Children and Their Meaning for the Mission of the Church in Our Changing World, Held at Sita Katharinastiftelsen, Osterskar, Sweden, from June 28th-July 2nd, 1968. Geneva: World Council of Churches, 1968.

Reuther, Rosemary R. *New Woman/New Earth: Sexist Ideologies and Human Liberation.* New York: Seabury Press, A Crossroad Book, 1975.

Reuther, Rosemary R., ed. *Religion and Sexism: Images of Woman in the Jewish and Christian Traditions.* New York: Simon and Schuster, 1974.

Revised Interim Report of a Study on the Life and Work of Women in the Church, Including Reports of an Ecumenical Conference of Church Women, Baarn, Holland, and of the Committee on "The Life and Work of Women in the Church" of the Assembly of the World Council of Churches, Amsterdam, 1948. Geneva: World Council of Churches, 1948.

"Revised Report of the Structure Committee Approved by Central Committee, 1971." In *Central Committee of the World Council of Churches, Minutes and Reports of the Twenty-Fourth Meeting, Addis-Ababa, Ethiopia, January 10th-21st, 1971*, pp. 136-188. Geneva: World Council of Churches, 1971.

Rosaldo, Michelle Zimbalist. "Women, Culture, and Society: A Theoretical Overview." In *Women, Culture, and Society*, pp.17-42. Edited by Michelle Zimbalist Rosaldo and Louise Lamphere. Stanford, CA: Stanford University Press, 1974.

Rossiter, Margaret L. *Women in the Resistance.* New York: Praeger Publishers, 1986.

Rowbotham, Shelia. *Woman's Consciousness, Man's World.* London: Penguin, 1973.

Runice, Robert. "The Community of Women and Men in the Church." In *The Community of Women and Men in the Church Study: The Sheffield Report*, pp.20-23. Edited by Constance F. Parvey. Geneva: World Council of Churches, 1983.

Rupp, Leila J. *Mobilizing Women for War: German and American Propaganda, 1939-1945*. Princeton: Princeton University Press, 1978.

Russell, Letty M. *The Future of Partnership*. Philadelphia: Westminster Press, 1979.

—. *Human Liberation in Feminist Perspective—A Theology*. Philadelphia: Westminster Press, 1974.

Sappington, Roger E. *The Brethren in the New Nation: A Source Book in the Development of the Church of the Brethren, 1785-1865*. Elgin, IL: Brethren Press, 1976.

—. *Brethren Social Policy, 1908-1958*. Elgin, IL: Brethren Press, 1961.

Sayers, Dorothy L. *The Mind of the Maker*. Westport, CT: Greenwood Press, Publishers, 1976. Originally published by Harcourt, Brace in New York, 1941.

Scharffenorth, Gerta, and Thraede, Klaus. *"Freunde in Christus werden. . .": Die Beziehung von Mann und Frau als Frage an Theologie und Kirche*. Gelnhausen, Berlin: Burckhardthaus Verlag; Stein/Mfr.: Laetare-Verlag, 1977.

Schmidt, William J. *Architect of Unity: A Biography of Samuel McCrea Cavert*. New York: Friendship Press, 1978.

Scholder, Klaus. *The Churches and the Third Reich*. Vol. 2: *The Years Disillusionment: 1934, Barmen and Rome*. Philadelphia: Fortress Press 1988.

Schweitzer, Wolfgang. "The Bible and the Church's Message to the World." *The Ecumenical Review* 2 (1950):123-132.

Second World Conference on Faith and Order, Edinburgh, August 3-18, 1937. Edited by Leonard Hodgson. New York: Macmillan Co., 1938.

Sexism in the 1970s: Discrimination Against Women. A Report of a World Council of Churches Consultation, West Berlin, 1974. Geneva: World Council of Churches, 1974.

Sharing in One Hope: Reports and Documents from the Meeting of the Faith and Order Commission, 15-30 August, 1978, Ecumenical Christian Centre, Bangalore, India. Faith and Order Paper, no. 92. Geneva: World Council of Churches, n.d.

Sittler, Joseph A. "Called to Unity." *The Ecumenical Review* 14 (January 1962):183.

Skoglund, John E., and Nelson, J. Robert. *Fifty Years of Faith and Order: An Interpretation of the Faith and Order Movement*. New

York: The Committee for the Interseminary Movement of the National Student Christian Federation, Department of Faith and Order Studies of the National Council of the Churches of Christ in the U.S.A., The Commission on Faith and Order of the World Council of Churches, 1963.

Slack, Kenneth. *Nairobi Narrative: The Story of the Fifth Assembly of the World Council of Churches, 23 November-10 December 1975*. London: S.C.M. Press, 1976.

—. *Uppsala Report: The Story of the World Council of Churches Fourth Assembly, Uppsala, Sweden, 4-19 July, 1968*. London: S.C.M. Press, 1968.

Slater, Mary Louise. *Future-maker in India: The Story of Sarah Chakko*. New York: Friendship Press, 1968.

Soderblom, Nathan. *Christian Fellowship or the United Life and Work of Christendom*. New York, Chicago, London, and Edinburgh: Fleming H. Revell Co., 1923.

"Space to Grow in . . .": Report of the European Regional Consultation of the Community of Women and Men in the Church, Bad Segeberg, Federal Republic of Germany, 20th-24th June, 1980. Geneva: World Council of Churches, 1981.

"Statement from Third World Participants." Sheffield, England, 15 July 1981. Unpublished document in the personal files of Melanie A. May, Lombard, IL. A revised version of this statement is published in *The Community of Women and Men in the Church: The Sheffield Report*, pp. 96-98. Edited by Constance F. Parvey. Geneva: World Counicl of Churches, 1983.

Stendahl, Brita. *The Force of Tradition: A Case Study of Women Priests in Sweden*. Appendix by Constance F. Parvey. Philadelphia: Fortress Press, 1985.

Stockholm Conference 1925: The Official Report of the Universal Christian Conference on Life and Work Held in Stockholm, 19-30 August 1925. Edited by G. K. A. Bell. Oxford: Oxford University Press, 1926; London: Humphrey Milford, 1926.

Study on the Community of Women and Men in the Church. Geneva: World Council of Churches, 1978.

Tanner, Mary. "The Community Study and the unity of the Church and renewal of human community." In *Towards Visible Unity: Commission on Faith and Order, Lima, 1982*. Vol. 2: *Study Papers and Reports*, pp. 153-165. Edited by Michael Kinnamon. Faith and Order Paper, no. 113. Geneva: World Council of Churches, 1982.

Tatlow, Tissington. "The World Conference on Faith and Order." In *A History of the Ecumenical Movement 1517-1948*, pp. 403-441. Edited by Ruth Rouse and Stephen Charles Neill. Philadelphia: Westminster Press, 1954.

Temple, William. *Essays in Christian Politics and Kindred Subjects*. London: Longmans, 1933.

——. *Nature, Man and God*. Being the Gifford Lectures delivered in the University of Glasgow in the academic years 1932-1933 and 1933-1934. London: Macmillan & Co., 1940.

Third World Conference on Faith and Order, Held at Lund, August 15th to 28th, 1952. Edited by Oliver S. Tomkins. London: S.C.M. Press, 1953.

Thoburn, James M. *Life of Isabella Thoburn*. Cincinnati: Jennings and Pye, 1903.

Thompson, Betty. *A Chance to Change: Women and Men in the Church*. Philadelphia: Fortress Press, 1982.

Till, Barry. *The Churches Search for Unity*. Harmondsworth, Middlesex, England: Penguin Books, 1972.

Tillich, Paul. *Systematic Theology*. 3 vols. Chicago: University of Chicago Press, 1951-63.

Tomkins, Oliver S. Foreword to *The Fourth World Conference on Faith and Order, Montreal, 1963*. Edited by P. C. Rodger and L. Vischer. Faith and Order Paper, no. 42. London: S.C.M. Press, 1964.

Towards an Ecumenical Consensus on Baptism, the Eucharist and the Ministry: A Reply to the Replies of the Churches. Faith and Order Paper, no. 84. Geneva: World Council of Churches, 1977.

Towards Visible Unity: Commission on Faith and Order, Lima, 1982. Vol. 1: *Minutes and Addresses*. Edited by Michael Kinnamon. Faith and Order Paper, no. 112. Geneva: World Council of Churches, 1982.

Towards Visible Unity: Commission on Faith and Order, Lima, 1982. Vol. 2: *Study Papers and Reports*. Edited by Michael Kinnamon. Faith and Order Paper, no. 113. Geneva: World Council of Churches, 1982.

Tracy, David. *The Analogical Imagination: Christian Theology and the Culture of Pluralism*. New York: Crossroad, 1981.

Trible, Phyllis. *God and the Rhetoric of Sexuality*. Philadelphia: Fortress Press, 1978.

Troeltsch, Ernst. *The Absoluteness of Christianity and the History of Religions*. Translated by David Reid. Introduction by James Luther Adams. Richmond, VA: John Knox Press, 1971. Originally published under the title *Die Absolutheit des Christentums und die Religionsgeschichte: Vortrag gehalten auf der Versammlung der Freunde der Christlichen Welt zu Muhlacker am 3. Oktober 1901. Erweitert und mit einem vorwort versehen*. Tubingen: 1929.

"Unitatis Redintegratio." In *The Documents of Vatican II*. A new and definitive translation, with commentaries and notes by Catholic, Protestant and Orthodox authorites, pp. 341-366. Edited by

Walter M. Abbot. Translated by Joseph Gallagher. New York: Herder and Herder and Association Press, 1966.

Uniting in Hope, Accra 1974: Reports and Documents from the Meeting of the Faith and Order Commission, 23 July-5 August 1974, University of Ghana, Legon. Faith and Order Paper, no. 72. Geneva: World Council of Churches, 1975.

Uppsala Report 1968: Official Report of the Fourth Assembly of the World Council of Churches, Uppsala, July 4-20, 1968. Edited by Norman Goodall. Geneva: World Council of Churches, 1968.

Uppsala to Nairobi, 1968-1975: Report of the Central Committee to the Fifth Assembly of the World Council of Churches. Edited by David Enderton Johnson. New York: Friendship Press, 1975; London: S.P.C.K., 1975.

Vischer, Lukas; Borovoy, Vitaly; and Welch, Claude. "The Meaning of Catholicity." *The Ecumenical Review* 16 (October 1963):24-42.

Visser't Hooft, Henriette. "Aus den Briefwechsel mit Karl Barth 1934." In *Eva wo bist du? Frauen in internationalen Organisation der Okumene: Eine Dokumentation*, pp. 14-19. By Gundrun Kaper et al. Gelnhausen, Berlin, Stein Mfr.: Burckhardthaus-Laetare Verlag, 1981.

—. "Eva wo bist du?" In *Eva wo bist du? Frauen in internationalen Organisation der Okumene: Eine Dokumentation*, pp. 20-32. By Gundrun Kaper et al. Gelnhausen, Berlin, Stein Mfr.: Burckhardthaus-Laetare Verlag, 1981.

Visser't Hooft, W. A. *The Background of the Social Gospel in America.* Haarlem: H. D. Tjeenk Willink, 1928.

—. *The Fatherhood of God in an Age of Emancipation.* Philadelphia: Westminster Press, 1982.

—. *The Genesis and Formation of the World Council of Churches.* Geneva: World Council of Churches, 1982.

Ware, Timothy. *The Orthodox Church.* Harmondsworth, Middlesex, England: Penguin Books, 1963.

Wartenberg, Barbel von. "Participation in the Oikoumene: Relfections on Women's Participation in the Sixth Assenbly—Vancourver: A Model." *The Ecumenical Review* 36 (April 1984):156.

"We Listened Long before We Spoke": A Report of the Consultation of Women Theological Students, Cartigny, Switzerland. Geneva: World Council of Churches, 1978.

Webb, Pauline. "The Word of Life." *The Ecumenical Review* 35 (October 1983):345.

Welch, Sharon D. *Communities of Resistance and Solidarity: A Feminist Theology of Liberation.* Maryknoll, NY: Orbis Books, 1985.

What Is Ordination Coming to? Report of a Consulation on the Ordination of Women, Held in Cartigny, Geneva, Switzerland, 21st-

26th September, 1970. Edited by Brigalia Bam. Geneva: World Council of Churches, 1971.

What Unity Implies: Six Essays after Uppsala. World Council Studies, no.7. Geneva: World Council of Churches, 1969.

"What Unity Requires." In *Breaking Barriers, Nairobi, 1975: The Offical Report of the Fifth Assembly of the World Council of Churches, Nairobi, 23 November-10 December, 1975,* pp. 57-69. Edited by David M. Paton. London S.P.C.K., 1976; Grand Rapids: Wm. B. Eerdmans for the World Council of Churches, 1976.

What in the World is the World Council of Churches? 2nd ed., rev. Geneva: World Council of Churches, 1983.

Women Priests: A Catholic Commentary on the Vatican Declaration. Edited by Leonard Swidler and Arlene Swidler. New York: Paulist Press, 1977.

Women and Catholic Priesthood: An Expanded Vision. Proceedings of the Detroit Ordination Conference. Edited by Anne Marie Gardiner. New York, Paramus, Toronto: Paulist Press, 1976.

"Women and Men in Community for Humanity." In *The Community of Women and Men in the Church: The Sheffield Report,* pp. 96-97. Edited by Constance F. Parvey. Geneva: World Council of Churches, 1983.

Women and Men in the Church. Syosset, NY: Department of Religious Education, Orthodox Church in America, 1980.

Women and Priesthood: Future Directions. A Call to Dialogue from the Faculty of the Catholic Theological Union at Chicago. Edited by Carroll Stuhlmueller. Collegeville, MN: Liturgical Press, 1978.

Woolf, Virginia. *Three Guineas.* London: Hogarth Press, 1938; reprint ed., Harmondsworth, Middlesex, England: Penguin Books, 1977.

World Council of Churches Central Committee, Minutes of the Thirty- Third Meeting, Dresden, German Democratic Republic, 16-26 August 1981. Geneva: World Council of Churches, 1981.

World Council of Churches Central Committee, Minutes of the Twenty- Ninth Meeting, Geneva, Switzerland, 10-18 August 1976. Geneva: World Council of Churches, 1976.

World Missionary Conference, 1910: The History and Records of the Conference, Together with Addresses Delivered at the Evening Meetings. 9 vols. Vol. 9: *World Missionary Conference, 1910.* Edinburgh and London: Oliphant, Anderson, & Ferrier, n.d.; New York, Chicago, and Toronto: Fleming H. Revell Co., n.d.

Zabriskie, Alexander C. *Bishop Brent: Crusader for Christian Unity.* Philadelphia: Westminster Press, 1948.

Zander, L. "The Ecumenical Movement and the Orthodox Church." *The Ecumenical Review* 1 (Spring 1949): 267-276.